The Life of Lee

The Life of Lee

LEE EVANS

MICHAEL JOSEPH
an imprint of
PENGUIN BOOKS

MICHAEL JOSEPH

Published by the Penguin Group
Penguin Books Ltd, 80 Strand, London WC2R ORL, England
Penguin Group (USA) Inc., 375 Hudson Street, New York, New York 10014, USA
Penguin Group (Canada), 90 Eglinton Avenue East, Suite 700, Toronto, Ontario, Canada M4P 2Y3
(a division of Pearson Penguin Canada Inc.)
Penguin Ireland, 25 St Stephen's Green, Dublin 2, Ireland (a division of Penguin Books Ltd)
Penguin Group (Australia), 250 Camberwell Road,
Camberwell, Victoria 3124, Australia (a division of Pearson Australia Group Pty Ltd)
Penguin Books India Pvt Ltd, 11 Community Centre,
Panchsheel Park, New Delhi – 110 017, India
Penguin Group (NZ), 67 Apollo Drive, Rosedale, Auckland 0632, New Zealand
(a division of Pearson New Zealand Ltd)
Penguin Books (South Africa) (Pty) Ltd, 24 Sturdee Avenue,
Rosebank, Johannesburg 2196, South Africa

Penguin Books Ltd, Registered Offices: 80 Strand, London WC2R ORL, England

www.penguin.com

First published 2011
8

Copyright © Lee Evans, 2011

Picture of charity cricket match copyright © *Plymouth Sunday Independent*.
Every effort has been made to trace copyright holders. The publishers will be glad
to rectify in future editions any errors or omissions brought to their attention.

The moral right of the author has been asserted

For the protection of the privacy of individuals concerned, some names have been changed.

Set in 13.75/16.25 pt Garamond
Typeset by Palimpsest Book Production Limited, Falkirk, Stirlingshire
Printed in Great Britain by Clays Ltd, St Ives plc

A CIP catalogue record for this book is available from the British Library

ISBN: 978-0-718-15618-3

www.greenpenguin.co.uk

MIX
Paper from
responsible sources
FSC
www.fsc.org   FSC™ C018179

Penguin Books is committed to a sustainable
future for our business, our readers and our
planet. This book is made from paper certified
by the Forest Stewardship Council.

Acknowledgements

Thank you to all my family and friends. I really appreciate your encouragement and support. I love you more than you know.

This book is dedicated to little Maxwell Evans – the sole inspiration for this story.

Contents

1. In the Beginning

It wasn't the greatest of starts. In fact, things were pretty rocky for me at the beginning. As if arriving on earth with a hole in the heart wasn't enough already, when I was born on 25 February 1964 at the Bristol Royal Infirmary, I was also named Cassius Clay Evans.

Now, that's fine if you're a strapping lad from the Deep South who's destined to grow up to be undisputed heavyweight champion of the world. However, it's not so brilliant if you're a scrawny kid from Avonmouth who's fighting for something else altogether – his life.

Being an obsessive boxing fan, Dad was keen to mark in his own special way 25 February 1964, the day Clay knocked out the seemingly invincible Sonny Liston to claim the world heavyweight title. So passionate was Dad about boxing, the moment I was born he hot-footed it up the corridor from the waiting room where he had been glued to the TV, demanding that I be named after the new champ.

Luckily, Mum flatly refused, thank goodness. I'm not suggesting that Cassius isn't a decent enough name, but even the great man himself changed it to Muhammad Ali a little later.

Fortunately, Dad's other passion was rock'n'roll music, and so I was named Lee after Jerry Lee Lewis, the manic, piano-playing rocker. Looking on the bright side, I'm very glad he never listened to Grandmaster Flash and The Furious Five, or Dave Dee, Dozy, Beaky, Mick and Tich.

This is the story of how that small, shy, sensitive boy from a run-down council estate near the Avonmouth dockyards of Bristol and a travelling family of performers stumbled quite by accident into the heady world of show business.

Regarded by anyone I came into contact with as hailing from a different planet, I had a simple longing to be accepted. Life for me always felt like an unexpected turn of events that merely conspired to exacerbate my bewildered state of mind. A naturally quiet, enigmatic, gangly, fuzzy-haired, goggle-eyed scruffbag, I just wanted to blend into the background as best I could. Ironically, trying to do so only made me stand out from the crowd.

My dad was a performer who worked the South Wales and West Country club circuit, eventually sharing the bill with some of the most famous and talented performers of his generation. As a child, I led a kind of secret, dual existence, flitting between show business and the real world. In the realm of loud, excessive, sometimes over-dramatic, insecure show people of all shapes, sizes and persuasions, I was always under strict instructions from my parents to be seen but never heard. I became The Invisible Boy.

All the while, stage folk would talk openly in front of me about all sorts of things that children shouldn't normally hear. But, through it all, I was unwittingly soaking up everything I witnessed. A loner, I fostered a clandestine yearning to be noticed, to be a part of all the excitement that was going on around me.

At nineteen, I rushed into marriage and was immediately expected to provide. But faced with never really fitting into the conventional workplace, I was forced under pressure to fall back on what came naturally: show business.

Eventually, when my back was to the wall and all else had failed, I got an act together based on what I had seen as a kid and entered a talent show. To my astonishment, I found very quickly that it felt better out on stage than it did dealing with the harsh realities of bills and rent payments. I stepped on to a magical platform where, miraculously, all my troubles melted away and everything suddenly seemed possible.

Looking back at my adventures now, I have come to feel that, to an extent, I have triumphed over my background. I have hurdled quite a few barriers and undergone an amazing journey. I've got a beautiful wife and a wonderful daughter. And I've still got all my own teeth. But the truth is, all I have ever been looking for is peace and acceptance.

I'm getting ahead of myself, though. Let's go back to the very start, just after my parents wisely dropped the idea of calling me Cassius Clay.

Even though I now had a more commonplace British name, I was still blighted. Afflicted with that hole in the heart, I was for several years seen as the weakling of the family. I suppose that underlined to me the sense that life was going to be a bit of a struggle and that I would always feel a bit detached from everyone else. My illness only heightened the feeling that, from the very beginning, I was somehow different.

When I was tiny, of course, I didn't know about the illness, having only just taken my first gasps of air. I was too young, only one step up from a sperm really, at the time. I could have died right there on the table and not known much about it, if it hadn't been for the hefty ward nurse at the Bristol Royal Infirmary who promptly scooped me up and, with a face that could crack nuts, sternly informed my mum in a thick, unforgiving West Country accent that she was taking me away to let the doctors have a look because there was 'something wrong'. With that, she swiftly left the room, leaving my mum in stunned silence, exhausted and confused as to what the problem could possibly be and feeling that her baby might not actually return. Eventually, I was returned to Mum, who was allowed to take me home. I still needed lots of monitoring, though.

My dad was the son of a very hard and tough Welsh ex-miner who later became a drill sergeant in the army. Dad complained that Granddad never really gave him any credit for anything. His attitude was, 'If you get knocked down, you just have to get back up again.' Even though Dad joined the army to please his father and signed up for the boxing team, that still didn't cut it with Granddad. I think this informed Dad's whole outlook on life. My mum shared his sense of not fitting in. She was the daughter of an Irishman who left her to be adopted in Bristol. Subsequently, she suffered constantly from feelings of abandonment.

So from a very early age, I realized things weren't

exactly going to be a bed of roses around here and somehow I always knew I was different. That feeling was only heightened by my parents, a couple who always seemed to be at war with the world.

Anyway, after the first few years, my condition slowly improved. But there were still the regular bus journeys every week to Bristol Royal Infirmary, a much-cherished day off school and away from the grey, dull housing estate, as the bus took Mum and me through leafy Fishponds and the excitement of the busy Bristol city centre. As a scrawny five-year-old, I relished the attention from what seemed like angels, the beautiful nurses with their crisp, clean, blue uniforms and tender looks of concern. Then there was the routine examination by the doctor, the cold stethoscope that made me jump every time he placed it on a new part of my chest. 'Mmmm, mmmm? Mmmmm, Mmmm.' I thought, 'Surely I deserve more than "mmmm"? That's a perfectly decent chest, that is.'

My height was taken, and my weight. Then, after the examination, the doctor would hand me a lollipop from a jar on his desk, smiling as if giving a chimp a treat. You could tell from his face that he thought we were an unfortunate family. As he told me I'd done very well, he'd ruffle my hair with his hand. Then you'd see him secretly check to see if it was now dirty while he gave some quick words of advice to Mum, never to me – after all, I was the one who was 'ill'.

My illness was never mentioned around our flat. The only indication I got that something was wrong was whenever I decided to run around the lounge. Then Mum would quickly snap at Dad to make me stop. She would argue with Dad, accusing him of not keeping an eye on me. 'Why?' I wondered. 'What could possibly happen?'

But I always knew there was something not quite right with me, and so did all the other kids where we lived. It's funny, kids can smell a defect a mile off, and whenever there was a game of football on the green at the front of the flats, involving all the kids from around the estate, suspiciously, I would always be the first to be picked for a team, just so they could laugh at my ineptitude.

My brother Wayne would do his best to look after me. 'No, come on you lot,' he would remonstrate loudly, pointing meaningfully to his heart. 'Let him go in goal.' In response to which there were always lots of disappointed groans. The cruelty of kids knows no bounds.

I loved the England World Cup-winning goalie Gordon Banks and wanted to be just like him. I would dive all over the place. For no reason whatsoever, even when the ball was up the other end, I would go through a whole mock situation where I saved the ball by heroically throwing myself across the goal and tipping the ball round the post to the roar of the crowd. Then, of course, whenever the actual ball would come anywhere near me, I would miss it completely. I've always had the same effect on footballs whenever I go near them. They veer away from me as if we were two negative ends of a magnet being forced together.

Whenever the play went up the other end, a couple of the kids from the estate would get bored, and their attention would turn from the game to me. Adhering to the age-old stereotype of bullies picking on the weak, they would first of all check to make sure Wayne was up the other end of the pitch. Then they would find it hilarious to dare me to run around in circles. I would immediately oblige, knowing full well what would happen: my blood pressure would rise and mid-run I would suddenly grind to a halt and collapse, dropping like a stone on the spot, much to the amusement of the two lads.

I used to collapse all the time: on the way to school, during lessons, at break times. I was quite famous for it at school, and it became a bit of a challenge for other kids to see if they could get me to pass out. I did it so often, they called me 'Rubber Legs'.

I was once dared to go and ask Emma Baker for a kiss. Desperate to please, I jumped at the chance. This was slightly nerve-racking, as she was a girl I fancied very much – well, who didn't? Emma Baker was the best-looking girl in the whole of Lawrence Weston Junior School, easy, by a long chalk. Her sunny blonde hair danced around her perfectly smooth face and her massive deep-blue eyes were the size of the moon.

Goaded by a handful of giggling boys, I strutted across the playground towards Emma Baker in the extra-large school shorts that Mum had promised I'd grow into. Of course, I secretly relished putting on a bit of a show. I knew it was something they were scared to do, and that made it all the more enjoyable and risky. I was doing OK until I got to the point where I had to say something to her. When I actually stood face to face with Emma Baker, I suddenly came over all nervous. That raised my blood pressure, I felt my legs buckle and bend beneath me, and before I could even pucker up, everything went black. I slumped to the playground floor, not an unusual occurrence and a highly amusing one for the gathered audience of laughing kids. I lay there dreaming of Emma Baker.

Manic energy has been a characteristic of mine ever since. Indeed, it is a trait that has served me very well as a performer. But my whole life, people have constantly advised me to slow down or sit still – something I find impossible. If I ever have to undergo the torture of having to sit still for more than a second, I have a habit of jerking my leg up and down. It's like an automatic spasm. I refuse to sit still, which is a constant frustration to my wife.

Over the years, she has tried desperately – without success – to get me to stop for just a moment, to take a break from working and relax. She has, thank God, given up on booking any more holidays. That became too stressful and demanding for her because of my inability to sit on a beach or lie by a pool. She would book a holiday to get some rest, but come back a nervous wreck, in serious need of a couple of weeks away. Maybe one day I'll learn how to relax. But, for now, even thinking about it makes me feel anxious.

It was typical of my younger self that I would instantly agree to do whatever the bigger kids demanded of me. If they'd asked me to swim the Bristol Channel dressed as a sponge with a pocketful of bricks, I would – like some unquestioning nodding dog on the back shelf of a Ford Cortina – have at once assented to the request. When you think everyone is automatically against you, when you're seen as the school's resident idiot, you will do anything to be accepted. All the ridiculous things I agreed to do as a kid were in some way connected to this apparently futile quest for self-esteem. The problem was, the more I gave in to their ludicrous demands, the less they respected me. Being an outsider has helped my stand-up no end, but back then it was much more of a hindrance than a help.

I was desperate to be a dude, but was – sadly – always much more of a dork.

Welcome to the world of Lee Evans.

2. The Lawrence Weston Estate

I always felt that our family never fitted in anywhere. When I was growing up, it seemed as if we were living in our own world; you might call it 'The Evans Bubble'. There was never any money and somehow we always felt cut off from the people around us. Mum and Dad feared the outside world. We always had the sense that it was us against them. We were perpetual outsiders.

When I was a small boy, we lived on the very margins of conventional society. Part of the reason I always felt insecure as a child is that, because of Dad's peripatetic job, our family was constantly on the move. We rarely stayed long enough for me to feel settled in one place, as we travelled from one town to another. The one location where we did spend a lot of time was Bristol, where I was born. I lived there for eleven years, though there were frequent breaks when we followed Dad to his summer seasons all over the country. I remember, when I was little, we moved into a flat above a doctor's surgery in the city. At that stage, Dad worked on the bins. We all shared a bedroom that overlooked a bus stop. Dad always had trouble with the curtains. They weren't hooked on to the rail properly, and so one end would keep falling down. He hated it when that happened because the buses would stop outside, and he always thought the passengers on the top deck could see into our flat.

One morning he was woken by a familiar noise as, one by one, the hooks at the top of the curtain pinged off the rail. Angry and frustrated, Dad climbed out of bed and stomped in a rage over to the window. He picked up the curtain and climbed up on to the window-sill, attempting to hang the curtain back up. We all watched as Dad, mumbling obscenities, tried desperately to re-hang the curtain. He had just stuffed the last piece of curtain up between the rail and the pelmet when he stumbled and, to break his fall, grabbed both curtains, tearing them away from the rail and away from the window. Dad stood there in the window, holding fistfuls of curtain and completely naked, face to face with the passengers on the top deck of a bus that had just stopped outside.

We had no living room, so the doctor would let Dad, Wayne and me, still in my mother's arms, sit in the waiting room to watch the TV, which was permanently left on for the patients. It was a ridiculous scenario. Here was this family sitting there, Dad stinking to high heaven having worked on the bins all day. We were surrounded by people who had come to see the doctor for all sorts of ailments, and Dad would chat to them all. A man might walk in, coughing and spluttering, and Dad would ask, 'You all right, mate?'

'Flu, I think,' he would reply.

'Well,' Dad would advise, 'it's probably best you go home, take a couple of aspirin and stay in bed.'

'You think?' he'd ask.

'Well, that's all he's going to say,' Dad would answer, pointing towards the doctor's door.

Or if Dad was trying to watch the news and someone entered the waiting room and started moaning because he'd hurt his arm, Dad would start tutting and giving him a look. He would put his ear closer to the telly, as if trying to hear what the newsreader was saying. Living there was not really what the doctor ordered.

So, not long after, we left the flat above the doctor's surgery and moved on to the Lawrence Weston Estate, a large housing estate in Avonmouth that was, to say the least, rough and ready. We were the dispossessed, continually ducking and diving in a generally hopeless attempt to make ends meet. We were trying to get by – by any means necessary. Potentially, we were the ASBO generation long before ASBOs were even a twinkle in an authoritarian Home Secretary's eye.

As kids on that estate, we were like baboons at a safari park. If anyone left anything lying around, we'd have it. But our incessant monkeying about only alienated us further from mainstream society. These days, everyone goes on about middle-class this, middle-class that, but we didn't know what middle-class people were or what they thought of us because we didn't know any. There were times when we felt like travellers, moving from place to place without ever putting down roots. We never got any respect – and ever since then I've spent my whole life searching for it.

The Lawrence Weston Estate was like the Wild West. It was, for example, the sort of place where arson was an occupational hazard. On one occasion we were awoken in the middle of the night as a fire had started in the airing cupboard of one of the downstairs flats. Mum said it could have been started deliberately as residents would 'accidentally on purpose' set fire to their flats – 'Oh dear, I've dropped me match on the floor. I must quickly run to the shops, and by the time I get back the flat will be well cooked. That's a new lounge before Christmas right there!'

As long as you could prove it was an 'accident', then the council would come in and redecorate for you. That was nice if you liked woodchip wallpaper throughout and the whole place decked out in magnolia. But, if you ask me, that's just asking for snow blindness. And if you brushed up against it, you could end up with a whole armful of splinters.

The residents of the devastated flat would be temporarily re-housed while the council went in to rip out all the fire-damaged items. Then the problems really began – a brimming skip was just asking for trouble. The workmen would fill it with the contents from the flat, and overnight it would all disappear. You'd see the amazement on the council workers' faces; they filled the skip up with stuff, then when they returned the next day, like magic, it was completely empty. You could see them all scratching their heads and mumbling to each other, 'I could have sworn I filled this thing up.'

'Yeah, I saw you do it.'

You would look on in amusement as residents crept out after dark to see if there was anything of value in the skip, before they quickly darted back indoors, holding a slightly worse-for-wear picture or a table. Basically, the goods would be taken from the skip outside a fire-damaged flat and redistributed around different residences on the estate. Either that, or they were removed by the local kids, me included, carried round the back of the sheds and fashioned into ramps for our bikes to go over. A kitchen door on which to practise our Evel Knievel impersonations? Yey-ha!

Nothing was wasted on the Lawrence Weston. It was recycling before that word was even invented. Weeks later, you would call for a friend, his mum would ask if you'd like to come in and wait, and as you entered you'd be surrounded by stuff that you recognized from another flat. It was quite obvious that the picture of Prince Charles hanging on the wall had scorch marks all round the frame. Even Prince Charles looked confused by it all.

Like every close community which had no money, we would all come together on a big night. Someone would bring along illicit booze, someone else would come with fags that had fallen off the back of a lorry. We really knew how to party. It was great way of forgetting the daily grind.

Take New Year's Eve, always a memorable occasion on the estate. It was the one night when everyone really went for it. The thing to do on that night was to go outside on the stroke of midnight with any implement and make as much noise as possible. All the residents would gather at the entrance to the flats in a small hallway just by two rows of bins. Everyone would grab a bin-lid and wait for the moment. It must have looked like the musical *Stomp!* just before a performance, with everyone holding bits of garbage, waiting for the off to smash seven bells out of any poor inanimate object. Then, suddenly, you would hear a faint voice wafting from across the estate.

'Haaaapppy Neeeew Yeeeaaaar . . .'

It felt great to celebrate. God knows what we were actually celebrating, given that we had bugger-all! Nevertheless, it was good to feel like part of the community. Perhaps that's what we were celebrating – the fact that we all seemed to be in it together, helping each other whenever we could. It may have been considered by some as a shit-hole of a council estate, but it was our shit-hole of a council estate – and we were going to revel in it together!

And we would go nuts, banging our makeshift instruments and shouting at the top of our voices. Mum would be right in front of me, smashing a bin-lid on the concrete floor with one hand, fag in the other, shouting, 'Happy New Year!' I loved it. There was a genuine sense of belonging, of being one big (more or less) happy family, celebrating together. It was a rattling good show.

Then everyone would end up at someone's flat for a drink and a knees-up. We kids would be either still out on the street or gathered in another room, playing. Even when it got to the early hours of the morning, and I was physically exhausted, I refused to admit I was tired. When I was five or six, I'd be asked constantly if I'd like to go up to our flat to bed, but there was no way – I might miss something! Even after all the other kids had either fallen asleep or collapsed and been carried off to bed by their parents, I'd be sitting quietly in the corner of the kitchen, listening to all the grown-ups chatting. I learned so much about life from just staying there inconspicuously, observing the adult world.

By now, they would be very drunk and at the stage where local grievances began to surface. One particularly memorable New Year's Eve, I was watching with interest as two neighbours begin to get more and more irritated with each other – nothing major, just the usual 'You don't keep your piece of the landing as tidy as everyone else's'. At that moment, I caught sight of Doreen, another neighbour, a short, hunched, scruffy woman with small, beady eyes and a pointy nose. Doreen liked a drink, I think, and was already unsteady on her feet. She suddenly flung her arms in the air and announced: 'Bollocks to this. I'm off to the toilet.'

Nobody took any notice, but just carried on arguing. After a minute or two, there was an almighty scream from the direction of the toilet. Everyone stopped what they were doing and listened, a look of concern on their faces.

'Doreen?' enquired Mum.

Everyone rushed out of the kitchen. I followed and found them all gathered around the toilet door. 'Doreen? You all right, love?'

'Mo, I am MOT aff might!'

'Have you got a problem in there?'

'Me teeff aff gom bown the bog.'

'Let's have a look.'

'Well, how can you fee from vere? The frigging boor's shut.'

'Then open the door. Silly cow.'

Doreen opened the door with some embarrassment and stood in the entrance, swaying and hanging on to the handle to steady herself. Poor Doreen had lent over the toilet at the same time as she pulled the flush, and her teeth had fallen into the bowl and been whooshed away. Looking at her face, I personally thought they'd jumped ship.

'Quick!' shouted Dad, taking charge. Everyone bundled down the stairs and out into what was now daylight, and over to the manhole cover that serviced the flats. Dad lifted the cover as everyone gathered round.

'You lot,' he ordered a couple of us kids. 'Go and pull all the flushes and turn on all the taps.' We raced off. Beginning at the top flat, we started turning as many taps and pulling as many flushes as we were able. We then ran back downstairs to the waiting crowd at the drain hole.

Doreen emerged from the flats and staggered over, swearing all the way. 'Buddy peeth! They're too loose anyway, ssshhhlipping all ober me gob.' She arrived at the hole and squeezed through the crowd. Looking into the gaping maw, she moaned through her gums, 'Sssstufff em, they'll be in the Avon by mow.'

Everybody watched in nervous expectation as the water gushed from the pipe into the T-junction that took the waste and sewage away. 'I think they might be halfway to Avonmouth by now, Dor . . .'

Doubt was seeping into the gathered crowd. 'Put the lid back on,' said Doreen, disconsolately. People began filing away dejectedly, back into the flats.

Dad picked up the lid and was about to drop it back into place. 'Wait!' he shouted. Everyone ran back to look down the hole. And there, poking out of the gushing outlet, were the smiling teeth – or were they in fact grimacing, having been apprehended trying to make good their escape? Either way, they were edging themselves slowly

out and about to fall into the T-junction. With no concern for health and safety – we had never heard of those
words back then – Dad reached down and snatched them
up.

Picking off the debris and wet toilet paper, he handed
them to Doreen, who, without hesitating, popped them
back into her mouth.

'Cheers. Now where did I put me drink?'

And, with that, she staggered quite nonchalantly back
through the crowd and into the flats, leaving everyone
stunned.

That kind of incident was commonplace on the Lawrence Weston. We existed on not much at all. I suppose
some people might have seen us as outlaws or even
crossed the street to avoid us because of what we looked
like. But they didn't know anything about us – we did our
best with what we had. We had no knowledge of any
other way of existing. Life may have been tough, but we
just got on with it.

And if we picked up a painting of Prince Charles along
the way, so much the better!

3. My Family

That feeling of being excluded from the mainstream was drummed into me from birth by my dad, a man who gave the impression that he was constantly at odds with the world. In those days, his favourite gesture was to look up the sky, tut and say, in tones dripping with sarcasm, 'Thank you very much . . . for nothing! Someone up there doesn't like me very much!'

At times, he was not an easy person to have around. He was forever fuming about the hand fate had dealt us. He wrestled with the feeling that he would never be accepted and constantly railed against his lowly status. He felt that everyone else was having a fantastic time at a party to which he had not been invited.

The trouble with Dad was that because he was constantly expecting to be attacked, he was forever on his guard. Convinced he was always being persecuted, he carried around an almighty chip on his shoulder. He also lived with an overwhelming fear and loathing of authority. An ex-teddy boy, he would refuse to back down if he believed he was right.

But then, in the blink of an eye, he could be your best mate and a funny, loving father. He was hilarious at times. The problem for Wayne and me was knowing how to tread that tightrope. We could never tell which way Dad was going to turn.

When he wanted to, he could charm the birds off the trees – although there weren't many birds, or trees for that matter, on the Lawrence Weston. When Wayne and I were small, Dad was still working on the docks. But he gradually started to pick up more paid work in the evenings, singing in pubs. Like the two generations before him, he had the Evans singing gene. When my granddad belted out 'Land of My Fathers', tears would fill his eyes. 'Hear that,' he would wail, 'that's proper music, that is.' My great-great auntie was also an amazing singer, who played on the Welsh and English music-hall circuits. Performing was in the Evans blood. Even though it took me an age to twig, I suppose it was really no surprise that I eventually ended up on stage.

Late at night, Dad would come back from his shows, burst into our bedroom clutching a handful of pound notes and regale us with tales of that night's performance. It may only have been a show in a pub or a club, but to us it seemed like an impossibly glamorous universe that existed only on the telly. At those moments, the glittering world of showbiz briefly entered our grotty flat. We felt that, just temporarily, we were touched by magic. It seemed as if there might be a way out of the drabness of the estate. It felt like there was hope.

The glittering world of showbiz might have seemed light years away from our humble council flat but, strangely, it kept knocking on our front door. The two apparently irreconcilable worlds collided – one dark and desperate, the other seemingly shiny and out of reach for us mere mortals. It may have appeared impossibly remote, but I suppose I was already getting a glimpse of the glitter.

I still vividly remember the first time I saw Dad perform. I must have been six or seven. Wayne and I stood clutching Mum's hand at the back of a pub as he came on stage. Suddenly – kapow! – he started singing and we were mesmerized. We couldn't believe how brilliant and how powerful he was onstage. He was like a force of nature, a second Tom Jones. He could blow a crowd away with the sheer potency of his performance. It was as if he was saying to the audience, 'You're going to have this and there's nothing you can do about it. We're going to blast the roof off!'

Dad appeared to be releasing all his pent-up anger. It hit you in the pit of the stomach with a rare energy. It was electrifying. To see all these people transfixed by Dad was an extraordinary experience and such a departure from the mundanity of our daily lives. His word was law at home, and his magnetic performance only added to the potent myth of his god-like domestic status.

But then, on other days, the mood in our flat could be decidedly dark. Often, reality would bite the morning after a show. There was never enough money and Dad would soon be worrying about bills again. His simmering sense of resentment often boiled over into the most fearful rages. He had a ferocious temper – and unfortunately, probably because of her background, so did Mum. When they went at it like cat and dog with helmets on, Wayne and I would cower in the corner. We wanted to be anywhere other than in the midst of that horrendous row.

When aroused, Dad's temper would possess his whole

body. He was like the Incredible Hulk – although he turned red rather than green. It was like living with an angry traffic light. Then, just as quickly, the rage was gone, leaving him exhausted, wondering what had happened and apologizing, as if the fury had gripped someone else entirely. We lived in a state of constant fear about when he would next blow his top.

Dad's rages only added to our sense of being outsiders. Because of his insecurities, he would drill us never to ask for anything. Whenever we met someone new, we were taught to say 'please', 'thank you' and – above all – 'sorry'. We were never allowed to connect properly with anyone, and that made us feel cut off from the world. That's why I kept myself to myself as a child, terrified of stepping out of line. I would play the fool, but only to mask my innate shyness. I lived in mortal terror of standing out from the crowd, in case I was doing something wrong. I was a textbook misfit. If there was an instruction booklet on how to be one, I could have written it.

Dad was never far from snapping. When he was at home in Bristol, he was unable to relax properly. He was always irritable, always fretting about where the next meal was coming from. His mind was constantly plagued by anxiety. He would sit in the chair bouncing his leg up and down, biting his nails, moaning or shouting at the telly. In his presence, you were constantly treading on eggshells.

Whenever I was out and about with him as a kid, I always felt things could flare up at any moment. His mood fluctuated wildly. Sometimes Wayne and I walked down the street with him having the time of our life. But it would only take one tiny incident for him to explode. He had no blue touch paper – he was a spontaneously com-busting rocket. He would never just let it lie. He was like a Jack Russell; once his teeth sank into you, they were never going to let go. That was the prevailing storm force in the house when we were kids – and it left us feeling bewildered and bedraggled.

Dad viewed the world through cynical, angry eyes and had a sardonic way about him that could be hurtful. It was not nice to witness in those days. But, seen from afar, his rages must have seemed quite comical. So people would often be doubled up with laughter at his desperate, self-defeating attempts to gain respect.

You knew when he was about to blow a fuse because his whole body would change. A spasm of irritation would cross his face and he would stretch his neck for-ward, pulling his shoulders back. Then he would bunch up his fists so tight that his knuckles would turn white. At the same time, his wild glare was magnified by thick glasses that made his eyes look like rolling hubcaps on a clown's car. The final tell-tale sign he was about to blow was that he would calmly push his glasses back up his nose with his finger. Then – boom! – 'Right, that's it!'

And he was off.

Terror would permeate every part of my body at those moments. It wasn't just Dad's fury that scared me, but the sounds that always accompanied his eruptions. Hearing Mum desperately screaming his name over and over a few feet away – as if she were the increasingly unhinged corner-man standing behind the ropes at a prize fight – only seemed to inflame his demons even more.

These outbursts would always come out of nothing.

A perfectly innocent remark would set Dad off on an expletive-laden excursion into the land of the red mist. It was as if I had pulled the pin from a hand grenade or flicked an angry switch. Nowadays I would find it really funny, but back then it was pretty scary.

If we went anywhere by car, for example, there was always the risk of an explosion. Once behind the wheel, in an instant Dad could metamorphose into a raging bull. As we drove along, we would watch him change from a mild-mannered, hilariously funny man into a shrieking maniac. Mum would sit, terrified, in the passenger's seat next to him, living in fear of the next flare-up.

I remember on one occasion, some smart-suited commuter driving a flash motor made the terrible mistake of inadvertently cutting Dad up at a roundabout. That was it. Dad was instantaneously livid. His anger went from nought to sixty in about two seconds.

For Dad, that perceived slight was like a gauntlet thrown at his feet – there was no way he'd let anyone get away with that. 'I'm gonna kick that bloke's teeth in as soon as he stops,' he muttered, with barely suppressed rage.

As Wayne and I cringed in terror on the back seat, Dad became consumed by the idea of following this commuter all the way back to his house and having it out with him. After half an hour of frantically pursuing the guy home, we watched on in horror as Dad jumped out of the car, his blood still boiling. The innocent commuter parked up on his drive, only to be confronted by a snarling Dad leaping out of a nearby privet hedge.

'Who are you?' the guy asked.

'Never mind who I am, who's this?' Dad replied, holding up his fist threateningly.

The poor, unsuspecting commuter – whose only mistake in twenty-five years' driving back and forth to work had been unwittingly to cut up this nut case – then received a punch up the pinstripe on his own driveway. Blood dripping from his nose, he was only able to mumble, 'What was that for?' as Dad stormed back to our car.

'Nobody gets away with cutting me up!' replied the Incredible Hulk – sorry, Dad.

But just ten minutes later, he would be back to being riotously funny. He would spot a helicopter overhead and take on the guise of a policeman, pretending to talk into his crackly radio or swerving on to a grass verge as if in pursuit of a rogue terrorist.

He also had a very loud laugh – you couldn't sit with him in public because it was too embarrassing. *Round the Horne*, *The Goons*, *Hancock's Half-Hour* and *The Bonzo Dog Doo-Dah Band* were always on in our house – like they were on a loop – and he would sit in the lounge laughing uproariously. Then, a click of the finger and – boom! – he would explode again.

That was life with Dad. It was always lively, and you never quite knew where you were. It was like living on the slopes of Mount Etna. It was beautiful and sunny at times, but you were constantly living in the shadow of the volcano and you could never quite be sure when it would next erupt and engulf everything in its path. No wonder I grew up a nervous wreck!

*

The other huge character who bestrode my childhood was my elder brother, Wayne. Although he is only two years older than me, he would always fearlessly spring to my defence – and sometimes get a beating for his troubles from much bigger lads.

But we were very different characters. I was constantly on edge and would always think of the worst-case scenario, whereas Wayne was the life and soul of the party – he had much more of a 'live and let live' disposition. He has always been a very funny man to be with and would constantly play jokes on me when we were growing up.

For instance, when we were teenagers and Dad was out working the pubs and clubs in the evening, Mum would like to go with him, leaving us alone in the flat. One time, Wayne got hold of a copy of the film *The Exorcist*. After watching it together, unbeknownst to me, he sneaked into our shared bedroom and loosened the legs of my bed. Then, when I got in that night, my bed shifted violently across the room, just like the girl's in the film. After the bed finally settled, all I could hear through the darkness was Wayne giggling uncontrollably.

Then there was the old 'Lee, look out, there's a car coming!' gag he used to love to pull. He'd shout that to me every time we crossed an empty road together, ensuring that I would always leap into the air with shock while he would fall about clutching his sides with mirth. It usually had the desired effect.

Feeling flush one day when we were about twelve and ten, Dad bought us a couple of small fishing rods, as well as all the bits and bobs one might need for a spot of angling. Not a massive fan of fishing, I did ask if I could have the money to spend on something else – like a giant bag of sweets – but was outranked by Wayne's more elevated position. Wayne and I got on pretty well, we always liked to banter and laugh together. But there was never any doubt about who was the senior partner in our relationship.

Early the next morning, the decidedly more excited Wayne and I quietly slipped out of bed and began preparing for the day's fishing with the newly purchased kit. Wayne readied the rods out in the hall, priming them with floats, hooks and weights. 'It'll save messing about when we get there,' he whispered through gritted teeth.

As Wayne set up the rods, I was ordered to make sarnies for later on in the day. I made Wayne the snack he liked best, cheese and onion crisp sandwiches, and then prepared my own favourite: a thick layer of tomato ketchup between two hefty slices of bread. But I had no intention of waiting till lunchtime to eat it. I was eager to have it for breakfast. Once the intoxicating scent of that ketchup had wafted up my hooter, I just had to start munching on it as soon as possible. There was no thought about what I might have for lunch. Once the olfactory receptors in my nose were stimulated and sending signals to my belly, it was curtains for that ketchup sandwich.

Closing the back door carefully, so as not to wake Mum and Dad, we loaded up for the long walk across the vast field to the reservoir. As usual, I seemed to be the designated packhorse, the one who had somehow ended up having to carry most of the stuff. 'Come on, hurry up,' Wayne groaned at me, before disappearing off carrying only his rod. He left me looking like a walking display stand at a fishing show, with a tackle box, two fold-up chairs and a fishing rod all hanging off me. But, at the same time, my hand conveniently slipped into a carrier bag and located my tomato sauce sandwich. There and then I decided I would have a chew on it during the long walk across the field.

I rattled around the flat to where Wayne was already waiting impatiently to cross the road over to the field on the other side. With the beautiful-smelling sandwich bobbing around in front of my face, I staggered along the short front garden path, weighed down with all that stuff. I joined Wayne at the kerbside, and he held his arm across to stop me – Mum and Dad always told him, 'Whatever you do, look after Lee.' We looked both ways, up and down the road. Nothing coming. But I wasn't paying much attention. I was too busy concentrating on taking a bite out of my delicious sandwich, so I left the Green Cross Code to Wayne as we stepped off the kerb.

As we reached the middle of the road, right on cue, Wayne turned to me and did his customary 'Lee, look out, there's a car coming!' joke. As usual, for dramatic effect after shouting, he darted off to the other side of the road and the safety of the pavement. I, of course, by now knew his little game and decided this time I wasn't going to fall for it – after all, how could I run anyway with all the weight I was carrying? So I stood my ground in the middle of the road, looking at Wayne and triumphantly taking a big bite from my sandwich. With a mouth full of ketchup, I laughed at him, waving the slices of bread in front of my face, scoffing at his little game.

'Buuuuuttttt . . . Theeeeerrrree's aaaaaa caaaaaarrrrr, Leeeeeee . . .'

BAM!

I had never heard the story of 'Cry Wolf'.

And I never saw it coming. The car thudded into my side, and everything went black. According to Wayne, I bounced off the front of the vehicle, flew ten feet into the air, completed a full flip, then swallow-dived to the ground. I landed with a crash, like a sack of spuds, on my back twenty feet away from the car.

Wayne looked on, stunned. He was rooted to the spot as the driver, an elderly man with white shoes, grey hair and beard, climbed distraught from his car. Stumbling along the middle of the road towards me, he began crying out, 'Oh my God, sorry, I wasn't looking where I was going, I'm so sorry.' He reached down to where I was lying on my back in the road, surrounded by fishing tackle and with my eyes firmly shut. Suddenly he stopped, pinned to the spot, and his jaw dropped open. Wayne told me later that the poor man's heart must have skipped a few thumps. My face appeared a terrifying mess, completely soaked in blood.

The man fell to his knees. Crouching over me, he began swaying, moaning and wailing, 'What have I done? Oh God, look what I've done!'

Wayne snapped out of it, ran over and stood looking down at the man knelt over me. Wayne was angry with him. 'All right, mate, give it a rest. Lee? Lee? You all right, mate?'

I flapped my eyelids open, the blue sky and clouds came into focus and there was a white-haired man hunched over me, raving and rambling on about God and stuff. I looked down and saw that his palms were facing the sky. 'Oh my God, oh my God, what am I going to do?' he shouted. For a moment, I thought I must have died and gone to heaven.

I remember thinking, 'Oh no, if I'm dead, Dad's going to kill me!'

I began frantically feeling parts of my body, checking to see if I was all in one piece. My face felt cold and wet. I wiped it with the back of my hand. Then I held my hand to my face to take a look.

Blood! Lots of it!

A cold chill ran right through me. My face must be mushed, I thought, that's what this bloke is moaning about. Alarmed, I sat bolt upright in the road, stared at the man and screamed for my life. The man looked at me for a moment then began screaming back at me. That scared the living daylights out of me, because now I didn't know who or what he was screaming at. I thought that maybe my face was in an even worse mess than I'd thought, puréed perhaps. So I screamed even louder back at him.

While we yelled at each other there in the road, instinctively I brought my hands back up to my face and felt the cold blood dripping down it. Reacting instantly, I pulled my hands away and looked down at them, drenched in bright red liquid. Wait a moment! Ever so gingerly, I licked the end of my fingers. Ketchup!

I stopped screaming and looked up towards Wayne for help. He had already twigged about the ketchup and smiled knowingly. He dropped his fishing rod to the floor and buried his face in his hands, perhaps out of relief that I was OK, perhaps to hide his giggles. The man looked at Wayne, then at me. Puzzled, his screaming petered out into a small whimper and then fizzled out into silence. He knelt there for a moment, quietly scrutinizing my face. Then his big grey bushy eyebrows locked together in the middle of his forehead and his tiny ice-blue eyes narrowed to the size of pinheads. He dipped one finger into the ketchup covering my hands and licked it. A look of fury suddenly crossed his face, as he realized he'd been duped.

But I didn't wait around for his reaction. Knowing I would be in trouble, I jumped to my feet and ran home at full speed, leaving a trail of fishing tackle, fold-up chairs and a rod behind me.

Wayne said the old man got even more angry after that, clambering back into his car, ranting on about bloody kids not crossing roads properly and smearing themselves in ketchup and giving decent citizens like him a right old shock.

I never went fishing again.

But for days afterwards, Wayne couldn't stop laughing about it.

So that was the environment I grew up in. A place full of anger and hardship, of scrapes and accidents, but also of love and laughter. We scrabbled around on the margins of society, but we also had terrific fun – just as long as no one cut Dad up when he was driving.

4. The Outsider

As Dad slowly became more established in the world of show business, he left his job at the docks and began to travel all over the place for bookings. We went with him, frequently having to move schools before returning once more to Bristol. One year, he was doing a long summer season in Blackpool, and Mum managed to blag Wayne and me into the local school for the last two months of Dad's run.

As we were hauled up in front of the local education authority in an oak-panelled room, Mum pleaded on our behalf with one of the tweed suits. He sat there, resting his leather elbows on the desk and looking down his nose in dismay at these oiks who had somehow talked their way into his office.

Irene Handl-style, my mum adopted a fake posh accent and said, 'Ah, for the life of me, I think school places are vital for their education.'

Wayne and I looked at each other thinking, 'Education? What's she on about? There's not a brain cell between us!' I was eight years old, but I remember it like it was yesterday.

Anyway, we got into a school. The second day I was there, the teacher, Mrs Taylor, set the class a test, but a test on work I had no idea about. As Mrs Taylor gave out the test and all the kids around me fell into silence with eyes down, I just dipped my head so no one could see me, and I began crying.

The next day, Mrs Taylor gave out the results. A scary cross between Ann Widdecombe and Miss Ewell, the terrifying teacher from *Please, Sir!*, she called out one by one the names of all the children in the class, followed by their marks. Filled with dread, I waited with a knotted stomach, willing her not to call out my name. She called out the last person's name and mark, but didn't mention my score, which I knew must have been atrocious. To my great relief, she just carried on with the lesson.

But then an interfering busybody of a boy put his hand in the air. 'Yes?' enquired Mrs Taylor, smiling and exposing teeth stained red by the generous amounts of lipstick smeared on to her thin crimson lips.

'You forgot the new lad.' He pointed at me.

I wanted to run, and to keep running all the way home to where Mum was. I didn't want to tell her that I'd failed, that I wasn't liked, that I didn't fit in – she would have told me to go back, to stop being stupid – but I just wanted to be with her, where I felt safest. When she wrapped her arms around me, I felt like nothing could hurt me and in those moments nothing else mattered.

I began sweating. I felt alone.

'Yes,' Mrs Taylor said, smug, calmly rising from her seat. She swaggered around her table, nose in the air. Without looking at me, she demanded I come to the front of the class.

I rose nervously and quietly walked up to her.

'Stand up there, Lee Evans, let us all see you,' she demanded, pointing at the top of her desk.

I stepped hesitantly on to her chair and on to her table at the front of the class, head down, hands clasped in front of me, and waited.

'What you are looking at,' she began, strolling magisterially between the desks towards the back of the class, 'is a disappointment, a failure in every sense of the word.' She turned back, staring at each child as she passed. 'This young man . . .' she carried on.

I don't know why I did it – it was an automatic reaction – but I began miming, mouthing her words as she spoke and impersonating her swagger behind her back.

The class began to giggle. Mrs Taylor swivelled round and looked daggers at me. I immediately reverted back to my submissive little schoolboy act. She stared briefly at me with suspicion, then resumed from where she had left off. 'This young man is a prime example of a failure . . .'

I began imitating her again, this time with more exaggerated movements. The other kids couldn't help themselves; they knew they shouldn't, but the whole class burst into laughter. I got carried away. I didn't know it yet, but this was a good crowd and I was going well.

I was so intoxicated by their laughter that I didn't notice Mrs Taylor standing next to me, glaring. Then, all of a sudden, I felt her beside me. I stopped and slowly turned. There she was, looking up at me. Face clenched, eyes raging and blood-shot, prim, lacquered hair waving about like the wild woman of Borneo, she exploded hysterically. 'Get to the headmaster's office now!' she shouted, straining the last words out of her empty lungs.

I got the cane that day, but I learned a very useful defensive tool that would stay with me for the rest of my life. I wasn't aware of it at the time, but one day I would even get paid for it. That's not to say it's right – if everyone did it, there would be anarchy. But I realized that at last I'd found something at which I could excel.

I never really conformed at school. I had so few positive learning experiences as a pupil that I can more or less recall each and every occasion I was stimulated. When my interest was piqued, it was as if I had awoken momentarily from a comatose state. I felt enthused, excited, but then we would have to change schools and move on. And just as suddenly as it had begun, it was over and I was out of kilter again.

The problem was, Dad's job meant we were always on the move. As he got busier as a performer, we were constantly shifting from place to place. I was at school in Bristol one term, Southport the next, then Eastbourne, Blackpool, back to Bristol again, then eventually to Billericay. So I got used to thinking that things were always going to be temporary – friends, school, where we were staying.

There was never any time for teachers to include me in what was going on, show me how their system worked. How could they? I was never around long enough. So I kept safely out of the way, reclusive, sitting at the back of the class, the new boy, retreating, wandering around in my own imaginary world.

Agonizingly shy, I would sit there all day in the classroom, heart pounding away, face flushed and sweaty, head bowed, trying not to make any eye contact, just staring blankly at the workbook that was put in front of me, in complete confusion and terrified of being mocked. I've always been odd. I'm just not part of the system, the mainstream, the establishment, the norm. I've always been the weird boy at the back of the class.

But if you point me out, the focus is thrown without warning towards me, and I will play the clod, the goofball or the klutz, stumbling in at the wrong time from the sidelines to disrupt. So used am I to being the oddball, I actually feel safer there. On the edge is good. It's a nervous reaction, I think, a kind of physical, mental, automatic form of self-defence. If I am suddenly thrust out in front of some lights, I'm like one of those Duracell battery-operated rabbits. I'm off. I never stop.

For as long as I can remember I've been out of step with everyone and everything that's going on around me. It's the void where I feel safest. That day in Mrs Taylor's class, I just did what came naturally. I wasn't even aware I was doing it.

All I knew was that suddenly I was accepted, regarded. I didn't understand it at the time, but comedy by sheer accident would become the vehicle into which I would channel all the stuff I saw and felt. It would be a zone I could visit where no one could tell me I was doing something wrong. Comedy would become the one place where I was able to fit in. I found real life a struggle. Only on stage did I feel at home.

5. The Early Days

The Lawrence Weston was the only constant in my life. We'd go back there after every summer season and it was the place where I did a lot of my growing up. The estate backed on to a wide, barren piece of scrubland, interspersed with parking facilities for lorries, allotments, ditches and streams. But mostly it was wasteland awaiting developers' careless drawings. Sandwiched between this vast space and the sky was a huge chemical works. Beyond that was the point where the M4 motorway – which went from east to west – met the M5 – which went north to south. It was known throughout the estate as 'the gift shop', for reasons which will become clear.

When I was nine or ten, I would sit for hours at night staring out across the blackness of the field at the sprawling chemical works, which was lit up like a giant fallen Christmas tree. I would pick out cars' tiny headlights travelling along the motorway and follow them, trying to predict which way they might go. I was able to tell whether they were going north or south by the fact that their lights either turned red or remained white – hey, there wasn't much on the TV back then! But I'd also invent the people who might be in the cars, where they were going and for what reason. I would even act out the conversations that might be going on inside the car while sitting on the windowsill of my bedroom.

One whiff of snow would always cause a large crop of road accidents – I never understood why no one ever did anything about that treacherous junction. Every year, without fail, I would watch from our bedroom window the distant blue flashing lights of the police, fire brigade and ambulances. Clustered around a smoking heavy goods vehicle, they would be cutting some poor bugger out of the cab, always at the exact same black spot, the lethal Avonmouth turn-off. That was the junction the heavy goods lorries took to get them down to the docks, either to drop off their loads or pick something up from the foreign container ships.

There was never a long gap between the accident actually happening and the alarm being raised. Someone had a constant eye on the motorway in the winter months, particularly when black ice was on the road. For the usual suspects prowling around the estate, this made conditions ripe for potential booty.

There was no siren or alarm bell – somehow we just knew, we felt the buzz across the estate. It was like a gold rush: grown men still in their slippers, young boys trying to get there before anybody else, a few women with hair still in rollers, a horde of residents all shapes and sizes running full pelt across the back field, jumping over the tall scrub grass towards the motorway, desperate to see who would grab the first pickings from the over-turned load scattered across the carriageway.

To be honest, I wasn't too enthusiastic about the stuff that came off those trucks. The most I ever got was a big box of over-sized men's Y-fronts that Mum used to clean the flat with for more than a year. So my full-speed running was more of a 'let's take a wander over and see what there is'. By the time I got there, anyway, it was usually too late. Like a bunch of hyenas, the locals had by then well and truly stripped the carcass of any real meat.

As you approached the scene, you would pass a line of men, women and kids, all walking back across the field, each one enthusiastically clutching their bounty. A young boy would be struggling towards us fighting to hold on to an industrial-sized tin of something with no label on. 'Pineapple chunks!' he would shout as he passed, face all flushed with excitement.

'What are you going to do with that? It's massive!' I'd say.

'I don't know yet, but I'll find something. Perhaps pine-apple pie,' he'd reply as he staggered back to the estate.

Now more curious to see what the truck was actually carrying, I walked to the edge of the field. From a sloping embankment there, you could look across at the full extent of the accident on the motorway. A lorry would be lying on its side like a dead whale. It had obviously come around the turn-off too fast, hit some black ice and kept on going till it hit the barrier, turned over and strewn its load. Its now-empty boxes were sprawled across both sides of the motorway and the driver's cab was sur-rounded by the blue flashing lights of the emergency services trying to free the poor truck driver. They were all far too preoccupied to bother with the scavengers forag-ing around the trailer for loot.

'Bollocks.' I turned round and looked down. At the bottom of the bank, a young man was stamping his foot on the soggy grass in anger. Surrounded by boxes of cigarettes, he was frantically scratching his head as he tried to figure out how to carry the pile he'd made of about two hundred packs of fags.

'What's that?' I shouted down to him. It was just to make conversation really – I could see he was hacked off.

'Piss off, Evans, you runt. They're mine!'

The flashing blue lights and a crashed truck on the motorway always interested people on the estate. Yes, they wanted to see if there was anything of value to nick, but they were also curious about the accident itself – maybe they could do something to help. It might sound morbid, but I think it brought a bit of excitement to an otherwise uneventful day.

But on one occasion there was an accident that stopped me going across the field ever again.

It was about seven o'clock in the evening – I remember the time because *Space Nineteen Ninety-Nine* was on the telly. I loved it, but not enough to miss a lorry crash. When the word went out that another one had toppled over, I made my way across the field, as always a little late in getting to the scene. But this time it was different. As I approached the usual large cluster of flashing blue lights, I could hear the muffled sounds of the emergency services barking orders to each other in the distance.

I was puzzled. There wasn't the usual mischievous giggling from the looters. No one had even passed me with anything. Perhaps there was nothing on the truck. I could only see the outline of people silhouetted by the white floodlights set up by the fire service. Everyone just seemed to be standing at the edge of the field looking down the embankment. Eager to see what was going on,

I ran the last few yards, squeezed through the crowd and peered down.

The lorry had been travelling so fast, it had smashed through the barrier and rolled down the bank into the massive ditch between the motorway and the field. The emergency teams were desperately trying to cut the driver from the smashed and dented cab.

Unfortunately, the cattle trailer the truck had been pulling wasn't getting the same attention. It lay on its side, having been violently twisted. The whole back panel had peeled away like the lid of a tin can. Cows lay dead or dying in all sorts of odd shapes around the scene. They had obviously been thrown from the trailer.

I was only about ten at the time, and it was difficult for me to fathom. As I watched the emergency services busy concentrating on the driver in the cab, I was confused as to why they were completely oblivious to the desperate, stomach-churning cries from the animals. Couldn't anyone else hear that blood-curdling noise?

One cow lay on its stomach, struggling to stand, but was too injured, and so it just bobbed its head back and forth. Meanwhile, there were cows still packed in the cattle trailer. Their body heat and panicked breathing spurted vapour and steam out through the air slits along the sides of the trailer. It merged with the rest of the heat generated by all the bodies and hung in the air above, creating a sort of dry ice. It was a dramatic, intense scene.

I looked around at all the people just staring down at the poor animals and found it difficult to understand why no one was being affected by the sound of their crying. I couldn't help myself. I tentatively began taking small steps

41

down the grassy bank towards the trailer. I didn't know what I would do exactly, but I thought maybe I could go and hug one of the animals and talk to it.

But as I stepped forward, a car screeched to a halt on the motorway, and two huge men dressed in lumberjack jeans and boots jumped out of a plain white van. The driver shouted down to me, 'You, get back!'

Then, as he turned to a policeman and began talking, the other man efficiently opened the doors at the back of the van, took out two long cases and began walking down the embankment towards the cattle trailer. In a workmanlike fashion, he placed the two cases side by side on the grass and flipped open the lids. He revealed – and this was quite obvious to me as a boy obsessed with comics and American cop shows – the two parts of a gun. He took the pieces out of their cases and began assembling them, checking the barrel and trigger system as he went.

Now I knew what was going to happen. The other man descended the grassy bank and was handed the gun by his friend. He swung it under his arm, cradling it on his wrist, pointed at the ground. He inserted the pack into the gun and slammed it in with the palm of his hands. It was loaded. I knew, as I'd seen them do it on the TV.

It was a shock to me at ten years of age to watch that man with the gun stand over the first cow that lay in front of him. There was panic and fear in the animal's eyes, and the others back in the trailer started to get restless. They were moving and shifting around.

They knew.

As the man lifted the gun and cocked it, I turned my

head one way, then the other. All the people were just staring down at what was going on. Why weren't the grown-ups going to do anything to help that cow?

The cow looked up in terror at the big man. It began trying desperately to get to its feet but, because of its injuries, it was impossible. My gut wrenched, and I wanted to run down the embankment, but I knew I wasn't allowed. I didn't know what to do.

The man pointed the gun at the cow's head. Its eyes widened with fear.

It knew.

I knew.

I turned and ran. I ran as fast as I could, stumbling over the knobbly grass, a huge shadow in front of me cast by the floodlights back where the crash was. I didn't want to hear the sound of the gun.

I just kept seeing the look of helplessness in the cow's eyes. My lungs began to burn, I was running so fast. But still I wasn't able to run fast enough. I heard the crack of gunfire. It stopped me in my tracks. I was confused. It didn't sound like the guns you hear on the TV. This was a small pop. I knew it was the gun, but I couldn't help thinking, 'What a crap gun sound.'

I stood silently in the middle of the field, trying to make sense of what had just happened. The twinkling yellow lights of the motorway stretched out before me. The bright full moon gave the dark, ominous clouds that sailed across the sky a silvery-blue silhouette. I looked towards the flats, our flat, on the estate. I was in no hurry to run home. All I could do there was sit in my bedroom and think about what I'd just seen and heard. I felt content to stay where I was, on my own in my remoteness in the middle of this field.

I looked back at the illuminated, surreal scene of the accident, the tiny outlines of people moving around the top of the embankment and looking down into the ditch.

'Pop!'

I jumped. I'd heard another one. I put my fingers in my ears, so I couldn't hear any more and tried to make myself feel better by thinking I wasn't a part of it, like I was looking down from a distant Olympian height. But then I rolled to my knees and began crying uncontrollably.

'Why couldn't I have done something? I didn't do anything!'

It was some time before I could go to bed at night without staring up at the ceiling partially illuminated by the distant lights of the motorway and without thinking about the plaintive look in that animal's eyes.

Another childhood incident that had a profound impact on me happened soon after, and it was an experience that rammed home to me the fact that my family appeared to hail from an entirely different planet.

People often ask me the same question: what was your first break in show business? Well, it might not surprise anyone to hear that it was in actual fact a ludicrous, completely voluntary appearance in an item which topped the bill of the local evening news in Bristol.

It was 1974, the time of the industrial action that swept through the country faster than Arthur Scargill's hair on a motorbike. It was bad enough coping with the power cuts inflicted on us by one lot trying to get their own back on

Ted Heath, let alone having to deal with the rotting stench of waste after another lot – the rubbish collective – voted for an all-out strike.

So, after some cursing and ranting about how if he ran the country he could do it a damn sight better than those bastards in Downing Street, Dad came up with the cock-eyed idea of taking the rubbish to the local dump ourselves.

The bins downstairs on the estate were bulging over with stinking refuse, and everyone in our flat was gradually losing their upper-arm strength from continually pushing the well-packed rubbish down into our kitchen bin.

There were no bin bags then, so we emptied as much stinking waste as possible into carrier bags, boxes, even our pockets, then loaded it into Dad's Ford Cortina and headed over to the tip. It wasn't far away, about three minutes in the car – I could walk it in fifteen.

We arrived at the gate to a small but vocal welcoming party. A few members of the transport union were picketing the gate. A local news crew was there, too. Reporting on such a small-scale demo didn't exactly push back the boundaries of investigative journalism, but the way they were acting you'd have thought we'd just arrived at the gates of the Gaza Strip.

As soon as we pulled up, the bloke with the microphone was banging on the car window, shouting at my dad: 'Will you be going in, what's your name, are you local, are you fed up with the unions?'

'Who the bloody hell's this clown? Piss off, you twat!' Dad didn't even give him any eye contact.

The bloke with the microphone hustled towards the picket line. 'We think he will try to cross the picket line,' he shouted down the lens of the camera.

Dad turned and stared down at me for a moment through his trademark thick bottle-end glasses. I could see that journo bloke had riled him. His eyes widened with mischief. They looked huge. 'Wait 'ere, son. I'm just going to have a quiet word with the nice man on the gate.'

He got out of the car and I watched him barrel up to the small crowd of protesters standing around a burning oil drum, some with home-made placards calling for more pay. I saw Dad standing in front of the men. As he delivered a flurry of jabbing hand movements and lots of pointing at the gates then back at the car, I could hear his muffled shouting – something about 'I'll kick your something head in and I will stuff it where I can't quite remember.' Dad was still working at the docks at the time, so perhaps the bloke in charge knew him. But wherever Dad was offering to stuff it, he obviously thought it worth opening the gates.

Dad bowled back to the car and got in. 'Everything all right, Dad?' I enquired fearfully.

He laughed and did an impression of W. C. Fields. 'Son, we're goin' in.' He proceeded to sing 'The Dambusters' as we pulled off at full pelt through the gates and into the tip. We bobbed and bounced at speed along rows of piled-up waste, followed by the man with the microphone and the crew of one in their ATV van. We came to a stop and the news van pulled up alongside us. The man with the microphone and his crew jumped out and began setting up their tripod.

'Take no notice, Lee. Whatever he says, just ignore him,' Dad muttered.

I began unloading the rubbish from the car. The camera was set up and the man with the microphone began talking into it, as Dad and I carried boxes round the back. Dad began doing funny walks and pulling faces over the reporter's shoulder, while I just kept my head down.

That night after tea, Dad gathered us all round the TV to watch the local news, just to prove to Mum that we were telling the truth and that we were actually filmed at the rubbish dump that day.

The news began and we all got excited during that little teaser bit at the beginning about the forthcoming stories on the programme. There was that man with the microphone and, sure enough, Dad and I could indeed be glimpsed in the background, stumbling around amongst the rubbish, holding boxes. ''Ere we are. Look, there's us!'

Every time an item came on the news, Mum was unable to cope and kept running out of the room, a nervous wreck. 'I can't watch, Dave,' she would say, flying out with a tissue to her face.

We had to wait until right at the end of the news, but it did come on. Unfortunately, it wasn't what we were expecting. It was an item about the state of the country and how there was an emerging underclass of deprived people who were relying on the discarded waste of the poorest neighbourhoods. It went on about how we were turning into a Third World country, how the most disadvantaged people were suffering so badly that these blighted beasts had begun to scavenge among the disgusting waste grounds of our rubbish tips.

I didn't really know what my first ever TV appearance meant. It certainly didn't indicate that one day I might have my own BBC series. But Dad seemed angry as he got up to leave the room and kicked the dog on the way out.

The dog – a mongrel called Dougal – always had a resigned look on his face as Dad approached. He knew what was coming. The dog accepted he was an essential part of Dad's failed anger management course.

6. Fireworks

Life on the Lawrence Weston was always on the chaotic side of shambolic. Despite the fact that Dad was getting more work as an entertainer, he only earned a pittance and we still existed from hand to mouth. We led an almost feral life, dressed in other people cast-offs and living off whatever food we could muster.

The funny thing was, although there was crime on the estate, I never felt threatened or uneasy. There was the odd scare, but it was always taken care of by the older boys who were very protective towards the younger ones. It was a close neighbourhood. If there was a break-in, Dad would tell us, poking his fork at us for emphasis while he ate dinner: 'If anyone got in 'ere, I would kick the shit out of them.' He was scary when he said it, but it made me feel a lot safer, knowing he would confront them and not me.

Most of the residents would know whodunnit anyway. Through the various channels of gossip, everyone knew everyone else's business. Without ever involving the police, it was always taken care of.

An example of how protective the older boys were was one evening when my mate Jeff and I were playing a game of football after school. The local flasher came out of nowhere and pulled his pants down in front of us. Jeff shouted across the main road to his house and his two older brothers were out quick as a flash, so to speak, chasing after him across the back fields, shouting at the top of their voices, 'Come 'ere, you dirty bastard . . .' Suddenly, from nowhere, there was a gang swarming the estate looking for him. Luckily for that flasher, they never caught him. If they had, he would definitely have had a cauliflower bean bag, as Jeff's brothers, Keith and Pete, were rock hard. They returned saying, 'If he comes back, gissa call, and we'll kick him right in the rucksack. He won't flash any more – he won't even have a dim light!'

The estate was always buzzing with activity. At weekends, we would be out the back of the flats in a small play area. It was nothing special, just some swings, a see-saw and a roundabout, but to us it was Thorpe Park. Competitions would always be on the go between the various kids from all over the estate.

It's amazing how fearless you are when you're a kid. You never believe anything will happen to you when you're out playing. One game involved pushing a swing as high as possible and then leaping off, trying to wrap it around the top crossbar. Unfortunately, one on-looking kid got a bit too close, and the swing hit him full on the head – bosh! – knocking him into the middle of next week. They carried him off to hospital. But the next day, he was back at the playground, his head all done up like a mummy. To me, he looked just like the Invisible Man.

'God!' I exclaimed. 'You all right?'

'Yeah. Me mum just shouts that me bandage is in the way and she can't see the telly.'

'Well, take it off! You're invisible, ain't you?'

'Piss off, Evans.'

I think that's what he said – I mean, it was muffled.

Then there was a kid who got too near the see-saw while about ten lads were going mental on it. He trapped his leg underneath it – you could hear the snap right across the estate. He was back the next day too, playing football on crutches.

Bonfire Night was always a massive occasion for us. Every year, the estate would stage a bonfire the size of which would make the Great Fire of London look like a carpet burn. The mammoth bonfire construction would begin in earnest weeks in advance, presenting every house and flat on the estate with an annual opportunity to ditch the rubbish the dustmen wouldn't touch with a barge pole. So it mostly consisted of old tyres, paint cans, sump oil, aerosol cans, old couches and chairs piled and stuffed into a framework of surreptitiously lopped-down local trees. At that time of year, all the trees in our area looked a bit sorry for themselves, like they'd been roughed up by gangs of local youths armed with saws and choppers, who would set out across the fields to gather not just branches, but whole trees from miles around.

By the time we'd finished, it was like a Brazilian rain-forest clearing. I pitied the trees; you'd see them there with chunks missing, trying to do a Bobby Charlton-style comb-over to cover up the gaps. A bunch of kids would drag all the wood back and then await directions from Keith, an absolute master of bonfire building and a real leader amongst the boys on the estate. He would order a bunch of kids to erect the wood into a tepee shape as tall as a large semi-detached house. The bonfire structure was so big that we could climb inside it and roam around at will. It was so densely packed with branches and household tat that you could even lose your friends in it. You could hear them shouting, but you'd spend twenty minutes trying to track them down, like a potholer squeezing through the gaps to find his mates.

Unable to afford any sort of firework display, residents would club together and purchase a small box of standard fireworks. Of course, somehow a few of the kids would produce a couple of the ones the grown-ups didn't want us to have. We found all that 'reading the instructions and standing well back' bullshit boring, so we burnt those. A bunch of us would hang around outside the newsagent's for hours waiting for a grown-up we knew and accost them to go in and buy a Jumping Jack or a couple of bangers. Even having just one banger would be a thrill. It would be carefully stowed under my bed for weeks prior to the big night, hidden away from my parents. Then, every now and again, I would retrieve it from its hiding place and stare at it, excitedly envisaging a bang loud enough to create a shockwave visible from space. I could imagine people on distant planets asking each other, 'What the hell was that?'

As we all stood around watching one of the grown-ups methodically go through the whole rigmarole of following the Firework Code, without warning someone would throw a lighted Jumping Jack at our feet and burst out laughing as we all scattered in a panic, the firecracker leaping and throwing out sparks on the floor. I would love to wrap a polythene bag around a stick, set light to it and watch it drip, drip on to the grass. It made a kind of laser sound as it dripped. In my mind, I was a bomber pilot dropping ordnance.

Then, after all the grown-ups had got bored and shoved off, the action would really start. A kid would rush up as if he had news of a gold rush and reveal under his jacket a box of shooting fountains. These were fireworks that when lit shot out different-coloured fireballs with such force that, if aimed at a charging rhino, they would drop him on the spot. And in the hands of a bunch of fearless kids, these babies were lethal weapons. They were our equivalent of rocket-propelled grenades.

The most fun game was to light your fireworks all at the same time and let battle commence. It amazes me now that no one got seriously hurt, because these things were flying all over the place. If a ball of red-hot flaming gunpowder hit you, it just seemed to bounce off.

But, then, fate is strange. There we were, being complete maniacs with these fireworks, and it was a young girl innocently standing next to the bonfire who got seriously injured. As we fired balls of gunpowder at each other, I glanced over at the bonfire and spotted Debbie, one of the prettiest girls on the estate. She was standing near the fire, away from a group of girls. She was just looking into the now-glowing embers while her friends cheered us on and dared us to fire more accurate shots at each other. I stared briefly at her, thinking how beautiful she looked as she was lit by the glow of the fire, when suddenly there was an almighty explosion that engulfed Debbie in flames. Everyone stopped in their tracks. The whole mood changed in an instant.

Silence.

Then Keith shouted, 'Shit!' He ran over to Debbie, who was now lying on the floor, having been flung back from the fire by the blast and stunned. Steve shouted to two of the other kids to go and get someone. The boys ran towards the block of flats shouting, 'Mum, Dad . . . !'

I stood trembling as I looked through the crowd of kids now assembled around Debbie. She lay there smoking, her face and clothes all burnt up. 'What happened?' shouted someone frantically.

We all looked to Keith, who replied, 'Some idiot put a bastard aerosol can in the fire!'

Just as he said it, there was another huge bang from the fire. Everyone scattered, apart from a couple of kids who managed to drag Debbie a few feet further back.

An ambulance came and took Debbie away. I heard she went back to school eventually.

That incident certainly taught us a more sobering lesson than we ever learned from the Firework Code.

Some kids on the Lawrence Weston Estate had brilliantly inventive minds. Just like magic, every week a kid would appear with a new form of transportation.

There was the trolley made from pram wheels, some scaffold planks and some string, the skate with a board nailed on top that, without even thinking, we would ride down the steepest of hills, and old motor bikes that we would race across the back fields. Sometimes, we would try to emulate Evel Knievel by setting up a ramp made from a door, then seeing how many kids we could jump over. Happy times.

One day an old pram was found. It's difficult now to comprehend how these things – like an old motor bike or wheelchair – would turn up, but they always did. They were just left some place, and if you left something on the estate, the kids would have it away in a flash. If someone was throwing something away, then it was a given that you could do whatever you wanted with it, it was up for grabs.

It was decided that this new cast-off pram should be pushed really fast with someone in it. It was great fun watching the terror on someone's face, clinging on for dear life in this treacherous makeshift vehicle.

Everyone else had had their turn being pushed really fast by about five kids, going down a very steep hill with no means of stopping. Now it was my turn. But just as I slipped in, another kid, who had found a cardboard box, suddenly put it over my head. So I was now boxed in, which made it even scarier because I didn't know what was going to happen. It would just have egged those lads on if they'd heard cries of fear from inside the box.

So they began pushing. It immediately felt really fast, owing to the fact I could only glimpse the pavement through a small gap between my legs. There were two holes at the front of the box, and if anyone had looked through them, all they would have seen were two terrified eyes staring back. As I bumped and jogged around inside the box, I could hear through the laughter and revving tank noises that one of the kids, Jimmy, had picked up a bamboo stick. He then had the great idea of making it even more like a tank by pushing the stick through one of the holes.

I peered out to see Jimmy running beside the careering tank, trying desperately to find the holes with the end of the stick. The bamboo finally came through the hole and Jimmy let go, shouting, 'Lee, get hold of the stick, it's your gun . . .' I frantically tried to grab the end of the stick as it bobbed around in front of my face. Then the stick jammed into a pavement slab and jolted back into my eye socket. Aaargh!

The pain was furious. The pram stopped dead, its brakes being the inside of my skull, and I flew forward like a pole-vaulter – 'Look, Ma, no hands . . .' Up I went, still in the box and still in the pram, surrounded by five now-laughing, hysterical boys. I landed with a bang and just lay there, in the darkness, realizing I had a stick wedged in my eye.

I quickly shouted to the boys outside the box. 'Don't move the stick!'

I could hear their concern. 'What? What's the matter, Lee?'

'The stick. It hurts, it's in my eye . . .'

Jimmy looked under the box and, in a panicky voice, gave the others a quick diagnosis. 'The stick's in his eye.' Hearing the confirmation, I burst out crying. Suddenly, I heard Jimmy say, 'We've got to –'

'Got to what?' I thought, forgetting the pain for a moment.

Without warning, Jimmy pulled the stick from my eye and out of the box.

Instead of crying, I screamed in pain. But I emitted no noise – it was more of a primal scream. All the oxygen was pushed out of my lungs. I stopped breathing for a moment and lay there. I was pulled by my feet from the box and, upon feeling the daylight, I took a huge gasp of air into my lungs. I couldn't see anything; everything had just gone white. Jimmy picked me up and carried me home.

I wore a patch over my eye for months, and to this day still get bouts of intense pain at the back of my eye after writing for long periods. It always reminds me of that day.

Thanks, Jimmy.

The pram incident was typical of the sort of stunts we would pull on the estate. We were fearless. Another popular game was 'I Dare You'. Those must be the three most dangerous words ever spoken in the history of pre-pubescent boys. You throw down the gauntlet to any little bum-fluff bollocks under the age of sixteen when you say those words. You know he's going to do it for you or die trying.

Some scrawny kid with a dirty face who, having recently tired of pulling the legs off a passing insect, would randomly approach you. Holding a plastic bag in one hand, he would enthusiastically advertise that he reckoned he could put it over his head until he just about stopped breathing. Of course, this would draw a crowd, all eager to see if he really would nearly kill himself. Afterwards, he would actually be proud if we told him that he'd nearly died.

'You nearly died.'

'Did I? Did I nearly die? Fantastic!'

And if he didn't back up his boast, he would just get a bunch of groans. 'You said you were nearly going to kill yourself, but you didn't!'

I don't know why the government wastes millions of pounds of our taxes on employing scientists whose job it seems is to carry out some pointless experiment that will only answer the question 'How much more will our

research bill be next year?', when there have been kids –
or, as I like to call them, pioneers – mostly by the name of
Clive or Darren, who have been doing a great deal more
complex experiments on every housing estate across the
land since housing estates began.

They have been answering the real scientific questions
that will in time actually benefit our country, important
questions such as: ''Ere, Clive, if I put this gerbil in your
mum's microwave, do you reckon it'll burst?'

RRRRRRRRRRRGH . . . DING.

'Darren, look, it sort of melted!'

For some curious reason, every kid had some sort of
speciality, a party piece. The list was an endless litany of
sadism, physical abnormality and abuse.

'I bet I could eat that dog poo.' Even dogs would stare
in disbelief at that one.

'Let's see what happens when you put this firework up
that cat's arse.' (On firework night, the cats on our estate
were petrified, choosing to walk around with their backs
to the wall.)

There was always that tiny spud of a kid who could fit
his whole hand in his mouth. One lad round our way
could reach up and actually put his foot in his gob.
Another boy could turn his eyelids inside out, so he
looked like Fu Manchu.

'You could kick me in the balls right now, and I wouldn't
feel anything.' That was it, a line of foot-limbering lumps
was formed, and the spot-kicking aimed towards the seed
pouch began.

One day, while I was hanging around the swings with a
bunch of kids at the back of the flats, picking our noses,

smoking Consulate cigarettes and spitting, one of the lads suddenly announced, ''Ere we go. I got a beauty brewing up 'ere.'

Everyone was immediately excited, enthusiastically cheering and rushing to huddle around the boy as he quickly bent over. Then a cigarette lighter was produced and lit like a pilot light in readiness next to his backside. After a short pause during which the lad wiggled around, manoeuvring the air pocket trapped within, he gave a little heave and a push and – *Flbbbbrrrrrrrrrrooooww!* A gigantic fart was forced out through the narrow cheeks of his bum and a burst of fire shot out from the back of his trousers like a flame thrower illuminating our little faces – to massive cheers all round.

'I dare you to lick the end of this twelve-volt battery.' I saw a kid do this once, and as his tongue touched both pins of the battery, one side of his body jumped and his face contorted as if he'd had a stroke. Still, he earned a huge roar of approval and laughter from the gathered crowd. In fact, he couldn't wait to do it again.

Another time, when I was about ten, I was hanging around with some lads at one kid's flat. His mum and dad had gone out, and he produced a can of lighter fuel. His trick was to stand in the middle of the lounge, fill his mouth with gas from the can and blow it out of his mouth into the path of a lighted flame. This would then explode inches from his face, making it look like he was fire-eating.

Someone pointed at me and dared me to do it, a challenge that I, of course, accepted without hesitation. This was typical; as a child, I had no idea about an obviously dangerous situation. I was an idiot, a chicken brain, a banana head, a void, a dribbling dullard. That seemed to be my role in this world, that was my job. That's why he asked me. He knew I was odds on to mess it up. There was the fun right there, watching Lee the retard set fire to his monkey face.

I happily let the boy holding the can of highly inflammable gas jam it into my mouth. It worried me slightly as I had no control over how much gas was being forced into my face. My cheeks filled out quickly and felt as if they were about to burst.

But that didn't matter to me. I was more concerned at getting the laughs. The giggly mood in the room started to build as more and more gas went in and everyone gleefully anticipated what might happen to Propane Boy. I even began pulling funny faces, which was a defence mechanism, of course. I was, in fact, petrified, but luckily no one noticed. They seemed to find it increasingly hilarious as I sucked in more and more of the high explosives. Then a lighter was flicked on in front of me and a group of keen faces gathered in for a closer look.

That's when I got all confused. Perhaps I got carried away seeing them all staring at me. It felt good. For once, I was the centre of attention. I was in with the crowd, not standing on the outskirts of it. They were right there, right then, my friends.

But I panicked and stupidly opened my mouth too soon. The gas ignited in a deep whooshing sound and, instead of blowing out, I sucked in. I felt the hot flame draw into my wind pipe and chest. My eyes widened, and I just stared, stunned, into space, unable to do anything, frozen to the spot, mouth wide open, as I exhaled the blue flame and it wafted up my face.

Every kid in front of me dropped to the floor and rolled around with paralysing laughter, holding their stomachs in pain, as they watched first my eyebrows then my fringe singe and melt into powder. I was the Twisted Firestarter – but not in a good way.

Another favourite stunt was 'The Jump of Death'. Finding an abandoned motorbike and making it work again was the hard part. The easy part was finding some poor lemming with the brain density of a garden sieve willing to lay down his life for 'The Jump of Death'. That would be me.

It was quite simple. 'Evans, you're in "The Jump of Death".'

'Oh, all right then.'

Our proper, perilous, death-defying leaps were much more dangerous than Evel Knievel's – he had it easy! It was all done behind closed doors, so to speak. A discarded door was dragged over and hastily raised up at one end on a pile of breeze blocks. That formed the take- off ramp.

Then, the bone-rattling, wobbly bucket of bolts was driven full pelt by some mad hormonal fifteen-year-old across the back fields towards the rickety door ramp. He would launch himself and the heavy metal rust bucket into the air and hope to clear the line of petrified kids who had been volunteered for 'The Jump of Death' and were lying on their backs beneath. The object was to add another kid to the end of the line after each attempt, and try to beat the record for the number of lads cleared.

That was great in theory, but everyone knew that in practice, when the bike eventually clipped the final kid, the next chosen numb-nuts to lie down at the end of the line was going to get a motorbike full of sump oil right in the mush. That would, of course, be me, as I was always chosen as the last mug in the line.

So I would lie there, staring up at the sky, tensing up as the bike's screaming engine got closer. Everyone was just waiting for me to get it, but it was still an almighty shock to be on the receiving end of a darn good thumping from a trailing back wheel. As it brushed past my head, it left a skid mark longer than Lewis Hamilton's across my face, much to the amusement of all the other kids either lying next to me in the line or standing around watching.

I was the only kid who never got a turn on the bike. After it had hit me, I couldn't really see much. But my souvenir of the day was to go home and explain to Dad why I had a faceful of tyre marks that made me look like a miniature Maori tribesman. I was always the butt of everyone's bullying, but at least I was part of the gang and wasn't being ignored. A lifetime of feeling like an outsider had made me pathetically grateful for the attention.

So that was life with the lads on the Lawrence Weston. As you can see, scientists in search of proof of the Chaos Theory needed to look no further than the everyday existence on that estate.

7. Nanny Norling

We kids never had any money. But that forced us to come up with ever more inventive ways of finding it. We had a first-class education in the fine art of fund-raising as we spent our days and nights roaming the streets of the Lawrence Weston.

Len and Faith's paper shop was part of a parade of local shops on the estate. Next to the paper shop, there was a small supermarket, then a butcher's, and a fish and chip shop, which was a real cash cow for us kids as they would give you the money back on returned bottles.

We duly obliged by climbing over the back wall into the yard where they kept crates full of returned bottles. We would pass them over the wall to other waiting kids, then stroll round the front of the chip shop and, without batting an eyelid, inform the manager that we had a lot of returnable bottles. You could only do it once a week, otherwise the manager would get suspicious.

After getting the money, we would wait until just before closing, when we would go in and ask whoever was serving if they had any 'scrackling', which is stray batter that has fallen down to the bottom of the fryer and is dredged up by the cook in a huge spoon and kindly put in a cone of paper. They didn't mind as it was only fat and it would normally go in the bin anyway. Then we would sit on the wall outside, boasting to the other kids riding around on their bikes that we had not only made money that day, but also got a free meal.

Of course, a meal consisting of pure fat nowadays would be considered so unhealthy. Just looking at it, Madonna would scream in horror, collapse and shrivel into a steaming pile. But we loved it!

Across the street from the parade of shops was the Giant Gorham pub. It was certainly a rough place, but it had such an atmosphere that we'd get our entertainment every weekend by just hanging around eating crisps and mimicking the drinkers inside. We all sat there with the bottles of Tizer which one of the kid's parents had bought us to keep us happy outside while they got pissed inside.

For us kids, it was really exciting sitting about outside until eleven at night, watching people struggle out of the pub with blood pouring from their noses! Every weekend the Giant Gorham would put on entertainment. The resident band would have to back anyone unfortunate enough to be booked there to entertain the mostly drunk and disorderly dock-workers. After the guest acts had either died on their arses or been dismembered and sold off for parts, it was time for some of the locals to get up and have a go.

We would sit in the car park outside, enveloped in the beery cloud that emanated from the pub doors, drinking, eating, listening and watching the huge frosted-glass frontage. Through that, we could see the wobbly outline of animated figures inside who were lit up by coloured flashing lights. Every week, the usual suspects would climb on to the stage and have a go at singing with the band. It was not a pretty sight.

Then every now and then towards the end of the night, the doors would swing open and out would fall one of the locals, mumbling drunkenly and staggering up the road. For us, the big prize was Paddy. Paddy lived about a hundred yards from the pub and was well known to us kids as 'The Slot Machine'. He would stumble out of the pub at the same time every Saturday, as his strict wife ordered him to be home by twelve.

He would crash out of the doors and stand in the middle of the car park, swaying and rocking, like a sapling in a tornado. As he tried to focus on the route home, he would suddenly be surrounded by us kids. In order to get the slot machine to pay out, you had to say the magic words to Paddy: ''Ere, Paddy, you ain't got no money!'

To which he would shout back, slurring his words: 'Ieeev goh looooaaads a mawneee!'

All the kids would then buzz about his legs like manic flies. He would wave his arms around in the middle of us, like King Kong on top of the Empire State Building, trying vainly to swat us.

'You ain't got no money, Paddy, you spent it all,' we would taunt.

'I've got millions!' he would rant, delving deep into his trouser pockets and pulling out handfuls of change to show us the evidence in his clenched fists. 'See, you bastards!' He would then hurl the change, spraying it right across the car park floor. 'There, look, I'm loaded!'

We would frantically dive on the floor, fighting each other to be the first to get the silver coins. Paddy would weave away off home to his wife to explain why he now had no money, leaving us like pigeons pecking away at the tarmac. We would huddle up to compare our riches.

Some of the kids would then run to a call box about fifty yards down the hill and with the change make random calls to people. I listened in to a call a couple of times.

'Is that Mr Walls?' they would ask.

'Mr Walls? No, there are no Walls here.'

'Well, what's holding your ceiling up then?' the boys would shout and put the phone down.

Well, we thought it was funny at the time.

Because we never had any money, trying to find something that might make us a few bob was a major preoccupation on the estate. If it wasn't tied down, it was gone. And if something was going cheap, it would be already gone by now. Bob-a-job week was always extended to gissa-bit-more-a-job month, and a local character called Nanny Norling was just another way of getting in on some action.

An elderly lady, Nanny Norling lived in the very top flat of the block across from ours, and was to some kids a great source of income. I personally think she may even have been the first cash machine on the estate.

Initially, as a kid of around seven years of age, all I ever saw of Nanny Norling was her ominous, bony hand, the hint of her long, unkempt, grey hair that would wave wildly in the wind around her gaunt, ashen face, and the two small, pea-shaped eyes that would peer over the edge of her window box down towards us as we played beneath the flats.

Someone would notice her window open and, looking up, we'd stop dead still in anticipation as a hand would emerge and begin to be royally wafted around. It was a signal similar to the one they give at the Vatican when they have chosen a new Pope. This was our own, equally important, sign that there was going to be a major food drop.

The hand would retreat back into the open window and suddenly emerge again, but this time bulging with hard-boiled sweets. Then the palm would open like a claw-crane, letting the sweets cascade on to the courtyard below. We would watch them descend through the air, clucking away beneath like hungry chickens waiting for seed to drop to the ground.

We would run to the bottom of the flats, hands up ready to catch them, but alas, more often than not the sweets would smash uselessly into a thousand pieces on the concrete at our feet, rendering them into nothing but powdered sugar. It was the same with another food she liked to drop, fruit. The hand would come out, holding an orange or an apple. The hand would open and the fruit would drop. Even if you caught it from such a great height, it would splatter in your hands. But we still fell for it every time; it was as if we had been trained like chimps on a sort of 'press-the-button-get-the-banana' reward scheme.

Some of us kids knew that Nanny Norling was bed-ridden and so unable to leave the flat. Sad for her, but the advantage to us was that she always needed someone to make the trip to the corner shop for her essentials. So if her hand came out of the window and made a sort of regal beckoning motion – well now, that's where the real money was at.

When that happened, by God, the race was on. All hell broke loose – there might be five, six kids, maybe more, running up the stairwell towards her flat. Before you could say 'The Nanny Bank of Bristol', we would be banging at her door offering our services in exchange for some cash. It was mostly pennies, but it was still money.

I remember on one occasion, I was hanging around at the bottom of the flats, along with my brother Wayne and a couple of other kids, Tony and Alex, when Nanny Norling's window suddenly opened and the usual little wave summoned one of us up to see her. We shot a look at each other, like gunslingers waiting to see who would draw first.

I had never been fortunate enough to go on a Nanny shopping trip, as I was one of the youngest and never had the strength or the speed to get up to her flat before the others. But on this occasion there were only four of us, so maybe, just this once, the odds might be in my favour.

I needed no second invitation. I was off, with the three other boys, suddenly realizing I had legged it, in hot pursuit. As I made it to the entrance to the flats, though, I was grabbed from behind and pulled back through the doors, allowing Tony, Wayne and Alex to barge past me. I took off after them, as they fought tooth and nail up the stairwell. Suddenly, Tony lost his footing and fell on the first landing and Wayne and Alex fell giggling in a heap on top of him. This was my chance. Stepping over the hysterical pile, I was suddenly out in front. I had to take advantage of my lead – I knew it wouldn't be long before they were on my tail. This was survival of the fittest, and I wasn't that fit, so I needed to get a real head start.

As I reached the last flight of stairs, just feet away from Nanny Norling's door, my legs were on fire, my muscles burning from all the stairs I had galloped up. I took a quick glimpse over my shoulder to see Wayne bounding up behind me like a giant antelope. With all my energy, I put in a last, exhausting sprint along the passageway to her door, but Wayne was already on top of me.

We hit the doorway together in a human crash. Wayne popped forward through the unlatched door and into Nanny Norling's flat. I watched from where I lay and it seemed his upper body was going way too fast for his legs to catch up. The momentum propelled him forward and down on to a metal bucket that had been left in the hall. Crack! Wayne's nose hit the side of the bucket, splatting in as many directions as a compass.

Wayne rolled over and lay on the floor moaning, clutching what was left of his hooter, as blood oozed out between the gaps in his fingers. It looked like the only place he would be going was A&E.

I couldn't have cared less; I had my eyes on the prize. This was it, this was my moment, my time to shine, to bask in the sunlight that would lead to the Nanny Norling treasure trove and wealth beyond my wildest dreams. I snapped to my feet and slid quietly past the groaning lump that was Wayne. The treasure was mine.

I went to enter triumphantly through her living-room doorway, but, 'Nann—aaaargh . . . bollocks!'

A hand had grabbed my ankle and I was gone, whipped back out of the door without so much as a by-your-leave.

All that Nanny Norling must have seen was some scruffy kid appear, then just as quickly disappear from view. I was gone, sucked back through the door in a flash, like some demented cuckoo clock on the stroke of one.

As I lay sprawling on the floor beside him, Wayne quickly got to his feet, trying desperately to cup the blood now flowing like a river from his nose. I watched as he entered Nanny Norling's front room, cool as you like, as if butter wouldn't melt in his mouth, and say, quite calmly, 'Do you need something from the shops, Nanny Norling?'

I entered the room behind him, battered, exhausted and breathing heavily. I was too late. Wayne had secured the lucrative contract.

This was the first time I had been in the famous Nanny Norling flat. It was jam-packed with all sorts of odd artefacts, not unlike the set of *Steptoe and Son*. These objects had clearly seen better days. She had, it appeared, at some point fallen on hard times.

Up against the far wall of the front room was a four-poster bed where Nanny Norling lay. The mattress was thick and high enough above the window sill so that the poor old dear could, as she liked to, constantly stare out of the window. A huge grandfather clock loudly tick-tocked away at the foot of the bed, a cabinet with dusty, faded, black-and-white photos of men in uniform sat on a lace cloth across a chest of drawers, and by the window next to the bed was a stand supporting a bird cage with a small yellow budgie chewing frantically on a cuttlefish.

'Here,' she said, quietly holding out a bag of birdseed to me as I stood, crestfallen, after losing out to Wayne yet again. 'Feed the bird.' I fed the bird, gave her back the seed, and she handed me a sweet – one frigging boiled barley sugar was all I got for my troubles! Well, at least it was a whole one and not a shattered fragment.

Deeply disappointed, I followed Wayne down the stairs. His nose was still pouring blood, but what did he care? 'I got it, I got it!' he crowed to the others as we passed them on the stairs.

Wayne has that scar on his nose to this day.

But I still have the mental scars.

One year later, Nanny Norling died, or as Dad put it: ''Ere, Wayne, you know that bucket you caught your hooter on? Well, Nanny Norling has kicked it.'

I asked if her foot was all right.

When I say she died, she didn't actually die – well, not the first time anyway.

One of the neighbours called in a panic at our flat. She was crying, because she had gone into Nanny Norling's flat and found her lying motionless in bed. Mum and Dad and some other neighbours rushed over to Nanny's flat immediately. A few of us kids followed along too. By the time a few doors had been knocked on the way over there, quite a procession of people had built up.

When I got to Nanny Norling's flat, I had to squeeze gently under and through the legs of loads of people. The crowd led right down to the second landing. The door was open, with three, maybe four of the neighbours all trying to get a better look inside. I could just hear faint whisperings from the front room as I crept through the small hall, weaving in and out unnoticed by everyone –

they were all too concerned with Nanny Norling. I made it into the front room, and there was Nanny Norling lying completely still on her bed, face white as a ghost as if she had fallen into a bath of talc.

About eight people were around the bed, all doing their most convincing over-concerned whispering act and discussing what the best thing to do was. Have you noticed people will always say the same thing in those situations?

'I think it's for the best.'

'Yes, I think that's what she would have wanted.'

How do they know? She's dead!

Dad whispered loudly in a mock-respectful, authoritative voice: 'I think we should tie her mouth up.'

There were gasps from the gathered crowd. 'Tie her mouth up?' someone exclaimed.

'Don't be a fool,' remonstrated another.

'No,' replied Dad, keen to explain. 'I saw it on a programme once. If rigor mortis sets in, her mouth will be permanently jammed open like that. So we need to tie it shut.'

A voice piped up from the crowd, 'There's a few people round 'ere I'd like to do that to.'

Dad asked if someone would pass him a tea cloth from the kitchen. He took it and, with everyone looking on, he mournfully and carefully closed Nanny Norling's mouth. He asked another neighbour to hold it shut as he wrapped the tea cloth around her chin and up over her head, where he tied it in a huge bow. She lay there, like a giant rabbit, as everyone bowed their heads and said a little prayer. A couple of women began to cry.

I was sure I even saw a tear appear in the budgie's little eye.

I was confused. I was too young to understand. I didn't know what was going on. It was difficult to tell why you might tie a bow around Nanny Norling's head so she looked like a rabbit. Why was everyone so upset?

I heard the faint siren of an ambulance arrive on the estate. That must have aroused something in her because suddenly, without warning, Nanny Norling sat bolt upright in bed.

A woman fainted on the spot.

The room ignited with screams of terror. An atmosphere that just moments earlier was silent and solemn was now complete mayhem. The budgie fell from its perch, seemingly clutching its tiny heart with its wings.

Everyone stood terrified, dumbfounded, staring at Nanny Norling. It was like she'd awoken from the dead. She made a few odd faces as if she had a wasp flying about her mouth. She had no teeth in, which didn't help. It made her mouth look all concave. She produced some extraordinary noises that I had only previously heard on nature programmes. Her head jolted from one person to the next, her mad, staring, pea eyes darted about the room. She looked like a pinball caught between two posts as she flailed around in the four-poster bed.

'She can't breathe!' someone cried out.

'Well, no, she's dead,' shouted another.

'She's not dead, you idiot! Take that cloth off her head!'

Dad quickly ripped the cloth from Nanny Norling's head. She took a huge intake of air, paused for a moment and shouted: 'What are you trying to do? Kill me?'

In fact, not long after that, Nanny Norling did sadly pass on. No one knows if the trauma of that day contributed to it, but in my opinion, it surely couldn't have helped.

Even though we were so hard up, Nanny Norling managed to brighten up all our lives on the estate with her hand-outs, her exciting shopping expeditions and her exploding hard-boiled sweets.

I dedicate this chapter to the beautiful generosity of Nanny Norling.

8. X-Ray Vision

Despite participating in all these shenanigans on the estate, I still felt walled-off from mainstream society. It was as if all the real action was taking place in some far-off land, light years away from our life of grime on the Lawrence Weston.

As I got older, I started to yearn for something that might make me stand out. I wanted a capability that would command instant respect from others. So I decided that what I needed to mark myself out was a superpower. Then one day I got one. Well, sort of.

Dad was getting a lot more work on the club circuit by now and would often spend weeks away. The estate was getting pretty lively, which made me anxious. It was becoming increasingly rough. I only ever really felt safe when Dad was there. A superpower would stop me feeling so vulnerable. I imagined I could impress people by bending iron bars at will. So I'd lie in bed dreaming of amassing superhuman strength.

Whenever Dad was home, he'd like to go to Bristol town centre and visit a costume and make-up shop to stock up on tape and props, as he was now starting to incorporate impressions into his act.

For me, it was always the most exciting day of the year when I held my dad's hand and went up the Christmas

Steps, a section of the town centre with second-hand clothes shops, book shops, joke shops and music stores. One of the music shops was owned and run by Trevor, the drummer in the band Dad used to belong to in the old days when he was doing gigs around South Wales and Bristol.

I loved going up the Christmas Steps. About half way up, there was a joke shop that sold rubber masks, make-up glue, false hair and wigs of all colours and lengths. I would stand in the middle of the shop, quietly fascinated by the brightly coloured magic tricks, practical jokes, wigs and costumes, waiting for Dad as he had odd, work-related conversations with the even odder-looking bloke behind the counter. They would talk endlessly about dou-ble-sided tape, rubber noses and false facial hair.

As Dad chatted away, my eyes were drawn to a pair of plastic glasses in a bag that hung near the counter. 'X-Ray Vision' it said, in big red letters. There was a picture of a man wearing the glasses and looking at a woman. It appeared that he could actually see through the woman's dress to a skeleton underneath. I immediately snatched them from the rack and put them alongside the pile of stuff Dad had chosen to buy.

As the strange-looking man behind the counter cashed up all Dad's stuff and plonked it in a bag, I imagined all the things I was going to do with these X-ray specs. Per-haps I might look inside my own body to see how it worked, or peer through buildings. Best of all, I imagined that I would be able to see underneath the dress of every girl that came within my X-ray vision. My eleven-year-old hormones were going ape shit with X-ray excitement.

As soon as we made our way out of the shop and back into the hustle and bustle of the Christmas Steps, I was eager to give my powerful new glasses a field test. Dad was distracted by a shop window, so I delved into the white carrier bag and retrieved the equipment that would endow me with my new superpower. It would enable me first to dominate the school playground, and then the planet. I would be able to watch teachers through thick walls, see what other kids had in their bags and, mostly, view naked girls at my leisure without them even knowing it.

I frantically opened the packet and carefully placed the huge, plastic, super-powered glasses upon my small freckled face. To my dismay, I couldn't actually see anything. I looked around me at the buildings – nothing but fuzzy images. I took the glasses off and studied them. What was causing these powerful specs not to work?

Upon inspection, I found that they simply consisted of pieces of thin cardboard as lenses with red spirals painted on the front and a small hole in the middle over which a tiny piece of red nylon gauze was stretched and glued in place. I don't know if you've ever looked through your net curtains at home, but things do appear to be fuzzy and kind of X-rayish, I suppose.

But I couldn't give up. The spectacles had aroused something deep inside me. I no longer wanted to be the twat of the school, the odd boy, the one picked on for making strange noises to myself during class – well, OK, maybe that one. But I needed this new superpower to banish my reputation as the eternal loser. If I had this ability, the other boys who thought of me as merely the school buffoon would immediately see me in an entirely different light. I shall, I thought, see into their minds, control the school, fight crime, even take over the universe.

I would no longer be viewed as the unwilling volunteer for the latest painful experiments – for example, I can boast that I was the first at my school to test out the agonizing pain of a dead leg from Alan Wilson, and the bumps from the entire Year Three. They swore it was my birthday, but unless I got the date wrong, they were sorely mistaken. Actually, I was sorely, they were just mistaken. No, if these boys knew I had the power of X-ray vision, I would be the most important, sought-after pupil in the school.

I kept the glasses on as we entered the next shop Dad wanted to visit. I looked at everything around me, bumping into every other person – much to the annoyance of Dad, who started to pull me along the pavement once we were back outside. 'Take those bloody glasses off, you look mad,' he fumed, before turning to apologize to anyone I bumped into. 'Lee, look where you're going.'

But I wanted to keep the glasses on in case somehow they suddenly started working. I persisted with the specs in the hope that the X-ray vision might kick in. I tried desperately to focus through the small pinholes. So determined was I that I refused to remove them for a week, stumbling around the flat in near blindness.

'Lee, take those bloody glasses off. You can't see your tea,' Mum would demand at the table. I'd take them off, but as soon as I was away from the table they were back on and I was crashing into things again.

Trying my luck at school, I'd lurk in the playground next to the girls on the monkey bars, attempting not to look too suspicious. Then, at the right moment, I'd turn round, bend down, slide my hand into my bag, whip out my X-ray specs and put them on my face. Closing my eyes, I'd pray that they would work. Then I'd slowly, nonchalantly turn round and stare at the girls through these huge black glasses with red spirals painted on the lenses.

'Piss off, Evans, you pervert!' they would shout. Even though the glasses didn't work, I made out they did, by saying stuff back to them like, 'Oooooh! I see . . .'

They would all jump from the monkey bars and run to the teacher on playground duty, and tell on me. 'Miss, Miss, Lee Evans can see our underwear!'

Word got round that Lee Evans had X-ray glasses and could see girls' knickers. At every break, I would aimlessly stroll around the playground, then suddenly pop up somewhere and put the glasses on in front of as many people as possible. Then I'd point randomly at them and begin laughing and saying, 'I can see what you're wearing, you know!'

All of a sudden, I was the most in-demand boy at the school. Overnight, I'd gone from loser to lord of all I surveyed. Other lads would sidle up to me and whisper, 'Evans, gissa go on your glasses.'

'No,' I'd respond authoritatively. 'If these land up in the wrong hands, God help us!'

That just made them want the specs more. I found myself in the desperate situation of for once being the kid all the other boys wanted to talk to, but for something that I knew didn't really exist. As I was a prize twit and not used to this kind of pressure, I soon buckled.

One morning, I was in the playground at break time

with a crowd of excited boys, all wanting a go on my X-ray specs and to look at the girls. I made some futile attempts at lying – I said that I'd buried them far away because the responsibility was too great a burden, and even that the government had come and taken them away to test them for possible use by our armed forces.

But it was no good. I quickly gave in to Big Chris Blake, the school bully. 'Listen, Evans,' he snarled as he gripped the lapel of my blazer. 'I need those glasses. I want to see some crumpet.' I duly took them from my inside pocket and gave them to him. He grabbed them and, projecting spit into my face, spat out the word 'Tosser' before running off, followed by a cackling crowd of equally Neanderthal boys.

It was over.

I'd had my moment of popularity, shallow though it was. Just as I was thinking how empty it felt being a mere mortal, bereft of any superpowers, the crowd of boys came rushing back towards me. 'Wait,' I thought, 'maybe the glasses worked. Perhaps they are coming back to lift me on to their shoulders with shouts of appreciation.' Er, no.

They stopped in front of me. Chris Blake pushed his way through the crowd. Even though he was still wearing the glasses and his eyes were covered in red spirals, I could tell he wasn't happy. He came right up to my face and slowly took off the glasses, revealing red, angry eyes. His head looked like a geyser about to blow. He threw the glasses to the floor and, without saying a word, punched me full in the face. Was I still part of the in-crowd?

Back to the drawing board.

*

That feeling of being a perpetual misfit ran throughout my school days. I could do nothing right. The more I tried to be in, the more I was pushed out. The only time I ever felt at ease was when I was allowed to daydream. For example, I could lose myself in art. Every year a charity would hang up on all our front doors clear plastic bags containing colouring books and crayons. For some reason, the charity must have thought drawing the dot-to-dot pictures in those books would stop us from scribbling on the walls. But the crayons just gave us the ammo to do so.

I would spend hours sitting, colouring and drawing. Ever since I can remember, entering the world of writing or painting has been a great escape. To me, it is the place I feel the safest. It's where I feel total freedom to express myself any way I want, without prejudice or worry.

I experienced a similar feeling of belonging when it came to music. At the Christmas Steps on that same day with Dad, I went into Trevor's music shop and suddenly I was surrounded by all types of drums and cymbals. It was difficult to take it all in. There seemed to be no gaps anywhere. You couldn't see the wall – every available space was filled with equipment: bass drums, kettle drums, gongs, all sorts of gleaming chrome stands that held cymbals, and entire drum kits hanging from the ceiling.

Trevor, Dad's old bandmate behind the counter, was a short man with dark features. I thought he looked like a skinny version of Engelbert Humperdinck. He and Dad were both enthusiastically slapping each other's backs, obviously two friends who hadn't seen each other for a while. When he broke off from hugging Dad, Trevor looked down at me, smiling. 'This your boy, Dave?'

'Yep, that's the younger one. The older one's at home. I'll tell you what, Trev, the older one can sing, you know. He's very good, he is.'

'What's he do?' Trevor enquired about me.

'Nothing. I think he's a bit shy, this one. He don't say much,' answered Dad.

Trevor turned round and grabbed something from behind him. Then he walked around the counter and knelt down next to me. 'I'll tell you what, have a go with these, young Lee,' he said, producing two drumsticks from behind his back and handing them to me. I held them in my hand, lost in awe at my brand-new possessions.

The words 'Trevor's Drum Store' were written in blue along the two sticks. They seemed to have a mind of their own, as if they were obliging me to bang something with them. It was the first time I'd ever felt any sort of urge to be musical.

From that day, I never wanted to put those sticks down. Every chance I got, I would slide off into my bedroom and construct a drum kit, setting up a rolled-up blanket to act as a bass drum, two pillows as tom-toms and a book in the middle as a snare. I tapped away for hours. I'd always liked my own company because it allowed my imagination to wander. I'm still the same today. I love nothing better than locking myself away for hours on end, doing something creative. Wait a minute – that's prison, isn't it?

When I played on my bed back then, it was like to imagine I was in a band. I would put on the old record player in my room and try to drum along to whatever was playing. They were mostly records Wayne had bought: T-Rex, Sweet, Gary Glitter. The one record I had bought was Cosy Powell's 'Dance with the Devil'. I would practise playing along to it so much, I had blisters in between my fingers. I reckoned I had found my instrument.

I was never any good at school. I always seemed to be someplace different from the rest of the class, always marooned in the world of my own imagination. Mentally, I would cut myself off. But when I got home and played with the drumsticks, my whole body would just relax, I was in my own eleven-year-old comfort zone. This was it. I sat drumming on a book, some pillows and rolled-up blankets, but in my mind I was playing in front of thousands at Wembley Stadium. I was a performer.

Thanks, Trevor.

9. The Wish List

It was slowly becoming clear that the one place where I felt at ease was as a performer. Experiences such as my humiliation by Mrs Taylor had demonstrated as much. As yet, however, I had no idea that I could parlay clowning in the classroom into a career.

I was still very much regarded as the odd one out by people on the estate and at school. From a very young age, I always knew that I was not the same as everyone else, and there were lots of things about me which I wished were different.

That continues to this day. I'm still haunted by a 'wish list' of things I long to do better. I wish, for instance, that I didn't think so much, but I can't help it – I've always had a very vivid imagination. It's a place I can go to, my own little world where I find the most solace. It's the spot I can hide in, where no one can find me. It's a sort of defence mechanism. My imagination takes over whenever I find it difficult to cope with the real world.

I am completely satisfied with my own company. When I was a college student, I might suddenly decide that – for that day – I was going to be from a different country. It was no specific country. I just adopted a fictitious language, and any time anyone spoke to me, I would really believe I couldn't understand them. I'd shake my head and hold out my hands, trying to explain to them in a ridiculous made-up foreign tongue: 'Eye aammmmaaa no frum eerrre. I know not?'

It was just the same when I was a young kid. I'd lose myself for hours, painting, reading or dressing up and acting out stuff. To anyone watching, I looked like a simple boy, but to me I was right there in the midst of my imaginative world.

I could spend hours alone in my bedroom either imagining I was somewhere else or acting out being someone else from a film or TV show I might have watched. I always yearned to be someone much better than me – better looking, more decisive and confident, stronger-willed.

So, as a young kid, I might spend days pretending to be in a car. I would commandeer one of Mum's dinner plates, hold it out in front of me like a steering wheel and, while making a car noise, walk around our flat. I'd only respond if someone called me, as you might a taxi. If I was asked to sit at the table, I'd drive there. When Mum shouted at me to sit down, I'd spend ages meticulously parking my imaginary car, opening the door and saying, 'Sorry, Mum, did you say something? I couldn't hear you in my car.' Or sometimes I'd lie under my bed refusing to come out, explaining it would be impossible as I was a trapped miner who had somehow managed to find a small air pocket.

At various times, I was also both Batman and Robin, and Steve Austin, *The Six Million Dollar Man*. I once stood for an hour at the bottom of our block of flats, clasping hold of the corner brickwork, literally believing I was the Bionic Man. I would warn anyone who passed by in a sort of strained American accent to 'Step . . . back . . . I . . . really . . . don't know . . . if . . . I . . . can . . . hold it . . . up . . . much . . . longer.'

All the girls loved Donny Osmond, so I enjoyed pretending to be him, too. I once become so convinced that I was Donny, I went to the sheds at the back of the flats, climbed on top of the rickety corrugated roof as if it were a stage and sang 'Crazy Horses!' to thousands of imaginary screaming girls at the top of my voice. I beckoned the crowd to join in. What I didn't realize is that, having got up there, I was unable to get down and had to call for help. Our next-door neighbour tried to help me down, but in doing so he fell off the roof and broke his leg. He told me that he hated Donny Osmond after that and could never listen to him again.

On another occasion, I held a beaten-up old umbrella and dived off the garages because I really thought the umbrella would suddenly pick up the wind, take flight and lift me high into the sky. Of course, I plummeted like a rock, landing in a bone-shattering heap on the floor below, with the umbrella turned inside out.

Whenever a crash-test dummy was needed, I would always be the first kid to volunteer my services – anything to please the crowd. But I'd have volunteered anyway for no other reason than my naive and foolish optimism. Basically, I was an idiot with the brain cells equivalent to an amoeba. Stupidity was my speciality. Some people might frown at that, but I was good at it and it was all I had.

My visions became more and more powerful. I pictured things so vividly, I had to take a look around me to see if others had seen them too. For example, when I was at school, the teacher might enter the room at the start of a lesson and, in my mind's eye, he might randomly turn into, say, a giant bear or a gorilla. Or, while seated at his desk, the teacher would without warning transform into a frog or a rabbit, particularly when the class had been ordered to be silent and told to copy something from the blackboard. At that moment, I would look up from my book and suddenly inanimate objects – desks, coat stands, chairs, an apple on the teacher's desk – would all start talking. And I wasn't even on tablets!

School was really a place where I just went through the motions. It never really meant anything to me as it never had the things I wanted. I found it boring, unexciting. The school wanted to teach me things I never wanted to learn, and the things I did learn I haven't ever used since leaving school. Somehow I have always been out of synch with everybody else, either because my family travelled around a lot and I never really had time to settle in any one school and grasp the curriculum, or because I was just plain stupid. I'm not sure, although the latter now sounds more convincing! So, as a young boy, the ability to lose myself within my own mind gave me the escapism I so badly needed.

All the same, I wish I were more educated. It was so frustrating feeling such a complete simpleton all the way through school. In the classroom, I would mostly sit like some spaced-out lobotomy patient, dribbling and staring into the ether, my small pea-like brain working overtime just to keep my vital organs going, wandering off into the land of dim. Whenever a teacher began talking or writing anything on the blackboard, I would gawp at it from the back of the class like a Neanderthal muttonhead.

Even worse for everyone and much to the annoyance of the teacher, I would sit there with my hair sticking out in all directions making the sorts of eeks, burps, honks, zip, zap and frigging zoop noises to myself that a highly medicated psychiatric patient might when the brightly coloured toys come out of the play-box. The other kids literally thought I was retarded.

This story might show you what sort of stupid kid I was – it certainly shows how I was always an oddball. One day in class I stumbled upon a way to make a high-pitched humming sound at the back of my throat, while at the same time being able to speak quite normally. It was a two-voices-at-once kind of thing. I managed to become so good at this new vocal dexterity that I declared myself a Zen master of the vocal chords, able with just a few movements of my rubbery lips and voice box to drive teachers close to insanity. They would get more and more angry and frustrated about where this odd, high-pitched humming sound could be coming from. When in full flow, it sounded as if there was a huge bees' nest some-where overhead.

In lessons, I'd sit like a simple kid, usually drooling, watching the teacher pause mid-sentence at the front of the class. He would raise one ear in the air, tilting his head one way, then the other, like a parrot. I had become so good at making my noise that the teacher would follow the sound through the air to the point of placing his ear inches away from my mouth. However, his suspicion was confounded when, thinking he had discovered exactly where the sound was coming from, he questioned me and I was able to speak quite normally while still making the annoying sound.

Keeping a dead straight face was, of course, vital for my little trick to work. If I appeared to crack for a moment, it would wreck the illusion. It was like my own little lie detector test.

I could push the teacher to the edge of suicide. Eventually, he would be standing rigid with rage on the spot at the front of class, shouting, 'Whoever it is making that ridiculous noise, stop it now, or I swear I will kill them. And don't think I won't. Beeecaaaause Iiiieeeeee will.'

I would, of course, be looking innocently over my shoulder and around the class, demonstrating that butter wouldn't melt in my mouth, while still making the humming sound. 'Yes,' I would demand, siding with the teacher. 'Who is making that idiotic noise?'

So one of my wishes is that I were not resident in the world of stupid.

But the 'wish list' doesn't end there. Ever since I was tiny, I have always yearned to be what I wasn't. I wish, for example, that I'd had more girlfriends. Not now, obviously – my wife would kill me! – but growing up. Perhaps my life would have somehow turned out differently if I'd been better-looking and known exactly what to say to a woman. But so bad was I with the opposite sex that I'd more or less given up on trying to acquire a girlfriend by the time I was into my late teens.

I wish I'd had more confidence too. I've always been an insecure person. I was a nervous child, suffering from eczema that would flare up whenever I got anxious. In addition, I wish I cared less about other people's feelings. That problem has dogged me my whole life. My wife has always complained that whenever we've been round to someone's house, I will spend the next three days agonizing over how I might have said the wrong thing or reacted inappropriately to something, even to the extent that I want to phone them up and apologize.

On occasions, I have sent letters or even sneaked out of the house without my wife knowing, driven back to the supposedly offended person's house and tried to say sorry. Of course, the poor, baffled 'victim' I'm trying to explain all this to has no idea what the hell this loon is going on about as he rants away on his front lawn.

'I'm sorry, but I've just got to apologize for what I said the other night,' I'd say.

'What the fuck are you talking about, you tosser?' he'd reply. 'Do you realize it's five o'clock in the morning? I'm calling the police now!'

As you can tell, ineptitude has been my constant companion. A lot of my earliest memories revolve around sport – or at least my total inability to do it. My rubbishness on the sports field of course only served to intensify my sense of being one of life's losers.

But you couldn't fault my enthusiasm. Ever since that doctor handed me one of those lollipops for the last time and finally gave me the all-clear that my heart had healed over, I haven't stopped running, jumping, diving and making sure I generally fall all over the place. Anyone who has seen my live show will know what I mean.

Once I had broken free from the chains that had constricted me for so long and I was allowed to run, I sprinted everywhere. We couldn't afford running shoes, so we had what we called 'daps', cheap shoes from the Bata shoe shop. I would even run to the hall to put them on quickly in the morning. Then I'd run out the door and didn't stop running until I came back for my tea that night. At long last, I was able to be as physical as I liked.

But it still didn't make me any better at sport.

To me, sport always felt like another obstacle, another excuse to be left out. One might think that of all the sports in the world, there would have to be at least one I could do. But there really isn't, not even welly-throwing, although I do now realize that it's best to take them off first before throwing them. Alas, I seem to have the unfortunate trait of what you might call physical Tourette's when it comes to any sporting activity.

I have literally been thrown off or out of more football fields, snooker halls, golf courses, darts games, fishing lakes, cricket pitches, sports halls, running tracks, ski slopes and ice-skating rinks than I could shake a stick at – and I probably wouldn't even be able to do that. I was once chucked out of a dog track for jumping the fence and making a dive for that rabbit. And just in case there are any dogs reading this, a good tip is, when that bell goes and the gate is released, run around the track the opposite way to all the other dogs and don't be freaked out when you eventually find the rabbit is suddenly running towards you.

My very first encounter with sport was miserable and it never really got any better. Sports day was always a particular disaster. To compensate for my inadequacy, I'd stand in the sack at the start of the sack race and, as soon as they blew the whistle, quickly jump out, put the sack over my head and run in the other direction.

The other kids always had the proper kit for football. I, on the other, would still be in my school shorts, wearing one white and one black trainer borrowed from Lost Property. (Lots of my clothes were also made by Mum, an avid knitter. The only problem was, when it rained I was suddenly carrying 400 pounds of extra weight.) But I didn't care, as long as I was picked to go in goal. I loved it, because I could dive everywhere. But when the ball actually came towards me, I'd panic and dive frantically in a random direction, letting the ball go straight into the net, to the massive groans of the other kids. After a few experiences like that, I was quite content to stand on the sidelines and make spaceship noises.

My first game of cricket didn't go too well either. I was finally picked to bat. I had never had the honour before, and so I was very nervous. When the ball was bowled at me, I swung at it with all the effort I could muster and, by chance, hit it. I opened my eyes and, turning round to see where it had gone, I noticed all the other kids scouring the air. I looked up and there it was, high in the sky. Now it was coming down, fast. A shout came from Pat Phelps on the far side of the field that the ball was his. Pat was, apparently, really good at catching. Not only could he catch balls well, but all the girls thought he was a catch as well, as he had really nice teeth.

So he was standing there beneath my ball, with his hands cupped up ready in front of him to catch it. I watched as the ball fell towards him. Resigning myself to returning back to the pavilion, I dropped the bat and headed off the pitch. At that moment, I heard Pat shout, 'I got it, I got it.' I knew he had it, he always caught the ball. I was as good as out. But then, all of a sudden, I heard, 'I got it, I gooooooaaarghmmmm?'

'What does that mean?' I thought. I looked up towards Pat, and he certainly did have the ball. It had gone through his hands and jammed itself into his mouth, knocking out most of his lovely teeth.

It was, I hasten to say, a complete freak accident, and that's how it was explained to his parents by our PE teacher – though I, of course, was never allowed near a bat ever again. But that was all right. I had moved on.

While at school, despite having the eagerness of a ball-chasing dog, I was never picked for any team. They didn't even trust me with the oranges at half time, deciding that it would be safer to place them on the side of the field at the ready before the game. This was so disheartening for me – the PE teacher would rather trust a fruit to supply itself at half time than to rely on me to be in any way involved in what some might think a simple task.

My main motivation for wanting to be a sportsman was that I'd noticed lots of girls from school would stay behind after hours to stand on the touchline and cheer on the boys' teams in football and rugby. So I believed it to be imperative that somehow I must put some shorts on and blag my way into anything resembling a school team. I lay in bed at night dreaming that one of the main players in the school football team would miss a sitter at a crucial point in the match, triggering anger and a near riot from the disenchanted, rumbling crowd of girls who would then begin chanting my name, as I reticently kitted up. Not stuff from Lost Property, mind, but from a major sponsor.

'Lee is under-rated,' they would chorus, 'he is not to be wasted. Let him on and win this game, and we'll definitely get butt naked.'

Well, a boy can dream.

10. The Hair Trigger

You know the phrase 'Stuff that up your arse'? Has that ever been done before? I can bear witness that it has. I saw it with my own eyes.

At weekends, Wayne and I would often walk across the back fields near the estate. It was always a bit of an adventure to visit the tip that was not too far from the flats. The lorries had spent all week bringing stuff in and dumping it there, and you never knew what you might get your hands on.

One day, when we were thirteen and eleven, Wayne and I were in the middle of the back fields. The only thing you could hear was the occasional cricket. We were weaving our way blissfully through the long wet grass when suddenly Wayne ducked down, covering his head with his hands. He turned and looked up at me, shouting, 'What's that?'

I thought it was another one of Wayne's wind-ups. I just carried on with my stroll. 'You do my head in, you do, Wayne.' But then, suddenly, something whizzed past my head, really fast. I turned towards Wayne, but he wasn't there. 'Wayne?' Where'd he gone?

A voice came from deep within the tall grass. 'Lee, get down.' Again, something else whipped past my head, closer this time, and cracked into the grass. I folded to my knees, curling into a ball. I waited there for a moment.

Not lifting my head – that stay firmly tucked between my legs – I shouted, 'Wayne, what was that noise? What you up to?'

'It's not me, you tosser. That's an air gun, that is. Someone's firing at us.'

I instantly began to sob. I was frightened. 'I want to go home.' I heard Wayne moving, and I lifted my head and saw him on his knees, peeking over the top of the grass, trying to get a better look. There was a sudden low thud as another pellet hit the wet mud next to him.

Wayne ducked back into the grass and looked over at me. 'There's a bloke over by the flats. I reckon it's him.'

I buried my head into the flattened grass and began crying into the soil below, confused. 'What have we done? I haven't done nothing, Wayne . . .'

I was snapped out of it by a muffled 'Bollocks to this.' I looked up and saw the soles of Wayne's daps shoot past me. He was making a run for it. I was on my own. I panicked, jumped to my feet and ripped after him. We ran across the field to the sound of the pellets whizzing past our heads and cracking into the grass around us.

Why does anyone fire a loaded gun at two small boys in the middle of a field? The only reason can be that this deficient twat has too much time on his hands. He has saved up his money from the labour exchange and bought a gun. Anyone who has held a gun will know that as soon as you pick it up and hold it in your hands, there is some kind of weird, overwhelming urge to fire it. It's something to do with an ancestral hunting throwback in our genes. Well, Charlton Heston over there was certainly a throwback.

It must have been quite a buzz that filled his meagre, uneventful day as he aimed at two live humans. Of course, when we started running for our lives that must have made it all the more of a thrilling prospect for him – moving targets! To him, we were just two little dots on the landscape that jumped, bobbed and weaved their way around the inside of his telescopic sight.

We managed to make it to the sanctuary of the back sheds near the flats, slamming our backs against the wall, hearts pumping faster than pistons. We were safe. Sniper boy, on the other hand, would have most likely chuckled to himself, shrugged his shoulders and thought no more about it. He probably moved on to train his sights on other parts of the estate and see how far a lead pellet could penetrate a shed door. Or perhaps he tried to hit one of the clothes-line poles, finding some delight in hearing the little distant ding as the pellet struck the galvanized steel.

Rumours on the estate soon alerted us to the identity of the shooter. He most certainly wouldn't have expected the two dots on the landscape, mere unconnected ducks at a shooting gallery, to arrive at his front door in the company of a rather larger, rather angrier dot: Dad. Nor would he have expected that loud thumping knock on his front door as he was just about to sit down with his wife for his tea.

I could smell the mixture of chip fat and gravy from outside on the landing where Wayne and I stood trembling with fear as Dad let go of my hand for a moment to give the front door a good hard thumping.

The bloke wouldn't have had a clue about who was knocking at his front door as he raised himself up from the dinner table. He would have no doubt glanced over at his wife, confused as to why anyone would be knocking quite so loudly at such an odd time of the evening. Now he was up, disturbed, he might even have picked up a bit of a march across the lounge. His anger was growing and he might have thought that on opening his door he would certainly give this persistent knocker a bit of an earful for banging so loudly at teatime. Muffled from behind the closed door, we heard him muttering, 'Who the hell is that who keeps knocking?'

As kids we were often drilled about the dangers of air guns. It was a difficult lesson to forget anyway, as Dad's glasses were a constant reminder of how he was shot in the eye while messing around with an air gun while serving in the army. 'I nearly lost me eye,' he'd tell us. 'There are still bits of lead floating about in it. I can see them go by sometimes. I can't watch the tennis any more and God forbid I try to do Spot the Ball.'

So we knew that whoever this bloke was, he was definitely going to get it. For Dad, this particular encounter was very personal, and I think that's why he wanted us there: to watch this man receive justice.

I looked up at Dad. His face was stiff and his top teeth were clamped down over his bottom lip. His eyes were like lasers, staring at the door. Because he was holding our hands, he hadn't been able to push up his big, thick, square glasses, and so they were hanging off the end of his nose. But I knew, when the time came, he would push them up with his finger, loading up before lift-off.

Then I saw the outline of the Air Gun Man appear behind the thick, frosted glass. Watching the figure fumble around for the latch, I felt sick as a wave of fear swept over my whole body. I hadn't seen him up close – he might be big and hurt my dad.

The door opened slightly and the man peered out from the gap. I could only see one eye and a nose. I wanted to run. I didn't know when, but I knew an explosion was about to happen . . .

'All right, all right, what you banging at me door for?'

'You got a fucking air gun, mate?' Dad snapped at him.

Before the bloke could even answer the question, Dad let go of our hands and pushed his way in through the door. Grabbing the front of the man's shirt, he held him in the air just inside his hall. Then he repeated the question, very slowly and deliberately.

'Tell me, have you got a fucking air gun?'

Wayne and I, unable to think of what to do, retreated a little back down the hall. I wanted to go home, but how could we leave our dad? Wayne did what he always did when he was stressed and unable to control a situation: he put his fingers in his ears. At least it cut out the sound, I suppose. Me? I curled up next to him.

But I still wanted to see what was happening, so I peered out from beneath Wayne's shoulder. Dad must have spotted the gun because we heard him shouting, 'This yours, mate?' The man just let out a sort of scared, whimpering sound. Dad knocked the door shut. Now that it was closed, it was a little easier for us. All we could hear were the muffled shouts from Dad and the odd little squeaks, moans and cries of fear from Air Gun Man. Through the frosted glass, we could only watch the two performing outlines of Dad and the man, frantically bobbing and weaving like a particularly noisy mime act. With one hand, Dad was holding the poor man aloft by the throat and, with the other, he was brandishing the gun. Dad shook it in the air.

'See this? I'm going to stick it right up your arse!'

I stared, frozen and dumbfounded. Wayne and I were fascinated. He took his fingers out of his ears and I pulled myself from underneath him and away from the wall. We stood, silent, hypnotized by the two silhouettes framed in the top half of the door as they gave a kind of Chinese shadow-puppet show behind the frosted glass. Lit by the light from behind them, the two figures in the flat were jostling each other, their arms suddenly shooting out at different angles and their bodies confusingly merging into one then suddenly splitting apart.

Then, out of nowhere, another character arrived, accompanied by high-pitched screaming. We saw the out-line of Air Gun Man's wife, arms flailing, head shaking, hair flopping this way and that, as she tried to quell Dad's rage. By now, it was getting difficult to tell what exactly was going on, but it looked like Dad was behind the man with the woman on Dad's back.

Then Air Gun Man began to let out a series of odd, guttural, animal sounds. In the confusion, someone must have reached for the latch because the door slowly swung open, revealing the appalling scene. Poor Air Gun Man's eyes stared at us, desperate for help, as we watched Dad quite literally trying to stick the end of the gun through the back of the man's trousers and, as he promised, up his arse. Never has Dad's hair-trigger temper been more evident.

But at least Air Gun Man was unlikely to take potshots at kids again.

Dad's explosions may have been scary, but they were also strangely reassuring. More often than not, they were designed to protect us. Nothing would rile him more than someone threatening his family. When roused, he would defend us like an enraged lion protecting his cubs. He was mad as hell – but on our behalf.

The downside, of course, was that Dad's temper so often acted as a barrier between us and the rest of the world. Life with him was often fun, mad even, but never dull. You lived in a permanent state of precarious unpredictability.

On another memorable occasion, he arrived at the flats blasting the horn and hanging out of the window of an open-top truck. He was waving his arms about like a demented schoolboy and had an upright piano tied precariously on to the back of the truck.

However, not long after the great cheery arrival, it quite quickly became clear that he had neglected to inform the truck driver when setting off from the second-hand furniture shop that the piano was to be delivered up five flights of stairs to the top flat. That fact wasn't even mentioned until it had been heaved off the back of the truck, lugged into the entrance to the flats and was resting on the first step of the first flight of stairs.

As soon as he grasped what the task entailed, the delivery man told Dad in no uncertain terms to stick that piano in a place far easier to reach than the top of five flights of stairs.

With the help of a few neighbours he had comman-
deered, Dad managed to crash, bang and shoulder the
piano, inch by painstaking inch, up the narrow concrete
stairwell. A lot of the residents were most keen to contribute their highly unenlightening advice as to how to do
it as we humped the massive wooden box up on to each
landing.

A door would swing open inquisitively and a suitable
member of the family was ushered out on to the landing
and press-ganged into joining the growing crowd of
movers. They became part of the entertainment for that
afternoon – well, it's not every day a piano passes your
door with a herd of people and a dog, all chattering, heaving and barking orders at each other.

I think on every landing someone found an excuse to
down tools for a rest. Cups of tea for all were served
from lots of different kitchens, stories were told, gossip
was caught up on, new friendships were made and a tune
was even played on the piano, before a voice would pipe
up, 'Right, up we go then.' Cups were gathered up, palms
were given a new coating of spit and the lifting would
start again. Eventually the piano was heaved into our flat
and found its new home in Wayne's and my bedroom, as
there was no other place for it.

It didn't stay there very long, however. One Sunday,
Wayne and I complained to Dad that there was nothing
to do. Dad suddenly shouted at us, 'You're bored? You
might as well throw the piano out of the window, then!'
Like a rock star who drives his Rolls Royce into a swimming pool, he just imagined it would be a laugh to go in
for a spot of wanton destruction.

We thought his idea was ridiculous until, to our amazement, Dad actually started smashing the piano up bit by bit and hurling it out of the bedroom window. It must have been an astonishing sight for anyone who happened to be looking out of the flats below to see random planks of wood and lengths of piano-wire shoot past.

We laughed our socks off, but I'm not sure the woman downstairs who stuck her nose out of the window and was narrowly missed by the piano on its way down was quite so amused.

The piano, while we had it, was always a focal point for spontaneous outbursts of expression in our flat. For example, I would be sitting quietly in my bedroom when the door would burst open and Dad would march over to the piano and play half an hour of kicking rock'n'roll. Then, as quickly as he had entered, he was gone. It might even happen late at night, when we had to be up for school the next morning. But his explanation would be that he'd thought of an idea and just needed to work it out on the 'Joanna' as he called it. If it was late, he would offer up a nursery rhyme to help us sleep, usually something very rude.

He would chant:

> 'There was a young man from Gosham,
> Took out his bollocks to wash 'em.
> His wife said "Jack,
> If you don't put em back,
> I'll stand on the buggers and squash 'em."'

Then Dad would say, 'Sleep tight,' and be off.

Dad's moods swung so wildly he was like the Scottish Highlands, manifesting all four seasons in a single hour.

With him, it was alternately sunny and stormy, and it taught me a great deal about resilience and tolerance. It showed me how I didn't want to behave. I realized that exhibiting that sort of unpredictable temperament was no way to live your life and opted for a more tranquil approach to the world. But we couldn't avoid it; that's what it was like living with Dad.

11. Jus' Like That

By the mid 1970s, Dad was getting a lot more work as a club singer. It cast a more optimistic spell over us. Our flat – once so gloomy and cold – now seemed much more redolent with wonder and hope. The sense of optimism began to feed our young dreams of a better life.

Dad was enjoying some success in the world of show business in the pubs and working men's clubs of Wales and Bristol. Those places were buzzing back then. They were the destination of choice for your average working Joe and Joanna's Saturday night out. They were cool, affordable places to take your wife if you were a working man.

In those days, there was a social club or working men's club on nearly every big housing estate in the industrial heartlands of Britain. In Manchester, Liverpool, Glasgow or Newcastle at that time, there might be one on every street corner. It was the time of the Beatles, Morecambe and Wise, Jimmy Tarbuck, Tom Jones, Engelbert Humperdinck, Freddie Starr, Gerry and The Pacemakers, Shirley Bassey, Mike and Bernie Winters and Hughie Green with his catchphrase 'Opportunity Knocks!' Those were just some of the huge stars that played the clubs back then.

The shows presented by the working men's clubs were to our family and millions of others across the country a spectacular departure from the daily slog. Plus, those clubs were a real breeding ground for some of the funniest performers who would go on to become household names, British institutions even. Singers, comics, magicians, jugglers, bands and groups of all shapes and sizes – nearly every night of the week they were jamming clubs to the rafters.

So, as youngsters, Wayne and I often went travelling with Dad. We would be there wide-eyed with awe and amazement as we sat backstage watching Dad and his fellow acts. Take the famous night I saw Tommy Cooper. Great is an over-used word in comedy, but it really does apply to a man I regard as a genius.

I had gone with Dad to a club called Blazers in Windsor. It was a glamorous venue that only booked top names. This particular night Dad was supporting Tommy Cooper, perhaps the leading comedian in the country at that time, adored as much by his peers as by the public. I loved him, and so Dad asked me if I'd like to go with him. It was only a couple of hours away from where we lived at the time, so Mum didn't mind.

Upon arrival, the manager of Blazers welcomed Dad, but he seemed agitated and nervous and kept going on about how long Dad could perform for . . . if required. Dad wondered why he was so worried about the timing and the manager owned up that Tommy Cooper was running late and that he was worried the fez-wearing funny man might not make it in time. A no-show by the most celebrated comic of his day could cause the good people of Windsor to become uncharacteristically rowdy and rebellious.

Dad did his allotted slot, while I sat as ordered, listening over the speaker in the dressing room. All the time, I was getting more and more nervous about seeing Tommy Cooper. I thought he was the funniest comedian on the planet and was fully expecting the dressing-room door to burst open at any moment to reveal him, but it didn't happen.

Dad came back to the dressing room buzzing. Sweating as usual after a good show, he plonked his props on the dresser. At that moment, the manager arrived in the doorway. He looked agitated; he was sweating too, but not in a good way. He that said Tommy was still an hour away and he really hoped he could make it on time, as the break before the comedian went on would only be half an hour.

Half an hour went by, and the manager extended the interval for as long as possible before the excited audience took their seats, buzzing with anticipation at the prospect of seeing their beloved Tommy Cooper.

Fifteen minutes passed. As every minute ticked by, I saw a year taken off the manager's life. The crowd at Blazers were not known for their patience: they pays their money, they likes to be entertained and on time. Every second it seemed the manager would appear at the door, more nervous than before. After another ten minutes, I began to really feel for him, as the audience, now fed up with waiting, started to sing 'Why are we waiting?'

As Dad finished packing up the last piece of his stuff, he looked at me and said, 'I don't think he's coming, you know, and there's going to be a riot 'ere.'

I looked up and suddenly saw the manager, now

nearing a breakdown, shoot past the door with his arms extended. 'Tommy!' he exclaimed.

I could hear Tommy Cooper in the hall. 'Am I late?'

'Nooooo,' replied the manager, without missing a beat. 'You're right on time.'

I couldn't believe I could actually hear the great Tommy Cooper. I sat frozen to my seat. I barely heard Dad, who suddenly felt he was in the way: 'Come on, Lee, out we go. Tommy needs this dressing room.' I rose from my seat and followed Dad to the door. He threw his bags out into the hall, and said to Cooper, 'I'm out of there now, Tom.'

'Thanks, Dave. How are the crowd?' asked Tommy.

Dad told the truth. 'They're great, but I think they're getting a bit pissed off.'

Tommy understood. 'Oh; all right, thanks. I'll keep me eyes open then.' He stopped in the doorway and looked down at me. 'Who's this?'

'That's my boy. Come on, son, out you come.' I walked forward, staring at what was to me a giant. That moment has remained etched in my memory ever since. This was a man who embodied showbiz: even chatting away off-stage, he oozed charisma from every pore. Wow, I thought, I'd love to be like that!

Tommy Cooper – yes, Tommy Cooper! – bent down and shook my hand. 'Hello, son. What's your name?'

I couldn't answer – I was too nervous. So Dad answered for me. 'Lee.' Then Dad ushered me out.

'Lee? That's a nice . . .'

Just then the manager rushed back into the hall. 'Ten minutes, Tommy.'

'I need a radio mike,' shouted Tommy.

Then the other door opened, and Tommy's son burst in, pushing huge travel cases on wheels. Tommy sped into action. 'Right, son, you know what to do.' With that, Tommy pulled a stick from one of the boxes and gave it to his son. The manager hurried back in and gave Tommy a radio mike.

As Dad gathered his stuff together, I watched Tommy through the door begin to get ready. He took his shirt off and put on a stage shirt and over his head he placed a microphone holder. He shoved the mike into it and began speaking. 'One, two. One, two . . .' I could hear the crowd going wild.

Tommy carried on getting ready and speaking into the mike. As he did this, I could see his son on stage prodding the back of the curtain with the stick while at the same time setting up a table.

'What's this? Where am I?' Tommy went on, as his son poked the curtain some more. It was fantastic. I could hear the audience laughing their heads off.

By now, Tommy Cooper had his trousers on and had set up some props. I watched, rooted to the spot. He carried on with the same routine for at least ten minutes. What amazed me was that he hadn't even walked on stage, and yet the audience were roaring with laughter at the mere sound of his voice. You could feel it backstage, right in the pit of your stomach. That was some talent.

Slightly flustered, he came out of the dressing room and walked to the side of the stage, all the time nervously checking his pockets. Suddenly, I heard the manager start to introduce him. As Tommy Cooper stood in a gap between the curtains, beams of spotlight trickled through, silhouetting his huge stature. The audience cheered even more loudly.

'Ladies and gentleman, Tommy Cooper!'

He whipped open the curtain and walked out into the bright lights. As the curtain flopped shut, all I could hear – even through the curtain that tends to muffle everything on stage – was a cacophony of clapping and laughter. It was the definition of a 'wall of sound'. Through a tiny gap in the curtain, I could just pick out a woman in the front row saying, 'Blimey, ain't his feet big?' It's safe to say that he stormed it.

That was a turning point for me. I spent the car journey home in complete silence. All I could think about was how funny Tommy Cooper was, but without seemingly trying. He was just funny. I played it over and over in my mind: Tommy Cooper walking through those curtains, and the roar of the crowd, the laughter. It was not polite or restrained, but uninhibited, bellyaching laughter. That's what I liked – when it actually hurt to laugh.

They were laughing because he was funny; in fact, they were even cracking up ten minutes before he came on stage. The mere prospect of his appearance was making them laugh – what sort of power was that? When he did appear, they were not cracking up at his lines because he hadn't said anything yet, but somehow they sensed his funniness. His mere demeanour was enough to set them off. They knew he simply had funny bones. I thought, 'How incredible that must feel, to have the audience eating out of your hand before you even walk on stage, to be so funny they're already your friends before they've even clapped eyes on you!'

I know now that comes from years and years of hard graft in the clubs and theatres up and down the country. I know now that Tommy Cooper probably felt really insecure about whether his show would catch fire that night I saw him. A comedian never forgets it if something doesn't work. Even when that crowd laughed at everything he did that night, he was probably wondering all the time if it was good enough, hoping right until he said goodnight that it would be OK. That anxiety is just part of a comedian's DNA. But what I saw of Tommy Cooper when I was just a kid touched me deeply. It was truly awe-inspiring. It planted a seed in my head which, over the coming years, was to grow and grow.

It's difficult to put into words what I felt that night. But it's that sense which has driven me throughout my life. It's the sensation you get from a performer who makes you feel all tingly inside, as if he has touched you in some way – whether it be through pathos or familiarity. You feel safe with him in front of you, and when he says goodbye, he leaves you with that infectious sense of something hopeful and wonderful.

There are precious few performers who can do this, who can speak to you personally, connect with something deep inside you and tickle your soul. I know that it's each to their own and that one person's illumination is another person's ignorance, but that's what drives me.

From time to time, people have accused me of walking about in a dream world, seeing things around me that others don't see. But, you know what, I don't care. I've never liked beige.

Tommy Cooper, Charlie Chaplin, Buster Keaton, Billy Connolly, Eric Sykes, Morecambe and Wise and Freddie Starr – they are just a few of the performers who have funny bones. They can make you laugh without saying a single word.

Bob Hope, Bob Monkhouse – anyone called Bob, really – they're the kings of the one-liners. They're brilliant in their own right, but they don't get to me in the same way as the Funny Bones Brigade. I always preferred Harpo to Groucho Marx. The natural comics exhibit an Everyman feeling and a sense of pathos that genuinely touches me.

I would rather be in that world than anywhere else.

12. The Beginning of My Life in the Theatre

No one ever went abroad for their holidays in those days. It was unheard of, reserved for the super-rich. For the majority of people, if you could get some money together, you might take your family to one of the many seaside towns and enjoy the summer shows, which provided a rare glimpse of glamour.

A big part of our childhood was spent travelling around the country for summer seasons with Dad. The shows back then were huge productions that would be considered unaffordable now. A typical summer theatre show company might consist of at least forty people, sometimes more. Once everyone had got to know each other, it became one big family, with all the ups and downs, trials and tribulations that entails. But as Mum always said, 'What goes on backstage, stays backstage.' Maybe the Las Vegas Tourist Board stole that phrase.

Once everyone got to know that Wayne and I were Dave's kids, we could hang around anywhere in the theatre and no one would move us on. Mostly they just ignored us and got on with their jobs. They were accustomed to all of us kids being around. The offspring of all the different acts would always get together to form a large gang.

We quickly found out that show people are more tolerant of the quirky kind of behaviour that 'normal' society might see as strange. They appear to have an 'us and them' attitude; they believe they conduct themselves in a way that the audience wouldn't necessarily understand. Everyone I have ever known in show business – whether a member of the technical crew or a performer – takes it for granted that the show is the most important thing of all. A lack of inhibition comes with the territory. If a performer walked about with a banana up his backside, no one would bat an eyelid, as long as the show went on without a hitch.

No one took any notice of other company members, say, having affairs, walking around with no clothes on, swearing, drinking, fighting, rowing. It was like you belonged to a small, private community. All sorts of odd antics were allowed within those walls.

I always found that funny. In any other job, certain behaviour would just not be tolerated. If you worked in a bank, for example, you would be fired on the spot if you suddenly got naked to change into your work clothes before serving at the counter. You would also be dismissed instantly if you were a labourer and you refused to work with someone who mixed up the cement carelessly and was making you look bad. Can you imagine a road digger throwing his drill down, storming across the dual carriageway and shouting: 'I refuse to work with inferior tools! If you need me, I'll be in the tea hut!'?

By the time I was thirteen, I'd already seen stuff that most people might feel I shouldn't have: nudity, drinking, swearing. And that was just me. Only kidding, I never swore – but I did drink in the nude.

Everyone loved the dancers – they would always spoil kids. I'd often find myself in the dancers' changing rooms during breaks or when a comic was on. I never intended to be in there, but they would always ask me in. If they saw me hanging about, I'd hear: 'Lee, Lee, come in 'ere and keep us company.'

I loved the dancers. They had a way about them. Maybe it's their training, but they always moved so elegantly, and their bodies were so lithe and beautiful. It never bothered them that I was there – they liked nothing better than to relax by walking around with hardly any clothes on. Funny, it never bothered me either.

The only weird bit was the dancers' make-up. From the stalls in a theatre, they look gorgeous and glamorous but, curiously, close up it looks as though they've had a fight at the cosmetics counter. The make-up looks like it's been applied by an uncontrollable weightlifter who's been sacked from his previous job stamping passports because of his nervous muscle spasms. But, on stage, the dancers have the appearance of angels.

I just adored hanging around backstage when they were performing. I would find a place to sit out of the way somewhere in the wings and just marvel as they kicked, jumped and danced, a smile permanently fixed on their heavily made-up faces.

When there was a big routine involving all the dancers, I would watch them gather excitedly at the side of the stage. There they would be, nattering about boyfriends, where they might be going after the show, or complaining about having to do a laundry run tomorrow. But as soon as the curtain went up, they would all be in their places, with bright smiles lighting up their faces and their over-the-top eyeshadow sparkling in the spotlights.

It was like a giant clock, where at certain points every cog would just click into place. It was run with military precision and punctuality, as they had to bring down the curtain at an exact time in order to be ready for the second show.

I would sit there unnoticed as the performers scurried all around me. Backstage was pretty crowded, but there was always a terrific buzz. Lots of stagehands would be dashing around because of the enormous number of scenery changes. Dancers were rushing off to get changed and then reappearing as something else. The frantic costume department was always the hub of everything.

Whenever a stand-up comic came on, that was the sign for the orchestra to slide out of the band pit to the nearest pub. They would always know when to come back – in fact, they were so punctual, the comic was able to time his act precisely by the reappearance of the brass section. All the while, the top of the bill would be rehearsing his lines, wandering about in a circle backstage, muttering to himself. Then the stage manager would call for the right lighting and the juggler would go on to whooping and cheering.

I was always transfixed by a certain bandleader, Mr Dubbs, a lively, small man sporting an obvious toupee and a worrying tendency to lose concentration at vital moments.

Syrups were rife amongst acts and crew in the 1960s, 1970s and the 1980s. It was all the rage to have your head de-slapped. You couldn't get away with it these days. Now the whispers are shouts. Upon meeting someone wearing a rug so obviously held on with carpet grips, people will drop to the floor and roll around with hysterical laughter, shrieking, 'Right, take it off now, you've had your fun.'

Anyway, back to Mr Dubbs, a regular conductor of orchestras in many a summer show on the circuit. He chose, very unwisely, to perch what can only be described as a bit of tormented roadkill on top of his head. It was definitely the worst-fitting rug I'd ever seen. It was so bad, it had 'Welcome' written on it. Sometimes you wondered if the wig was real and the bloke under it was false because the rug was a completely different colour to the rest of his hair that skirted its edges. It did things independently of him. For example, if he changed direction suddenly, the wig would somehow stay where it was – until he felt there was no one looking and it was safe to manoeuvre it back into place. Mum and Dad ordered us never to mention it, but that only encouraged us to refer it more brazenly.

Mr Dubbs had a strategic collection of four wigs, each one boasting hair of a different length. So he would always arrive at the beginning of the month wearing a closely trimmed wig on his head. Then in the second week, he would be seen wearing a slightly longer and not so tidy wig. By week three, you could see his hair had seemingly grown quite rapidly and was getting out of control. To ensure nobody had any suspicions, Mr Dubbs would be heard tutting a lot and feeling his hair as though frustrated with its unkempt style.

In week four, as soon as he entered the stage door, he always made a big show of informing everyone he met that he needed a trim. 'Hello, Bernie, have you got me dressing-room key? I'll tell you, mate, I need a hair cut.' Just to drive it home, if he met someone in the corridor, Mr Dubbs would sigh: 'Hello, Pete, I'm off to the hairdresser's tomorrow to get this lot cut off. Look at it – it's like a mane!' Then, to top off this ridiculous facade, he would return the next day wearing the shorter wig, and the whole charade would start all over again.

Anyway, I remember Mr Dubbs completely messed up one evening during the performance of Johnny Curtis, a very skilful juggler. The repetitiveness of doing the same thing every night can afflict anyone during a long run, and so instead of focusing on what was going on, Mr Dubbs's mind must have wandered that evening. Mr Curtis's climactic juggle was usually accompanied by a small stab from the drummer, who was in turn waiting for the signal from Mr Dubbs.

But, at that moment, the bandleader resembled nothing so much as a lobotomy patient. He was standing motionless at the front of the band, hands raised at the ready, as if trapped in some sort of time freeze. So, always keen to drum up laughs and break up the monotony, Mr Curtis hurled one of his balls in the direction of the bandleader. The ball bounced off Mr Dubbs's forehead, sending his wig in one direction and the ball in another. It bounced straight back to Mr Curtis who caught it with a flourish, made a bow and took in the well-deserved applause.

As the juggler lapped up more cheers, the embarrassed

bandleader surreptitiously retrieved his wig and placed it back on his head. Ta-da!

Of course, Mr Dubbs was a figure of fun and the source of many of the company's most sustained and raucous gags. But he added to the gaiety of nations. He was exactly the sort of extravagant show person who made me think, 'I want to be one of those!'

As a small, quiet, impressionable boy, I was in raptures about the lights and the music. It was precisely the inner workings of the backstage area that no one sees which interested me the most. Some people might suggest that when you see the secrets of what goes on, the spell is broken. But I just found it fascinating to see jugglers rowing under their breath with their onstage partners about how they'd dropped a club or even narrowly missed their target with a knife, or acrobats flinging themselves about the stage while carrying on a conversation about whom they might have slept with the night before.

I'd listen to the lighting operator take orders from the stage manager to create the right mood for, say, Cilla Black to sing her 'Liverpool Lullaby' – a song that would always make me cry. I'd also watch Cannon and Ball, and laugh my head off as Tommy carried Bobby offstage in his arms. Bobby was always a master of pathos. They would walk into the wings and discuss how good the audience were. It was so brilliant.

I loved to see Michael Barrymore disappear off the stage into the audience, accompanied by a huge roar, or to be enthralled by the obvious pain of Dailey and Wayne's physical routines. You couldn't see from the front of house, but from the wings it was clear that this pair, the funniest double act I've ever seen, were pushing themselves to the very limit twice nightly.

As a young boy eager to absorb every experience, I also found it entrancing to watch Larry Grayson, a very nervous performer, psyche himself up before his famous intro music started. Then he would walk onstage, dragging his trademark chair and receiving rapturous applause, looking as self-confident as you like, even though I knew moments earlier he had been petrified. It was that feeling of magic which was created when all the elements came together: the lights, the music, the make-up, the costumes.

No one noticed me, but I was taking it all in. I found it captivating. Like a sponge, I'd soak it all up. I'd stand there out of the way and watch Jimmy Tarbuck, Little and Large, the Black Abbots, Tom O'Connor, Jim Davidson, Leslie Crowther, Bert Cook, Dustin Gee and Les Dennis, Roger Whittaker, Val Doonican, Les Dawson, Tommy Steele, Norman Collier, Mike Newman, Shirley Bassey and Roy Castle (whose drummer taught me to play percussion backstage). Imagine what it would cost to reunite that bill today – admittedly, the services of Doris Stokes might be required for some of the acts.

I also remember as a young boy my chance meeting with Lord Delfont, the famous impresario who ran most of the summer seasons. I'd heard so much about him. I was sitting in my dad's dressing room when he entered with a large entourage. He asked me if I wanted to follow in my dad's footsteps.

'Not in a million years, Mr Delfont, it's too scary,' I replied. Little did I know!

He turned to my dad and said, 'I like what you do, Dave. Where have you been all my life?'

'Er, working for you,' came the reply.

I watched like a hawk and drank it all in. Every day, for me, it was a case of 'look and learn'. Years later, all that observation paid off. I never knew it, but by the time I finally came to perform myself, I was already fluent in the language of the stage.

13. The Move to Billericay

Despite finding regular work during the summer season, during the rest of the year Dad was still struggling to earn enough money just to get by. The trouble with show business is that it can consume you, if you let it. It's an alluring little devil, and, once hooked, some people become self-absorbed and narcissistic. They're always looking over their shoulder to see what the other guy is doing. They're constantly growling to themselves, 'Why aren't I doing that? Why aren't the breaks coming my way?' You can very easily become bitter, even resentful, if you let it get to you.

But to Dad's immense credit, he simply got his head down and worked hard – and one day he got us out of the Lawrence Weston for good. I'm not saying there's anything bad about the Lawrence Weston. I'm very proud of coming from there, but life on that estate was perhaps beginning to grind us down. Most of the arguments in our flat revolved around where the next rent money was coming from and the stress would obviously trickle down to Wayne and me.

So Dad took a risk and stepped on the first rung of the property ladder to try and give us all better opportunities in life. He had met a bloke in a club who said he had a house for sale, going cheap. Fed up with hiding from the meter man, Dad thought that if he could just get us into a house, then at least we would have something solid behind us.

But Wayne and I were still bewildered when Dad came home one day and said, 'We're off to Billericay.' We just laughed and thought it was a joke. We'd never heard of such a place – I mean, who moves to a made-up town?

The day we left Lawrence Weston for the last time was the most devastating day of my life. The night before, I'd said my goodbyes to my best friend, Colin, and my then girlfriend, Betty. I was just eleven, but I swore to her that I would remain forever hers until I was old enough to return and ask for her hand in marriage. I told her that, whatever happened, she had to wait because I would be keeping myself for her only. I do hope she's not still waiting because now I'm married to someone else and the missus would go mad.

The next morning, the car was loaded up with just our clothes. That's all we took. The furniture in the flat would stay – Dad said it was worthless anyway and we'd wait and try to get better stuff in Billericay. As we pulled away, I waved furiously to Colin through the rear window of the car until he was but a speck on the grimy, smog-covered landscape.

Wayne and I were uncertain of what awaited us. We'd done all that packing up before, when we went away on the long summer seasons with Mum and Dad. But this time it was for good. We were off to live someplace else and never coming back. I don't know why we were anxious – after all, we'd been on the move ever since we could remember – but I think it was because it was so final. During that entire stomach-churning journey into the unknown, I cried. In fact, I sobbed so much I feel asleep in the back of the car, utterly exhausted.

The slam of the car door woke me with a start. I must have slept for ages. I looked around and saw I was the only one left in the car – either we had reached Billericay or the car was magically driving itself. I looked up from the back seat and through the angled gap in the side window. The sky was a bright blue, with not a cloud to be seen anywhere. I slowly lifted my head and cast a glance outside the car. We were parked on a driveway. It led up to a white, painted, semi-detached, pebbledash house with a front door adorned with a small lion's-head brass knocker.

The garden was overgrown – no one had lived in the house for some time. I looked around at the other houses. They all looked exactly like ours, side by side, neatly laid out. These identical, clean, bright houses stood there in a seemingly endless row. They all had the same driveways on which sat gleaming cars, the same green lawns separated by small, tightly cut hedges and the same borders packed with colourful bedding plants. A man opposite pushed his mower across the lawn. All the while, he was keeping one eye on us. We must have looked to him like we'd just landed from another planet.

I climbed out of the car and damn near fainted at the amount of clean oxygen in the air. All I could smell was foliage – the wind was wafting through a huge tree that hung over the driveway. As I walked slowly up the tarmac towards the house, through the open front door I could hear the echo of my family's excited voices and clanking footsteps on the wooden floorboards. It was like stumbling into a dream world.

I stepped into the hall and looked around for everybody. Wallpaper hung off the walls, the floors were bare, a staircase climbed one wall and, straight ahead, a narrow passage led to a dirty galley kitchen where Mum had already got going. The kettle was steaming away, with cups, milk and sugar on the side. Whenever we wound up anywhere, it didn't take her long to make it feel like our place. She's like the SAS of homeliness: give her five minutes and you'd have thought we'd lived there for years.

'Hello, is your mum or dad there?'

I whipped round to see a tall, beautiful woman. She had a shoulder-length, fresh-from-the-local-salon hairdo, rosy cheeks, big, blue, happy eyes and a knitted white polo neck. She looked down at me kindly and proffered a tray with a teapot on it and what looked like cake. She smiled. 'I live across the way, I wondered . . .'

I froze on the spot and began stammering. 'I don't, I mean, what? Did you? I better get . . . Muummmmmmm?' She bent down, trying in vain to understand my Bristol pronunciation.

Suddenly, Mum was at my side. 'Can I help you, love?' Mum said, smiling at the woman. But I could tell Mum was giving this new face the once over.

'Hello, I live across the way. I wondered if you would like a cup of tea.'

I knew what Mum was thinking. She would have normally said, 'What? You think we can't afford tea?' But she didn't. She thought on her feet, adjusted really quickly and put on a very odd, mock-posh voice. The effect was spoiled somewhat by her broad West Country accent.

'Eeooooww, thot's verr neice awv you, thonk youuu . . . Aaan ef there's aneefine we caan do for yoo, yooo ownly av to ask.' Mum took the tray and nodded as if to say, 'All right, now leave us alone.'

The poor woman looked confused. She stared blankly for a moment at Mum then down at me. Then, lost in thought, she turned and scuttled off back up the drive. The man mowing the lawn stopped and watched as the lady trotted across the road, back to her nicely kept house. Mum looked up and down the street. You could already see a few net curtains twitching in the windows. We were in a new place, but still had that same old feeling of being outsiders.

Let me tell you a bit about Billericay. It's a small commuter town about fifty miles east of London on the way to the Victorian seaside town of Southend-on-Sea. Southend is the resort known for the annual influx of the work-hardened mass of London's East Enders, keen to blow out the soot and smoke for a couple of days with some fresh sea air. After doing well for themselves, those same East Enders often choose to spill out of London to join the new start-up towns that orbit the capital like planets, swallowing up smaller villages in the process. Billericay is one of these.

It's now part of Basildon, a newer, much bigger town. Because of its rail links to London, Billericay provides an easy option for City workers to settle within its relatively quiet suburbs. It offers local shops, badminton, bowls and dance classes, community centres and relatively decent schools. It's a place where one can live out the British dream of the two point four children, the wife and, if you do well, perhaps the four-wheel drive which the people of Billericay love to wash and polish on the driveway of a Sunday – the car, I mean, not the wife.

I've always thought that this prim and proper ambience is why Mum never really felt comfortable in Billericay. She had just left the tell-it-like-it-is attitude of the Lawrence Weston Housing Estate. To have then been placed slap-bang in the middle of quiet suburbia discombobulated Mum. Goodbye to the afternoons spent nattering with the neighbours in our kitchen, keeping an eye out for trouble, people banging on your door for help all hours, the impromptu get-togethers, the fights and the break-ins – and hello to a nearly silent, empty, well-kept house with lots of cushions, trimmed hedges and the smell of freshly mown lawns. To her, an upfront, in-your-face woman, it must have initially been torture.

Anyway, after the well-meaning, tea-tray-bearing neighbour had left, I followed Mum into the kitchen, where Dad stood with arms folded, looking triumphant. He turned to Mum. 'This is it, Shirl!' he shouted, clearly excited. I smiled, revelling in his exuberant mood. 'We've got our own house,' he continued, punching the air.

'Yeah, I've just met one of the neighbours,' Mum said, hesitantly. I could tell she was concerned about it. I had the same sensation. I felt as though we didn't belong. It was as if my sense of never fitting in had merely followed me from Bristol to Billericay.

But Dad was having none of it – for once, he obviously didn't share our qualms. He broke into a loud laugh. 'Yeah, well, wait till they get a load of us lot.'

Billericay, you can't say you weren't warned!

14. The Frisbee Flop Performed Without a Mat

Over the years, Wayne and I had developed a really good sense of recognizing and then quickly adapting to regional accents and behaviour. This skill manifested itself I suppose because we'd travelled around the country so much as kids. But also we seemed to have an uncanny ability to disappear into the background. If I'm honest, I'd always followed the lead of Wayne, who was and still is especially adept at reflecting like a human mirror what may be going on around him. Anyone who knows him will tell you that what he reflects back will be amplified. While tickling your funny bone, he'll show up all the things that the locals have never noticed before and will always draw a laugh.

There's a strange dynamic that goes on between Wayne and me. Wayne is a very funny bloke – everyone says it – but he's the type who is funny in a group. Wayne's the funny one, people tell me, you're the quiet one. That's how it works. I've always sat quietly in the corner with my mouth shut and been happy with my own thoughts, content to dream and fantasize about odd things.

Meanwhile, Wayne is much more open; he displays his humour there and then, and the bigger the crowd around him, the better. I wouldn't think of standing in a pub, as

Wayne does, trying to make people laugh. I try so hard to fit in, I appear idiotic by always struggling to retain some normality. Unfortunately, the less I conform, the more neurosis I feel and the more things go wrong.

And yet, paradoxically, I don't mind going on stage in front of an audience of thousands – an experience that, strangely enough, seems less scary than performing to my mates in a pub. If I can go over everything beforehand and rehearse what I shall say, then I don't mind getting up on the stage in front of a large crowd. Somehow, then, I can understand what I have to do. It feels right to walk out onstage, if I've already rehearsed it in my head. I feel safer there than I do off in the so-called 'real world'. Wayne, on the other hand, would never in a million years walk out onstage and tell jokes.

But in some respects we're very similar. Like me, Wayne feels safer making people laugh; it gives him a sense of security, of acceptance, of belonging, where there has always been in both of our lives a sense of constant change and fear.

I'm with you, broth, I know. You've never said, but I know.

Why else would I attempt to stand up in front of twenty thousand people at the O2 Arena? It's insecurity on a giant scale. Basically, I'm shouting, 'Hello, my name is Lee. Would you be my friend, please? I ain't got none.'

But I also think it's a kind of test that I must pass. That's all I've ever tried to do: to punish myself by taking this test. I have constantly told myself I'm not good enough and love to give myself a hard time. Sometimes, working so many hours, I've collapsed from exhaustion.

But I feel that's OK because it hurts and that's what I want. Trouble is, of course, that it's not very nice for the ones around you, those who love you. But if it doesn't hurt, then I don't feel I'm doing it right.

I think this eagerness to please has been a driving force in my life – with mixed results. On the positive side, it has opened up many opportunities because of my willingness to take part. But on the flip side, because I'm afraid to say 'No' sometimes for fear of letting people down, it has got me into all sorts of trouble. If you've read the book thus far, you'll know what I mean!

Anyway, as a child, it never took me long to blend into the background, as I'd try to avoid singling myself out as 'Who's the idiot?' It would only be a matter of minutes before Wayne had already made friends at the local school. It usually took me a little longer because of my shyness and my eagerness to please. I'd try to merge into the nearest wall, while Wayne was the life and soul.

My mother is the same. She can fit in and make friends wherever she goes. Perhaps because she was adopted as a child and didn't know who her parents were until she was a lot older, she learned from an early age to just blend in. But there is a difference with her. She can make friends very easily, but in equal measure she can make as many enemies. She has a very earthy, direct way about her which you either love or hate. She tells it like it is, and when the blood pulsing through her veins starts to boil, God help you! She is equally adept verbally or physically.

I knew something would happen on my first day at school in Billericay: it always did. I was eleven, so I was enrolled in the junior school on the other side of town. I dreaded it, because I knew what was coming. I was introduced to the class as I had been on numerous previous occasions. It was always the same. I was brought in like a hostage and made to stand at the front of the class, while the head teacher stood next to me, giving it the softly spoken, concerned introduction. But the clincher would be when the head asked: 'Lee, would you like to introduce yourself to the rest of the class?' At that moment, he'd basically painted a target on my back. I was now the hare at the dog track, to be chased at break time.

It was a good job I had a big bush of fuzzy hair because it hid most of my face. It always looked like I was peering out the back end of a giant poodle or some rare breed of farmyard animal, but that was a good thing because, by that stage of the introduction, my face had gone a bright crimson colour. I nervously fiddled with the strap of my imitation-leather school satchel, emblazoned with my name on the front. Then I let out a little cough and, while still looking down at my skinny white knobbly legs, I said in a broad Bristolian twang to the bunch of Cockney kids in front of me: "Aaargh roight, me name's Lee. It's gurt lush to be yer, like. Fanks fur aven I . . .'

For a few seconds, there was complete silence – even the teacher stared at me in disbelief. Then, and I knew it was coming, the whole class burst into uncontrollable laughter. Even the cut-out characters in the Harvest Festival picture on the back wall were killing themselves laughing.

Other kids always thought I was mucking about and putting a voice on. But they were soon convinced that was indeed the way I spoke, and because of my West Country twang, they would then think it great fun to call me, 'Farmer Giles', or 'Cow Pat'. This, of course, just magnified my sense of neurosis, of being different and self-conscious.

One effect of this neurosis was the fact that I would never go to the toilet at school. I'd go through all sorts of agonies rather than having to endure the embarrassment of using the school toilet. I would walk around the place with my head bowed and eyes directed at the floor. At break times, I would stand right out in the furthest corner of the playing field, mumbling descriptions to myself of what was around me and how I was feeling. Pacing up and down, I would repeat it over and over again, as if talking to a second party. 'Just stay here where no one can see you. Not long now, Lee, before you can go home. What am I doing here? I want to go home.' I was trapped in my own imagination, a destination I would seek out as a constant place of safety throughout my life.

Another form of self-defence was to say something without warning or let out a strange sound or voice, just out of the blue. I think I did that to throw the people around me, allowing things to take on a more anarchic, unpredictable mood and making them focus on that rather than on me. It was like chucking someone a curve ball.

In fact, that's how I came to break a kid's arm soon after starting school in Billericay. I'd arrived there two weeks previously, but already things had started to happen. It was like *The Omen*. One kid called me Inspector Clouseau, because everywhere I went havoc would ensue.

Let me just straighten something out: I never actually broke his arm personally – he did it himself. But if it hadn't been for me, it would never have happened.

As I've mentioned, I would spend break times standing at the far corner of the playing field, muttering away to myself like a Bristolian Rain Man, ignoring the rest of the pupils who crowded the field.

One morning, at the aptly named break time, I had this burning desire to put my blazer over my head and run around like I was a superhero. I'd always wanted to be a superhero. I loved to do that at my last school – remember the X-ray specs? – but it had taken me ages to pluck up the courage.

So, instead, I just paced nervously up and down next to the wire fence, not wanting to make eye contact with anyone. All around me, there were groups of girls skipping, and boys with bed hair and one sock up and one sock down, playing football with a small tennis ball. Either that or they were imitating film fighting. There were the familiar, high-pitched screams and shouts of enthusiastic excitement you get from any playground packed with kids at break time. I so wanted to be a part of it, but didn't dare join in.

'Hoy, Farmer Giles.'

''Ere it comes,' I thought. It was inevitable – it was only a question of when.

I'd thought if I could just make it through break time without anyone picking on me, it would be a first. The last school I was at, I hadn't even entered the classroom before I'd trapped the teacher's fingers in the door. So adamant and determined not to go to school was I, Mum had offered to take me down to the class herself. However, as soon as the teacher opened the door and I set eyes on all those other kids, I flipped and tried to run.

But the teacher and my mum simultaneously rugby-tackled me. Mum grabbed my waist, while the teacher held my legs aloft. Together, they struggled to push me into the class head first. To the other kids, it must have looked like I was levitating into the room. Every now and then, my head would pop round the door. I would stop crying for a moment, stare at everyone and begin again. Then I seized the door handle and, as the teacher was using the door frame as leverage at the time, it slammed right on her fingers.

A lot of parents complained that their children came home repeating swear words they had heard from the teacher that day, so she was reprimanded for that. Plus, it severely hampered her maths teaching; for the next two weeks, when she tried counting out on her fingers, she couldn't get past two. It was like being taught maths the Django Reinhardt way.

'Farmer Giles?' Yes, I'd heard that one before. It always meant the same thing: they're coming over to test me out, to see what I'm all about. I turned round, and there were two of them: one a chubby kid with a helmet cut staring straight at me – he could have modelled Christmas puddings and resembled nothing so much as a fat penis. The other was a weasel boy giggling over Helmet Head's shoulder like a demonic parrot.

'I can do the Frisbee Flop,' I said, blurting out the first thing that came into my head.

They looked confused. It was a nervous reaction from

me. I've used it before and it always gets the desired effect. Not the Frisbee Flop line, no – but I've randomly shouted all sorts of things in a futile attempt to avert various different crises. Saying 'Plums!' is a good one, or just point – it doesn't matter at what, it simple distracts people.

But at this moment it was the Frisbee Flop.

Mind you, I wasn't lying because I had, back in my bedroom in Bristol before I got to Billericay, been an avid watcher of the Olympics. In particular, I had been fascinated by the Frisbee Flop. I called it that but it is, of course, actually named the Fosbury Flop. It was a brand-new jump that had been invented by the American athlete Dick Fosbury at the Mexico City Olympic Games in 1968.

From an early age, I had been enthralled by a jump that – when the bar is removed from the equation – just makes you look like a nutter lunging sideways and landing on your back. In Bristol, I'd spent hours practising it by standing at the foot of my bed then suddenly hurling myself sideways. I'd keep my arms pinned to my sides, pulling a sort of startled face as I landed successfully on my back on the bed, the mattress cushioning my fall like one of those crash mats they have on the telly. Then I'd spring back up on to my feet and run around the small space, waving my arms and making an ecstatic crowd noise. I was good at that, having spent so long alone. I'd learned enough noises to put the BBC Sound Effects Department out of business.

But here's the cruncher: you definitely need a mattress to break your landing or it doesn't work. The hard ground doesn't cushion your fall nearly as effectively. This is what

I tried to explain to those two lads at school in Billericay, but Helmet Head immediately began boasting that he could do the Frisbee Flop too.

I didn't care – it wasn't a challenge or anything. I even tried to stop him. I stepped forward and said, "Ere, biss don't want to try that'un, my cocker,' in my Bristolian accent, but he pushed me back. His weasel friend stopped giggling for a moment and came right up close, touching his forehead against mine in a sort of slow-motion head butt. Then, while still staring at me all hard like, he pulled away and began giggling again.

I tried talking Helmet Boy out of it, but it was too late. He adopted a very serious demeanour as he took a short run-up. With the concentration etched on his face, he shouted out a guide to what he was doing.

'What . . . I . . . do . . . is . . . jump . . . then . . . curl . . . over . . . and . . .' SNAP!

You could hear the snap all the way across the county, because everybody on the playing field just stopped what they were doing and stared at us. I was standing next to Weasel, who'd stopped giggling and was looking ashen and stony-faced at Chubs writhing on the floor in front of us. After not pulling his flop off properly, he'd landed with his full weight on his arm, snapping it in two like a dry twig. 'Biss, eer, your arm's pointen in enover doirection, my cock.' As if he didn't know!

It was weird because he wasn't crying, well, not yet anyway. He just lay there, his face contorted, his mouth wide open, doing a kind of primal scream, like the telly with the volume turned down – presumably because he was in so much pain. I asked him, 'Should I gow and get a teacherrrr or summut?' But he didn't answer, he just finally flipped, inhaled and started screaming. I panicked and ran.

Weasel Boy and I watched as Helmet Head was taken away on a stretcher into an ambulance. I never saw him again, because soon afterwards I moved on to senior school. I wonder what happened to him. He probably became an Olympic high jumper.

Still, I'd made an impression. And, after that, nobody at the school ever messed with me again. They thought that 'Farmer Giles' possessed strange West Country powers to inflict damage on Essex lads without even trying!

But it didn't help me fit in. I'm afraid I still felt like the Odd Boy Out.

15. Raging Bull

The very physical sport of boxing was always described by Dad – from the well-upholstered comfort of his armchair – as 'a proper, working-class sport'. He believed that passionately – remember his initial desire to name me 'Cassius Clay Evans'? To punch home his point, he could sometimes get quite angry and animated in his defence of the sport. He would rise up and dance around the lounge, mock-boxing as if in the final round of a world title fight, hands up by his chin, head bobbing around like a demented chicken on 'wacky baccy'. He would throw the odd jab towards Wayne and me, who stood rooted to the spot in stunned fascination at his pugilistic demonstrations.

'Careful, Dave, you're going to knock something over,' Mum would carp, not even lifting her eyes from another one of her production-line jumpers, smiling to herself as she stared down at her rat-a-tat-tatting needles. It wasn't very often that we were all together as a family, and Mum always glowed when we were. She liked the noise and the banter that went on whenever Dad was home after months away.

What there was to knock over, God only knows. Dad could have set about our home like a man possessed with a large sledge-hammer and only succeeded in doing about two quid's worth of damage. We hardly had anything, so what he might bump into was anybody's guess.

'Boxing is a sport . . .' Dad would begin, stopping for a lug of his fag before moving around the room and beginning to gear up to his usual Churchillian 'I know what I'm talking about' speech. All blokes do it, in the safety of their own home, in front of the wife and kids. There they are Einstein, the great intellect that demands to be listened to. And, it goes without saying, if only the world leaders would consult them, they might learn a thing or two. If we could have afforded a phone back then, the world leaders would have been constantly trying to get through, but they would've had to join the queue to speak to the top adviser. Of course, as soon as all these blokes get out of the house and into the real world, competing with everyone else, they find they actually have a brain the size of an amoeba and would dump in their Y-fronts if confronted by so much as a local MP.

'A sport,' Dad would rattle on, his lecture now in full flow, 'that can, through sheer hard work, raise a man up from the absolute depths to the very pinnacle of our society. It is a sport that does not discriminate. It is attended by lords, dukes and even royalty, as well as the ordinary working man in the street.'

Dad boxed during his service in the army, and he thought it would be a good idea to drill it into Wayne and me. So every Christmas or birthday, there would be the obligatory pair of boxing gloves, inflatable punchbag, or – the one I liked because it didn't hurt so much – a boxer on a stick. Under the boxer's robe were two levers you pushed to make the plastic boxer throw a punch.

I hated boxing when I was a kid because it felt as if I always came off worst in the pecking order. As soon as the gloves were unwrapped at Christmas, I knew at some point that day I would have to reluctantly slip them on. The constant goading from Dad and Wayne would chip away at my pride and, not wanting to look weak in any way in front of Dad, I had to put up or shut up. It was a constant competition in our house, as Wayne and I tried to gain some form of approval from Dad.

I don't know if Dad encouraged it between us – in particular, the contest to see who was the toughest fighter. My efforts on the boxing front were always futile. Dad would look on as Wayne bashed the crap out of me. My brother had this incredible move that would catch me unawares every time. Mid-fight, as I staggered around the middle of our lounge, visibly exhausted, Wayne seized his chance. He would suddenly dart forward and with his leading foot step on my front foot, so I was trapped, pinned to the floor like a rat in a trap, unable to back off or go anywhere. Then he would bend forward and follow through with a massive head-numbing, over-arm punch that came out of the sky like a meteorite, thumping down on to the top of my head and leaving me seeing more stars than Patrick Moore on a clear night.

It was that same devastating punch Wayne would later use to massive effect to win fights at amateur boxing club level. After moving to Billericay, we both joined Berry Boys, a local amateur boxing club. By then things were definitely a little different for me. I'd learned to be a bit tougher; I was no longer willing to take a sucker punch from my big brother. Instead, I'd mastered the artful technique of dodging. I was brilliant at it. I could bob, weave and dance around the ring in my over-sized shorts in a way Fred Astaire would have been proud of, my skinny white legs bopping across the canvas.

Maybe I was now more determined because I was slightly older, or perhaps it was because I thrived under the rules and regulations of club boxing, under proper supervision, or maybe I just lapped up the camaraderie and fun of being with all the other boys at the club.

The sparring still hurt, but I had learned to defend myself a little better. I began to enjoy it – and my love of boxing was to continue into later life. I especially loved the discipline of the intense training sessions. I also relished the fact that all the fighters at the club had something to train for, namely, the boxing shows. These were organized by the Amateur Boxing Association and pitted fighters from different clubs across the county against each other. It was usually an evening event and always well attended, mostly by the families of the young boxers, who came to shout their support.

There was always a tense, edgy atmosphere to these occasions. This was made all the more important for the young boys fighting by the presence of some of the regular faces and characters well-known to the boxing fraternity, who had either been in the fight game for years themselves, or were retired trainers, all unable to keep away from the buzz of the ring. They were looked up to by all the young boxers.

Every competition was different. Sometimes it was a relaxed, casual affair, a few bouts held, say, at a local working man's club in the East End of London, where a ring was simply erected in the middle of the room. By the time the first bout punched off, the air in the club would be hot and heavy, laden with thick cigarette smoke that made breathing difficult. How the boxers managed the highly physical bouts with such short supplies of oxygen was beyond me.

The rowdy tables were full of mostly lively, rotund, sweating riff-raff, some getting so excited they would be leaping out of their seats. Somehow, in their heads, they themselves were in the ring, as they demonstrated by incessantly bobbing around, wiping and flicking their nose with the end of their thumb and air-boxing. All the while, they were shouting their genius instructions to the poor young lads who were actually doing it for real, battering hell out of each other in the floodlit ring.

Then there were the shows I preferred, held at a posh hotel somewhere Up West, where the crowd all dressed up smartly in dinner suits and dicky bows. It was still the same riff-raff, but it somehow felt more professional and glamorous. Instead of the air being thick with cigarette smoke, this time it was cigar smoke.

The reason I liked the posher dos was that the illegal gambling created a real buzz in the crowd. Before each fight, the men in dicky bows were placing bets on who might win. If you put on a good show and created some real excitement in the room, some of the tables would shout their approval and throw money into the ring for the young fighters. It presented an unexpected problem; frustratingly, you couldn't pick the money up from the canvas wearing boxing gloves. Even though you might try, there was only limited time to do so, as you were hustled out of the ring by the officials to make way for the next bout. My trainer, Jack, would scoop up the money from the canvas, and was always strangely flush when it came to buying rounds afterwards.

Because Dad was so often away working, he could only manage to come to a couple of fights. But he still saw boxing as – cue his lecture again – 'a good, honourable art-form, with proper high-minded principles and sportsmanship.'

Now, Mum had never been to a boxing match before, but one day asked a friend secretly to smuggle her in so she could stand at the back and see what all the fuss was about. This turned out to be a very big mistake . . .

Naively, Mum hadn't realized quite how violent a boxing match is, in particular amateur boxing, a completely different sport altogether to the professional boxing one might see on the TV. Amateur boxing consists of three three-minute rounds. As it's such a short period, the time is limited in which to score points, and so the two opponents are encouraged to go nuts with each other. To the discerning observer, it looks like two Rottweilers set on each other in a back alley.

Unfortunately, Mum only ever attended that one fight. She never saw Wayne or me ever fight again. Luckily, I wasn't on the bill that particular night – just as well, as I think things would have been worse if I had been. Wayne did fight that evening, though, and that was all Mum could take.

What took place that evening had never been seen at an amateur boxing match before and was never mentioned in our house again. The psychological and physical damage to some of those in attendance that night was immense – Wayne's opponent, his training staff and, most of all, the referee. As soon as Mum witnessed Wayne being punched in the face, it made her blood boil. Before you could say 'Raging Bull', she had climbed from the back of the room up over tables, chairs and people's heads, jumped straight through the ropes into the ring and leaped on to the referee's back.

It caught him completely by surprise. I'm sure he wasn't expecting a fuming, middle-aged women suddenly to pounce on him and cling on like a limpet while hitting him across the back of the head with a handbag and demanding, 'Stop that boy right this second from hitting my son in the face!'

Mum then tried to deliver an uppercut to the jaw of Wayne's opponent as she accused him of cheating. A tense, unnerving atmosphere hung in the air even after a team of bouncers extracted the fingers of her right hand from around the corner ropes and the fingers of her left hand from around the poor referee's throat.

Her attendance caused much distress for all concerned. As Mum was evicted from the premises, it was explained to Wayne and me in no uncertain terms by the powers that be that our mother would not be welcome at any other boxing event. Ever.

But it showed one thing: Mum cared deeply about us – to the point of trying to land a right hook on anyone she thought was threatening us!

That regrettable – but quite unforgettable – incident didn't put me off sport, though. In fact, quite the contrary. So desperate was I to be 'in' and impress the girls at school, I was mad keen to try any form of sport. I enrolled with every single after-school sports club. I didn't care – I signed up for basketball, football, rugby. Being Welsh, Dad always encouraged rugby, but I found out very quickly there was a slight drawback with that particular sport: it frigging hurts. Also, my teeth were telling me in unequivocal terms that they wanted to stay in my mouth. I remember thinking, 'All my ancestors are Welsh and Irish and all their favourite sports seem to involve getting your head bashed in.' So I passed on that one.

Instead, I tried out volleyball, badminton – big jokes for me, then a thirteen-year-old wazzock, with the use of the word 'shuttlecock' – and javelin. That was a very difficult sport to master. Sprinting like a nomadic tribesman down the runway and holding the javelin aloft, I approached the line that signified I had to give it a good chuck.

Whipping my arm back in readiness, I accidentally jammed the javelin into the ground behind me. As I tried to pull the trigger, so to speak, all I managed to do was throw myself backward in a heap on the ground. It would probably have been a very alluring sight for any girl who happened to be standing around gazing at the runway, but – surprise, surprise – there were none. The javelin was the same as any other item of sports equipment: as soon as I got hold of it, it became completely useless.

Now beginning to despair, I travelled further down the official list of sports with which, based on rigorous scientific evidence, girls might be enamoured. So I had a go at the pole vault. I realized it was not exactly a glamour sport, but I was desperate. David Beckham might be able to curve a ball into the back of a net from roughly five miles away, but can Mr 'Sexy Tattoo Stubbly Man' catapult himself up into the air clutching the end of a giant pole and pointlessly throw himself over a bar? I didn't think so. I can. Well, I can't, but I tried.

At the county sports day, I was the only one entering the pole vault that year – well, any year actually. But I was ready to take the inter-school athletics championship by storm and probably pull a few lassies in the process. Why? I had the advantage that no other kid in their right mind would go in for such a dumb-ass-monkey-on-a-stick sport. So being the only competitor, I was a dead cert for a win and the all-important gold medal that I thought I could wear round my neck and prance about with. If anyone should mention it, I would look down as if wondering what they were talking about, and then be completely surprised by the medal hanging there. I was convinced that glittering bauble would become my shiny lure for catching the birds.

At first, everything went exactly to plan. The sports day was very busy. It was bustling with parents who had come to watch their kids in various sports. Disappointingly, my plan soon took a bit of a knock as I noticed the girls-to-boys ratio was a bit lower than I'd hoped. But my reckoning was that once I'd grabbed hold of that pole and belted down that runway like a boy, scientists might surmise, propelled by a huge hormone imbalance, my pole in the air at a forty-five-degree angle, no girl would be able to resist me.

I got a lot of attention from the passing crowd, some girls among them. But I felt that they were showing interest only out of a morbid curiosity. They were just rubber-necking, eager to witness an appalling accident at the most dangerous stunt they would see for some time. I heard gasps during my purposeful, some might say crazed, run-up and my death-defying leap skyward. I picked up comments such as, 'Who's that nutter?', 'That's the Evans boy – he's berserk,' and 'What the f–?' It probably made a thrilling change from some of the more ordinary sports on show, and I certainly didn't disappoint the crowd.

I must have got caught up in all the excitement myself – I was lost in what athletes call 'The Zone'. However, as I raced towards the scarily high bar that I was supposed to soar over effortlessly, I began to think, 'I don't remember running this fast in training. Come to think of it, I don't remember ever doing any training.' It suddenly occurred to me that I had never done the pole vault before in my life. But by now it was too late . . .

I didn't have any time to see the reaction of the gathered crowd, but there was no doubting my ability to thrill and give the stunned assembly exactly what they wanted: a catastrophe.

As I approached the towering bar in front of me, with perfect timing I slowly lowered my pole. At exactly the right moment, I managed with stunningly good aim to jam the end of it into the little cup at the end of the runway and braced myself for take-off.

It must have been the way I was holding the pole because instead of launching me skywards as desired, the end of the pole caught me suddenly with a mind-numbing thud right in the bean bag. The impact gave me an instant udder full of cauliflower sperms and, instead of going up, I went down, down like a large bag of jelly. I writhed around on the ground for several minutes in complete agony. The assembled crowd were also in pain – from their sustained, rib-endangering laughter at my utter ineptitude.

Typical. The only reason I was driven to this was to relieve a little tension in the very area that took the full blow.

I bet Mr Beckham hasn't got cauliflower sperms. But, on the plus side, I can now curve one of my balls.

16. How to Win Friends and Influence People (With a Little Help from a Piano)

After a long time being the odd one out at school, a funny thing happened. All of a sudden I was part of the in-crowd. I know, amazing, isn't it?

I had noticed the piano on my first day at my new senior school. The reason it stuck out during that first morning assembly was that it was the only thing that day which I could relate to. A lot of the kids had already come through infants together, or lived for years in the same neighbourhood. But I didn't really know anyone, I'd only just arrived, so when I made my way to the back of the hall and sat near the piano, that made me feel a little less nervous. Somehow I knew that if I was near it, I could do something if called upon.

For some reason, the urge to entertain and divert attention away from my inadequate, idiotic self goes hand in hand with a very similar desire to dig a hole and jump in it. Those two conflicting forces have always battled each other deep inside the pit of my character. Whenever I'm faced with any form of threat or potentially embarrassing situation – and it could be something as simple as putting my hand up in class – I desperately want to run, to hide. But, at the same, there's another feeling that sends bizarre thoughts whizzing around my head and tempts me to blurt them out. Now, I call it performing. But the more stressed I get, the more these two urges struggle for prominence.

For years, I had odd, surreal and rebellious thoughts, but kept them locked away because I didn't want to be misunderstood and was worried I might say the wrong thing. And so I would just sit in class like your average lobotomy patient who's missed his day's medication. Not listening to anything the teacher said, I would simply be staring down at my empty book, fretting, hoping, willing the time to go by so I could get home and sit alone in the safety of my bedroom and dream some more. I would stay in my room practising over and over an Essex accent, having listened intently to other kids' conversations at school, so they wouldn't keep laughing every time I opened my frigging mouth.

The fact that the Wurzels entered the charts halfway through my first year at school in Billericay didn't help my cause one bit. That was it for me – I was from then on known as 'a carrot cruncher' and 'a Wurzel'. I had, according to my tormentors, a brand new combine harvester. I wouldn't have minded, but the bloody Wurzels were from Somerset, which is, granted, over that way, but actually nowhere near Bristol.

Then again, I always laboured under the disadvantage of thinking that I was slow in the head; that I was one banana short of a bunch; that one of my van doors was always open. But perhaps a more accurate description would be to say that rather than being behind everyone else, I was merely one step to the side of them.

I was away with the fairies at that time primarily because I found school so incredibly boring. Plus, I had been to so many different schools, been taught so many varying curricula and made so many short-lived friendships before having to leave again, that I didn't know where I was. I couldn't do any maths whatsoever, I didn't know any times tables – I didn't even know how many days there were in a month. To be honest, I could barely spell my own name. 'Is it, er, L-E-A?'

So the senior school in Billericay immediately put me in a special class out of the way of all the other children. It was called 'remedial'. There were about nine of us, and we all sat around dribbling all day long. The other dunderheads and I would stare in wonder at what we thought was a computer – in fact, it was a small wooden abacus. They gave us our own special teacher, but she can only be described as a prize dong-ding.

And that is how I spent the first year of senior school in the hidden-away-and-never-spoken-about lummox unit, rolling my eyes around my sockets like the odd-shaped wheels of a clown's car and making trumpeting noises with my lips. It doesn't really fill you with confidence when all the other kids find out you have 'special needs' – there is something especially malevolent about the cruelty of children. But then, one morning, something happened that seemed to change everything . . .

I was wandering through the main assembly hall, idling my way towards another lesson, when I stopped just to have a little peek over my shoulder at the huge brown beast of a grand piano that I had felt so comfortable beside during assembly. It was standing quietly in the corner over by the window, like a giant, brooding rhino.

The urge was too great. I looked around to see if anyone was nearby and made an instant decision. I hurriedly tiptoed over and opened the lid. I knew that if I was caught, I would be in serious trouble – for some reason, school pianos must not be played, it's against the rules. But the desire was just too strong. It had been ages since I'd played the piano; in fact, I hadn't tinkled the ivories since watching our own piano fly out of our bedroom window in Bristol.

It does feel so good to express yourself on the piano. It's something that's just irresistible to me. I love to play. It has nothing to do with your abilities – it's the affair the individual has with this magical box of sound. Once you cross the line and begin pressing, kneading, stroking and tapping along on its shiny smooth keys, you're gone. You free yourself to the sensation that travels from your head down your arms into your hands. Depressing the light wooded keys – on to which are fixed small, crafted and perfectly balanced hammers that exactly mirror your intonation on the copper strings – you make a sublime sound. Mellowed by the surrounding wood, the chimes caress and soothe your primeval soul. You become immersed in a place far, far away, where anxieties lift from your body. You get a feeling of freedom, as though you're entering a zone of nowhere-ness and –

'Shit, farmer boy, that's all right, that is.'

I snapped out of my music-induced reverie. Standing next to the piano were a couple of scruffy boys. Where did

My nan –
Edna Evans.

And my
granddad –
Evan John
Evans.

Granddad was a drill sergeant in the army during the Second World War.

Dad in the army, stationed in Bristol.

Nan, Granddad, Dad and his brother, John.

Granddad, Dad and Nan in Rhyl, Wales.

On my brother Wayne's lap, in Bristol.

Wayne, me and Granddad.

Uncle John, Auntie Eileen, Granddad, Nan, Wayne, Mum, Dad and me, staring at Dad's clarinet.

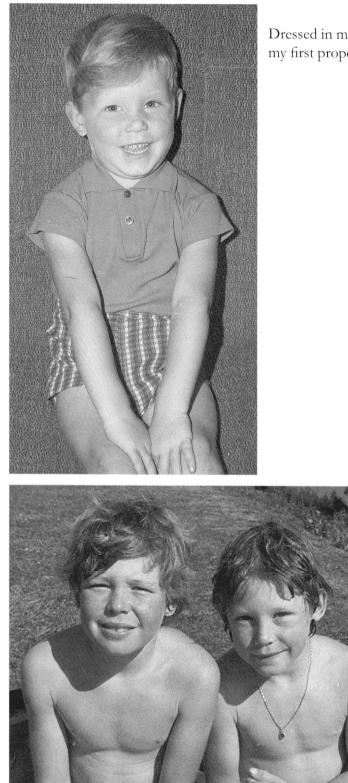

Dressed in my best clothes –
my first proper photo.

Wayne and me in Prestatyn, North Wales.

Me, on the far left, during a cookery class at
Lawrence Weston School, Bristol.

Me and Wayne waiting
for Dad in Blackpool
during the summer
season.

Great Yarmouth –
Dad's summer season
with Ken Goodwin
and the great
Mike Reid.

Learning the drums!

Me and Wayne wearing our obligatory boxing gloves that we got every Christmas.

First-year senior at Billericay School, aged thirteen.

With my mum on a day out
while Dad was away.

Having fun bunking
off school.

NAME.	Lee Evans		FORM	DV4A
SUBJECT	Art		SUBJECT TUTOR	
SET CSE / GCE		EFFORT B.	STANDARD	B+

COMMENT

Lee has much ability and generally works well. His work is bold, and imaginative and of a high standard. More work done at home would do much to improve his overall standard.

Billericay School

My art report – not too bad.

NAME	LEE EVANS		FORM	DV4A	TUTOR	
ATTENDANCE UP TO 22/ 6 / 79		288 / 338	LATE MARKS	25	DATE	25/6/79

FORM TUTOR COMMENT Lee is not making the necessary effort paticularly in such impotant subject as English and Maths. His future depends a great deal on his performance next year — I hope he realises this now and not when it will be too late. I am not happy with Lee turning up late so often — this is a point which employers look at !

HEAD A poor report, there is considerable room for improvement.

Billericay School

Overall assessment – not too good!

they come from? I panicked and immediately went into a little ditty in the key of D Major that I'd picked up when I was a kid and Dad used to sing it to Wayne and me.

> 'There was a young man from Gosham,
> Who took out his balls to wash 'em.
> His wife said, "Jack,
> If you don't put them back,
> I'll stand on the buggers and squash them."'

The two boys fell around laughing.

A door banged and Mr Nelson suddenly breezed into the hall. Mr Nelson was a short, stubby, balding man known for his extra-strict, take-no-prisoners attitude. He was hated by all the pupils because of his markedly sadistic streak. If he spotted a weakness in you, he would play on it relentlessly.

If he had an inkling that we were playing the piano without proper authority, then it would certainly be an instant caning for all of us, with no hesitation. If there was one thing that brightened Mr Nelson's day, it was a caning.

His little legs bowled at a determined pace across the hall, little feet tapping along the well-worn parquet flooring. He didn't say anything but stared with menace in our direction. Because of his infamy, we three boys froze on the spot, waiting for his notorious explosion of temper. It would only be a matter of seconds before one of us cracked under his laser-like glare.

'You see, boys . . .' I began, doing my best impression of a school prefect's posh accent. I thumped down on the keys of the piano before adding, 'That is what Mr Martin –' Mr Martin was a music teacher who Mr Nelson considered soft, arty and slightly effeminate, a frivolous waste of school time who only instilled indiscipline and rebellion. I carried on in what was becoming a bit of a Danny La Rue performance piece – 'calls an F Sharp.'

Luckily, it was working. Out of the corner of my eye, I could see that, like a robotic drone, Mr Nelson suddenly lost interest, looked away and carried on walking.

But as he approached the door on the other side of the vast school hall, I couldn't resist it; I began playing the Laurel and Hardy theme tune in time to Mr Nelson's footsteps. It was a highly risky move. He stopped with his back to us. Twitching, he sniffed the air and turned his head slightly, so we could see just one eye looking back over his shoulder at us.

The two other boys looked petrified. I could tell they were thinking, 'You've done it now!'

But, at that moment, I managed to rescue the situation. I flounced around the piano keyboard and continued, as smoothly as I could, 'Now, Mr Martin said to snap, snap, snap over to a nice E Minor that melodically would . . .' Still looking suspicious, Mr Nelson turned and left the hall. We were safe!

It was my lucky day. The two lads turned out to be two of the most popular pupils in my year, and they asked me to hang around with them. I couldn't believe it – they wanted to be my friends. They had older brothers in higher years who were quite hard. I was officially in with the lads.

Of course, I was still a numbskull, but, hey, I wasn't going to get my head kicked in – for a while, anyway! I would from now on be the funny punchbag, the butt of the jokes, the monkey boy of the group. Yes, I was considered the chump of my year and girls would still regard me as the loser's loser, but at least I could entertain people and I was happy with that.

Up to a point.

17. Trying (and Failing) to Impress Girls

There was no doubt about it, it was the life of Riley being a part of the main gang. It gave you a little respect and a taste of the finer things – yep, I was definitely getting used to the high life now. Already, I couldn't imagine how boring it must be not being one of the gang. If I had once more been consigned to 'loser' status, I wouldn't have experienced the joy of having fag butts pinged at my face while hanging out at the smokers' corner round the back of E block. I would also not have had the delight of receiving a shockingly painful random dead leg from Ben Coulter who, as I collapsed to my knees in agonizing pain, would laugh so hard, it would bring up a big blue vein that ran down his huge, dome-like forehead.

The main gang were popular because they made up half the school football team. I was an integral part of the celebrated side who came a close second in the regional inter-school championship. I didn't actually play in any games, of course, but I can only put their triumph down to the fact that I cut, bagged and brought on the oranges at half-time. I reckon I was also the main driving force in morale-building as, after showering, the whole team would subject me to a thousand stings by flicking their wet towels at my milky white skin. Just to see them all laughing like that, I felt I was the glue that held them together.

Naturally enough, the glamour of being a part of the football team did come with benefits: girls, and not just ordinary girls. The main gang attracted a certain type of wild girl, a girl who looked for a little more action and excitement than you might get from your run-of-the-mill social outcast.

This was a decided advantage. If I hadn't been in with the main gang, I wouldn't have stood a chance at all with these gorgeous, uninhibited girls. But now, being associated with the glamour boys, I had a sniff – at least, that's what I thought . . .

That's how I got to meet Jenny, the hottest girl in the school. There is no way she would have even looked at me twice if I hadn't been a member of the Alpha Male gang. OK, maybe she might have looked at me twice but only in the way that you might double-take at the sight of a zoo monkey sitting in a tyre rubbing his banana.

But I got my opportunity to drool over Jenny when I was hanging around E block by smokers' corner. I was trying to look impressed by a couple of hard cases, Barry and Steve, as they puffed away on their Number 6 cigarettes. They were boasting about their attempts to break the world record for the most masturbations in one evening while their mum was up the Mecca Bingo, when Jenny arrived with a couple of her friends.

She was searching around in her smart school bag when she suddenly looked up and clocked me. To me, she was a vision of unattainable loveliness. From the moment I'd first clapped eyes on her across the playground, I'd lusted after her from afar. She had the face of an angel and the body of a goddess. We were only thirteen-year-olds, but she already had ample breasts.

I couldn't believe she even acknowledged my existence, but at this moment she did. 'Gissa smoke, weasel breath,' she demanded – God, if only she knew how much I loved her!

I panicked. 'I don't have any, but I got some Polos,' I stammered feebly. As soon as I'd said it, I winced. In the pit of my stomach, I instantly realized that was the most ridiculous thing to have said – and she did, too.

'Don't be such a tit face,' Jenny sneered.

So I quickly tried to make up for it by desperately begging one of the hard cases, Steve, to sell me a cigarette. I emptied my pockets of all my change. Luckily, he agreed, thank God. However, he wasn't interested in my money alone – he would only sell it to me if I ate it.

I paused for a second, thinking his demand was a bit steep. But I was desperate, and at least I would have a cigarette to give to Jenny, albeit briefly. So I threw caution to the wind, handed over the money and took the cigarette. Barry and Steve were watching intently, clenched fists at the ready. If I didn't do what they said, they were poised to attack.

As I quickly proffered the cigarette to Jenny, her face changed. Her eyes softened, she shook her hair, rolled her lips like a giant succulent mangle, and slowly reached out towards me for the cigarette. I was mesmerized. As she put her hand around the cigarette, it was so sensual, so phallic, I could barely contain my excitement.

At that moment, though, I glanced over at Barry and

Steve and saw they were primed to pounce. So I snatched the cigarette from Jenny's eager grasp, stuffed it in my mouth and began frantically chewing it. Jenny looked at me for a long time in utter astonishment. Then she moved a little closer towards me, bringing her face right up close to mine. Her expression changed again, as she shouted in my face: 'You complete and utter prat!'

But even as she was shrieking at me, I couldn't keep my eyes off her porcelain features, now distorted with fury. At the same time, I couldn't help noticing that the delicate, smooth skin of her forehead had become furrowed and wrinkled from rage. The tip of her wonderful button nose had turned bright red with the blood rush. And the way her hair fell across her face when she shook her head in frustration at me was such a turn-on. My hormones danced around my body like a Russian Cossack group on a stag do in a pole-dancing club. God, she was incredible. I would have done anything for her. In fact, on one occasion I did . . .

I don't know if it was by design or just coincidence, but it seemed that every class the school stuck me in was disruptive. It always contained all the kids who either didn't want to learn or couldn't learn. Either way, it held all the pupils the school had just given up on, and I became one of them.

It's funny, maybe it's a survival thing, but kids like that can spot a weakness or a chink in someone's armour a mile away. That's why the stand-in teacher on that particular day didn't stand a chance.

I used to so look forward to English lessons, taught by

the much-loved Mr Cavendish. His methods were different from other teachers'. Unconventional, he seemed genuinely excited about the English language, sharing the power of the word with us dullards in the class. For example, he would never give us essays as he knew we couldn't even spell our own names, but preferred to involve everybody by physically acting out verse. He helped us understand what was on the pages of a certain book or play that us bunch of chowderheads would never otherwise have been exposed to in a million years. Even the most uni-brow, knuckle-scraping dribbler sitting in the corner – who would normally pass the time by pulling legs from a large stolen cow – would shut up and listen to Mr Cavendish.

Mrs Henford, on the other hand, was unfortunately well-known at the school for being a soft teacher, and if there's one thing that brightens up a class full of mutton-heads, it's a teacher who they can lasso, castrate and brand – any excuse not to do any work.

I sat at the back of the class, and on this day it just so happened I was sitting next to Jenny. She wasn't aware of it, but I was fixated on her every move. She didn't see me: she was too busy beautifully punching the boy in front of her in the back of his head for being – well, just for having a head. Good job she was punching him because if she'd looked round, she would have seen me staring at her like a psychopath. And no doubt she would have started on my head, even though it may have been a more challenging prospect as it was so much smaller in size, owing to its tinier brain mass.

"Ere.' I was snapped out of my reverie by Jenny. "Ere, twat brain.'

Dumbstruck, I stared at Jenny's exquisite face as she observed me for a moment, clearly becoming frustrated by my drooling incomprehension. I couldn't help it – my brain was drugged up in a love stupor.

I was confused because she was frantically trying to hand me a Bic lighter. 'Set fire to your book, ferret breath,' she demanded.

As Jenny whipped her head towards me for emphasis, her shiny black hair cascaded around her head like in one of those shampoo adverts. Then a mischievous smile spread across her massive mouth, and her angelic face turned red and devilish. 'Burn your book,' she hissed, slamming the lighter down on my desk.

Without thinking and still blinded by passion for Jenny, I took a quick glance up at Mrs Henford, who was having a dreadful time of it. She was pinned to the blackboard, on the receiving end of full-on abuse from everyone in the room. 'Mrs Cluck Cluck Henford. Cluck cluck cluck cluck.'

I looked back at Jenny. Aching to impress her, I automatically picked up the lighter and held my book aloft. Igniting the flame, I set fire to the pages. All the while, I stared at Jenny; it was like I was hypnotized by her beauty and sirens' voices were ordering me to do it because that's what Jenny had commanded. Suddenly, the book began to flare up, illuminating my hand with a wonderful orange glow.

I heard the sirens' voices, now singing in my ear: 'Jenny loves the fire, the magical orange flames. She loves you, Lee, too, she really –' Aaargh!

All of a sudden, I awoke from my trance and realized I was holding a significantly hot fireball in my hand. I looked to Jenny for help, but she was just cackling demonically and called out mockingly, 'You total turd head! Look, Miss, look! Evans is setting the school on fire!' The whole class began laughing derisively and getting out of their seats, ready to evacuate the room.

The fire alarm rang out around the school and through the window I saw other kids running past our classroom. I started to panic as smoke filled the room. Swiftly opening the lid of my desk, I shoved the now flaming book inside, slammed the lid shut and applied my full weight to it. There was a brief pause when I thought that by chucking the book inside the desk I might have suffocated the flames, but then black smoke and yellow flames began billowing out from underneath the lid. Hurling the burning book into the desk had only succeeded in stoking the fire. I was in serious trouble here.

Everyone started evacuating the room. From the middle of the scurrying crowd, Jenny glanced over her shoulder and gave me a curious look of puzzlement. I wasn't much good at this sort of thing, but I reckoned it meant she fancied me. There again, she may have just thought I was an utter wazzock.

Then Jenny was gone, swallowed up by the ubiquitous smoke as if exiting through a stage-managed cloud of dry ice. Now there was just me and Mrs Henford. Through the smoke I could see the teacher, still frozen to the same spot, mad eyes staring straight ahead in shock, mouth agog, traumatized, her fingers now gripped so tightly around her handbag it would take a team of surgeons to remove it.

With flames beginning to rise up around me, I was still glued to the lid of the desk. Unable to resist the urge to examine the carnage I had caused, I lifted the lid of the desk. At that moment, a huge fireball erupted out, singeing my fringe right up to my hairline and giving me an instant feather cut. I looked like a very charred, eyebrowless Neanderthal version of the lead guitarist from the very popular glam-rock band Sweet. Not a good look. Jenny was never going to fancy me now.

The moral of the story? True love can burn you. Or perhaps it's just 'Beware of pretty girls bearing lighters'.

On another occasion, which only underlined my status as a dork, I took on the challenge of fighting the school hard-man, Brian. I should have guessed he was tough – his nickname was 'The Karate Kid' – but I was ever-eager to impress.

As he approached me in the playground, we were instantly surrounded by a gang of lads shouting, 'Fight, fight, fight!'

I have to say, the shouting really spurred me on a bit. I felt encouraged by the whole thing; it began to rile my teenage hormones. Disconcertingly, though, Brian just stood stock-still, holding his ground and looking exactly like a psychotic turkey, parrot, scorpion thing. I was now just feet away from him and coming in at some speed, lungs burning, cheeks red, tears in my eyes from the wind. I wasn't quite sure what I was going to do when I got there but, boy, was I fired up now! I noticed, though, that Brian hadn't moved a single muscle during my massive run-up. He had just stayed exactly in the shape of his turkey, parrot, scorpion thing . . .

So I suppose I shouldn't have been that surprised when I was whacked by the most sickening scorpion sting – or was it a turkey attack or a parrot assault? The other kids told me afterwards that when I ran headfirst into Brian's fist, I looked like a jelly trifle that had been dropped into a clothes dryer on spin cycle.

On the positive side, after that initial blow I never felt another thing. It was as if Brian's fist hitting me repeatedly in the face acted as a general anaesthetic. I never even flinched when he threw me to the floor and began systematically showering my body with a serious of scorpion-like over-head kicks followed by a bunch of varied pincer-claw punches. I didn't even react when, according to one amazed onlooker, Brian threw me like a carrier bag full of feathers all around the playground. I never screamed once. Nevertheless, it's fair to say that I lost that particular fight.

Hours later, when I was finally released from the school sick bay, I found myself sitting outside Mr Nelson's office waiting to receive my punishment. I was by now an old hand at this cane lark. I looked over at my fellow miscreant, Brian, who was sitting on the other side of the corridor. I wanted to see how a karate expert might handle the pressure of a potential whack across the scorpion's arse. But Brian had his face tucked tightly into the wall, and I thought it best not to disturb him because, by the sound of it, he was sobbing. We all handle things differently, I suppose. I just took it that he must have been working through some kind of ancient Chinese blubbering ritual – I'm not sure, but he certainly called for his mum a lot. I would have tried it myself, but by now I'd had the cane so often, I had a backside that was starting to look like a Land of Leather sofa. So I used that as my strength.

Brian, it appeared, had never had the cane before, and so that's what made him cry like a baby at the prospect. After witnessing me receive a few whacks from Mr Nelson's special stick, I felt as though Brian admired my cool and blasé attitude to the pain. Maybe, just maybe, my stoical demeanour in the face of a heck of a beating gained me just a modicum of respect in the playground. I may have been a punchbag, but at least I was a brave punchbag.

The worst part of the whole experience, in fact, was getting home from school that evening. When I entered the house with a bigger black eye than a panda, Dad demanded I tell him how I'd got it. After I'd explained to him that I'd been beaten up at school, he started chasing me round the house, clipping me round the earhole and shouting, 'Never, ever, get involved in violence!' Then, just to ram home the point, he ran and kicked our long-suffering dog, Dougal.

Those anger-management lessons clearly weren't working.

Even as the school years passed, my relentless quest for a girlfriend went largely unrewarded. In fact, I'd only had one serious girlfriend in Billericay, Sue. She was nuts, even by my standards. It was a total mismatch. She, quite rightly, thought I wasn't the right one for her. She was one of those girls who craved danger. She needed someone to treat her badly, a moody bloke with misspelt tattoos and oily fingernails who smelled of leather. Sue wanted an out-of-control rebel who she could change – she was desperate to be the one who saved him.

But the rumour was, Sue went like the clappers on Red Bull and a pot of coffee. She oozed sex appeal. Every word that came out of her luscious lips indicated that there might be a shag in the offing.

I tried to explain to her that I could be bad, I could be rough, I could be savage, I could go like the clappers if required. If she really wanted, I could quite gladly punch her in the face. I could dress in moody leather, perhaps her dad's chamois. I could even fart my name in a menacing way, comb my hair the wrong way, put my clothes on backwards, if I could just have a shag right there in her front garden, right in front of all these trees, grass and her mum's special brass sundial.

Like the nutter I could be, I promised Sue that if she could wait five minutes, I'd be anything she wanted me to be. As my young teenaged hormones were on gas mark 9, just about to come to the boil, I'd have done anything just for a quick feel. I clearly knew the way to a girl's heart.

As you can see, it was no suprise that her parents hated me – not because I was a good-for-nothing roughneck who could flob a whole potful of phlegm. No, they loathed me because, in trying to create the bad-boy image, I failed miserably. I couldn't even be a successful lout.

For instance, I simply couldn't hold my liquor. After one ill-conceived night out at the local pub to try and save our relationship, Sue was so disgusted with me that she walked on ahead as we turned into her street. I thought my getting hammered was what she wanted, but there you go. She stormed into her house and I staggered after her. I pinballed my way down the hall into the kitchen.

There I found her at the kitchen table, arms folded, ferocious eyes glaring at me.

Through my blurry vision, I noticed to my horror that sitting across the table from her was Sue's very formidable hard-arse father. I was in big trouble. He had a face like a thunderstorm. I had unwittingly upset his princess, and he didn't like it one bit. He'd been looking for an excuse to have a right go at me ever since I'd been introduced to him. He had always thought I was a bit weird and not made of the right stuff. I was obviously not nearly good enough for his beloved daughter. From the other side of the kitchen table, he and his walking hairdo of a wife fixed me with a look as if I'd just kicked their cat's backside into touch.

'Sit down, Lee,' Sue's dad growled, menacingly tapping the chair next to his. They had been playing a quiet game of Scrabble before we'd walked in and now they wanted us to join in. That was going to be difficult, as I was really drunk and didn't know how long I could manage not to slur my own words – let alone make any up.

I slumped down into the chair. The room felt heavy and fuggy after the fresh night air outside. I suddenly came over all hot and shaky – alcohol has a tendency to really hit you hard as soon as your body comes to rest somewhere. All of a sudden, it realizes it's drunk and begins its own defence process by throwing out anything that isn't wanted. All the warning signs were there . . .

As they set up the game to include us, their nice blue-and-white Formica kitchen with soft-closing drawers began slowly to spin. I tried desperately hard to collect myself, to focus on the Scrabble board, but I could feel my stomach was on the move. Just as the doorman down the pub had asked me to leave, so the same was happening to my insides: the undesirable drunks and hangers-on were being asked to vacate the premises.

It came out with such force it surprised even me. More vomit gushed from my mouth than the entire batch the props departments made up for the film *The Exorcist*. It was a novel – and very unwelcome – method of redecorating Sue's kitchen.

After the lava flow from my mouth had finally ended, no one around the table had been spared the beer-soaked splatter of the old Hughie Green. It was like a technicolour bomb had just gone off. People sat around the table, their eyes peering out from face masks of 'Yo ho heave ho', staring straight ahead in stunned silence. As the tidal wave subsided, all that could be heard was the sound of dripping. Sue's mum's previously immaculately coiffed hair was now a blasted mess of barf, adorned with various unnamed vegetable chunks. Very gingerly, I looked around at her dad. I knew what was coming. His eyes narrowed and turned red with rage.

I landed in a crunching pile outside on the driveway. But that really didn't hurt as much as the dad's massive sucker punch that knocked me off my feet and propelled my limp frame through the chilly night air. I heaved myself up into a sitting position and, brain-dead and in double vision, tried to zoom in on Sue's enraged father standing just inside the front door. Even in that state, I could see that his whole body was shaking with fury and that his face was still covered in my minestrone.

'If you ever come here again,' he shouted, filling the air

with livid spittle, 'I swear I will smash your little retard head in, you tosser.' And with that home truth, the door slammed with such force it blew my hair up from five yards away. I wasn't definite, but I reckoned that would probably be the last I'd see of his daughter. No chance of a shag there, then.

18. Getting the Band Together

I couldn't really wait to leave school at sixteen. I felt that I was never any good at anything those poor teachers tried to drum into my dense skull. My sense at the end of it all was that I hadn't actually discovered anything new, apart from an obvious and deeper feeling of inadequacy than I'd had before. Anyway, I already knew what I wanted to do for my job. I told my dad after he had sat me down to ask me. I told him straight: I was going to be a musician.

I was surprised by his reaction. He was livid, dismissing it out of hand and telling me that would be impossible. 'You can't just be a musician!' he stormed.

'Why not?' I enquired. I was young and naive, of course, but I posed the question to him in my most exasperated voice. 'You are!'

I'd already had my first taste of the music business. While in my last year at school, along with my friend Bill, we had formed a band. Well, I say 'band' – there was just us, me and him.

Anyway, Bill played a mean guitar, and I would flit between a clapped-out electric piano, a second-hand bass bought from a junk shop and a set of drums borrowed from one of Bill's mates called Alan, a rich kid who lived up the road in one of the big houses on the other, better, side of the high street.

Bill's mum, an elderly, grey-haired lady, didn't like what we played. She fumed that it was too loud and too aggressive. As soon as she left the room, Bill would turn to me and say, really aggressively, 'It's not aggressive! It's gentle!' On the word 'gentle', he would smash his fist into the pillow in his tiny bedroom upstairs at his council house. We'd been confined to play there, strumming frustratingly quietly and singing in that sort of fake throaty whisper you do when you imagine that you're in front of a large, enthralled crowd. But one mistakenly played loud chord, and his mum's angry grey head would once more be poking round the door: 'Now I won't tell you again, William!'

If we were rehearsing at my house, we were allowed to set up the drum kit in our garage and go bananas. Plus, Bill was permitted to plug his guitar in at low volume. Although we had to keep the noise down because of the neighbours, we were amped, and so felt like a proper band. We could only play for an hour, though, before someone would be banging their fist on our garage door for us to shut the noise up.

I would bash away on the drums, while Bill tried singing over the top. Every now and again, he would shout over to me, 'It's good, ain't it, Lee?' his eyes wide and wild-looking. I would respond by banging even harder and sort of growling back at him over the drums through a face full of spots.

We actually sounded like a major pile-up on the M3 between a lorry carrying cymbals and another transporting zoo animals, but we thought we sounded fantastic. We began to take ourselves seriously by trying to look moody whenever we were out up the high street, combing our hair in various directions so it looked as though we'd just arrived on a motorbike. We'd hang around a lot smoking roll-ups and reflecting that the reason we had no gigs was because we were really a studio band – even though we'd never been in a studio.

So we mused that we could perhaps write our album in the garage. We just had to find two more people – hopefully with some instruments – and then we'd be a proper band. As far as we were concerned, we were going to be the next Beatles. Unfortunately, all we actually seemed destined to be was four Pete Bests, the bloke who dropped out before they made it big.

Bill had exactly the same ambitions for the band as I did. However, it was difficult to realize those as he could be a little unpredictable in nature. He might be perfectly gentle and amicable with you one minute, then the next he'd completely lose it. At band practice, he would suddenly slide into the corner and drift off into his own small world, tranced-out and fixated on his amp, which was turned up so loud it surely showed up on the Richter Scale in Brazil.

He'd gaze off into space like some absent-minded cabbage, strumming away on the strings of his guitar. He was cut off from everything around him like someone who had just been hit over the head with a large anvil, ungluing something in his head. He had the infuriating habit of constantly contradicting anything you said, just for the sake of being contrary and wanting an argument. He also had about as much patience as a great white shark on a case of Red Bull at feeding time and he loved to fight. Bill was a small stout lad, as solid as a pit bull on steroids, with a cow's-tail hairdo perched at the top of his forehead. He wore huge, thick glasses that magnified his mad, mischievous eyes, making them look like windows into the asylum without any bars.

What a guitarist Bill was! There wasn't a chord he didn't know. He was like Bert Weedon on amphetamines. During a number, his fingers would move continuously, rapidly reforming into all kinds of shapes, whipping across the frets in a blur, up and down the neck of his Gibson copy. When he really got going – watch out! – he was like a train with no leaves on the line and no brakes. But once he was on one, you didn't dare stop him. That would be like waking up an unhinged man while he sleep-walked. If you interrupted his flow when he was at full tilt on those frets, he was likely to rip your face off and use it as a joke mask.

The Cave Club was a much-coveted local venue in Brentwood, the next town along from Billericay. The club was a magnet for any budding musician; it introduced lots of new bands from around the area. So it was important that we somehow got a gig there. When we eventually had the desired four members of our band, we called ourselves THE ANONYMOUS FIVE. Even though there were only four of us, it sounded good, and if anyone asked where the other guy was we always replied that he liked to stay anonymous. Either way, people just smirked at our terrible explanation.

So there was Bill and me, Alan, the rich kid with his own set of drums – a great asset because his parents didn't mind us practising in the shed at the back of their house – and a guy called Rob. He was a real hottie, heart-throb type who stood around wearing dark glasses indoors, with his legs astride a large set of bongos, striking the odd pose while rhythmically bashing animal skins. He was all virile and strapping. Women loved him, so of course I hated him. He was chosen not necessarily for his musical skills – mainly because he had none – but for his looks. He was a real magnet for the birds. Me and Bill's somewhat crafty way of thinking was that Rob would churn the waters for us, and we could come and pick up the girls he didn't want, like hungry seagulls behind a fishing boat. Well, at least, that was the idea. It didn't work in practice – I remained resolutely girlfriend free!

As it was our very first gig, the booker at The Cave begrudgingly took a chance by letting us play there. He only shoe-horned us in after another band had cancelled at the last minute, catching us by surprise and allowing us no time at all to practise. We were lucky in a way. If the booker had known what we actually sounded like, he probably wouldn't even have let us open our guitar cases, let alone open 'Friday Night Is Band Night' – which was held, coincidentally, on a Friday.

I reckon it must have been Bill's relentless phone calls to the booker that somehow swayed it for us to play. Once Bill had the bloke at The Cave's number, he was like a pike on the end of a fishing line – he wasn't going to let go. He even called up impersonating an A&R man. I watched nervously, cringing as Bill got himself into character before making the all-important call to the club. Checking to make sure his mum had gone out, he kicked back on a chair next to the phone and sucked on a pencil so it might sound like a cigar down the line. With slight menace in his voice, he told the booker that he was calling from EMI and was advising the club to 'Quickly book us – them . . .' Then, knowing he had messed up, he got all frustrated with himself and began rambling angrily down the phone. 'I mean *them* . . . Shit! Look, book us or else, right . . . Balls . . . Sorry, I didn't mean *us* . . . Oh, freakin' hell!'

Struggling to keep control, Bill put his hand across the mouthpiece, looked over at me and wailed, 'I think I've fucked up 'ere, Lee.' Then he lifted his hand and shouted angrily, 'Well, I ain't Brian soddin' Epstein.' He proceeded to make his customary face, resembling an angry ape who had just been kicked in the bananas, calmed himself and started over.

Still in manager mode, he explained to the booker that there was a real buzz about these boys, and they would, funnily enough, be free this Friday. 'Well,' continued Bill, beginning to relish his new role as a music industry big shot, 'that is after shooting their video and finishing a brief, unplugged open-tuning session with The Clash.' He wasn't technically lying with that remark as his mum wouldn't let us plug in. 'And then there's a bit of a jamming thing to cut a new groove disk with The Pistols. Luckily for you, they'll be kicking around on Friday. But a word to the wise: be careful. If the fan club find out, then stick a helmet on.'

Eventually, Bill wore the booker down. I think he got so frustrated with the constant calls that in the end he just gave in. But who cared? The Cave gave us a rare chance to play live. 'I promise once you've seen us – er, them – play, you will never forget us – sorry, them.' Bill put the phone down and both of us jumped around his living room with excitement. Then slowly it dawned on us: we had never played live, never had everything up and running like you would if you were actually a band. The only live playing we had done was in rich Alan's garden shed. Basically, we were no better than your average set of garden tools.

Bill would be proved right in what he said to that booker: the club wouldn't forget us in hurry – but, unfortunately, for all the wrong reasons.

I am a dreamer, an optimist – always have been. Back then, I naively believed, like most kids do who have a band, that our group would be huge. I thought that with our superb musical skills and the tremendous songs written in Bill's bedroom, it was only a matter of time before the phone would ring and I'd be speaking to a record producer who had somehow been driving past and heard us playing in Alan the drummer's back shed. Forget the fact that this would have been quite impossible as the shed was way too far from any road. The whole idea was, in fact, ridiculous, but I imagined it happening anyway because I really believed that somehow or other my natural inclination was to step on a stage – I just didn't know how or why right then.

However, my expectations of music-biz stardom did begin to fade somewhat during that fateful, all-important gig at The Cave when – out of nowhere – a giant brawl broke out all around us. It was fearsome; it swept the entire room like a wild fire of violence, ending up resembling one of those saloon free-for-alls you see in Westerns.

But, I hasten to say, it didn't dampen my spirits one bit; no, it only momentarily made me fear for my life and shit my new, tight Sta Prest trousers. As the fists flew, my main concern was to protect myself from the rain of flying glasses and beer cans by using my bass guitar as a sort of umbrella.

That's when everyone, including Bill, seemed to just disappear. I looked around and realized I was on my own on the stage. All I could see were bodies, fists, bottles and chairs, all being thrown and landing here, there and everywhere. The whole room was heaving with violence and mayhem. My first reaction was to save my bass. I thought, 'If anything happens to that, Dad will kill me.' Then it occurred to me: 'Wait a minute, I'm going to die anyhow. So who cares?'

After The Cave Catastrophe, as it came to be known, the next band practice was a much darker affair. There seemed an odd cloud of doubt hanging over rich Alan's rehearsal shed. Things were different now, something was missing – well, Dave's guitar, for one.

Maybe Dad was right when he warned me about a career in music. I could hear his voice resounding over and over in my head: 'You can't just become a musician.' Now I wasn't sure if I even wanted to be a musician.

My expectations had been well and truly dented. I knew 'it' wasn't going to happen with that band – in fact, I didn't even know what 'it' meant. They always say you learn something from your mistakes. Wait a minute. If that's true, then how did 'Chico Time' get in the charts?

Well, I did learn something from my ill-fated spell with The Anonymous Five, something I hadn't really known before: that when I was on the stage, something changed inside of me. I felt better than I did when I was off it. I felt free. Even after all that violence started and everybody was running away, I stayed where I was. That was where I felt the safest, even as it was all going mad around me. I stood my ground because that's where I believed I couldn't get hurt. It's ridiculous, I know, but it was the real world that I'd never quite been able to fathom, whereas I 'got' the stage. So I simply stayed where I was.

I also learned that I thought differently from everybody else in the group. My work ethic and mental discipline were not the same as theirs. I couldn't even add up at school, but in the band I had an innate ability to separate each instrument, rearrange them, organize them in my head; I could tell each member to play something so that it sounded better when played along to a certain drum beat or bass line. I felt in charge.

Whether it was all the years of conditioning as a kid, sitting around theatres and clubs listening to music and watching performers, I wasn't sure, but it certainly felt natural to me. That experience helped me find a role in this world that didn't involve me feeling like an oddball, weird or excluded.

Alas, whatever 'it' was, it would have to wait. I thought, 'It may never happen.' But there was no doubt that my fleeting encounter with the experience of being in front of an audience planted something in my head. It thrilled me like nothing else. I'd crossed a line. I didn't know if it would ever come round again, but if it did, I'd be much better prepared the next time.

One thing was certain. I had changed and I knew that I was no longer destined to be a failure. If Mrs Taylor had been there that night, I would have blown her away.

19. The Art School Rebel

The band had kept my over-active head busy for a while, but now it was time to get real, as they say. I had left school at sixteen with a tiny pea for a brain and no qualifications other than the basic teenage trait of growing a face full of inflamed acne the size of which could be seen from space and a huge headful of fuzzy hair which a woolly mammoth would look at enviously and say, 'Wow!'

All I had to show for my time at school was an O level in art, a subject I loved and was reasonably good at, so it looked as though the only prospect for me was to . . . if perhaps I could indulge myself for a moment, to artistically connect . . . to dig deep inside my soul and collaborate. With the end of the frigging dole queue.

Margaret Thatcher was at the helm and driving us all mad. She was laying people off with a king-sized trowel and selling Britain off like it was a bring-and-buy sale. The country was experiencing a depression more gloomy than the Christmas Day episode of *EastEnders*. Mass unemployment reigned – jobs were definitely thin on the ground – and Norman Tebbit was telling us to get on our bikes. If I could have afforded one, I would have done.

I had no discernible talents apart from a good eye for drawing and painting – it was only the one eye, but it was a good one. Meanwhile, my school friends occupied themselves with fighting, smoking, dating and then shagging their hands. They say it was the growth of the thumb and the ability to grip objects that propelled man from his ancestral ape relative into the sophisticated race we are today. Need I explain what perpetuated that growth? The date is 4000 BC. We hear the echoes of frustration from a small cave entrance and just inside, lit by the flames of a burning fire, we see a hairy chunk of a man slapping himself in the groin area. 'That's nice . . . but if I could only grip it!'

Anyway, while my mates were putting their newly formed thumbs to good use, I was at home, busy creating stuff. Painting, drawing, modelling, that sort of thing. So by the time I left school, I'd managed to accumulate quite a body of work that I could take along to show the guy wearing a polo neck who was going to interview me at Thurrock College of Art and Design.

Art wasn't something I was ever intending to do, but I eventually discovered it was the only option I had. Plus, I had become pretty competent at it, so I thought, 'Why not? I've got nothing to lose.'

On the way to the interview, sitting on the bus clutching my huge art folder packed with my paintings, I really did feel that I was wasting my time. They didn't let people like me into art college. I was too rough around the edges. Art college was for the floppy-haired Hush-Puppy mob. You know, the ones that slope around all day wearing baggy jumpers and scruffy jeans; the ones that if you told one of them to piss off, they would simply tilt their head with interest, bring one arm across their diaphragm to support the elbow of their other arm so they could wave some pungent French cigarette inches from their lips and say in a pretentious turd-bag accent, 'Yeaaah? When, like, you say "piss owff", in what way do you actually mean "piss owff"?' The sort of people who go home early as they have to spend the evening stroking their beards.

Well, that's exactly how I turned out after six months. Yep, I was a fully fledged, beard-stroking twat who wore floppy jumpers, had bushy hair, wore odd-coloured socks and talked as if I needed everything to be somehow profound and meaningful. I had, as they say, had the operation. I was a bona fide art student.

When I first entered the art department of the huge college for my interview, I was immediately struck by the sheer array of art. The white-painted walls of the studio were filled with all types of work by the students, all at different stages of development. Some pieces hung around the walls, others sat there with bits missing, half finished. I thought I'd died and gone to heaven. This, I said to myself, is me, this is what I want to do.

I lumbered, mollified, across the studio and was beckoned over by a softly spoken hippy type, a good-looking man with long wavy blond hair and deep blue eyes, sitting at a large table. I unzipped my folder apathetically and laid my paintings out across the table before the man, who, it emerged, was Sam Benjamin, the head tutor conducting the interviews that day.

I sat and waited for his reaction, never making full eye contact. I just hunched over, staring at the floor and wringing my hands so tightly my knuckles kept going white as the blood was forced out of them. I expected him to say something disparaging. I'd made the mistake of showing some of my paintings to friends once, and they didn't get them at all. 'What is it?' they would whine. 'It doesn't look like anything I know.'

Plus, I was very self-conscious about the fact that I might not look very 'arty'. It had always been assumed on the council estate in Bristol and by the new friends I'd found in Billericay that art was something for the knobs and not us. I know it sounds ridiculous, but that's how it was. The only way the kids I knew expressed themselves was through their fists. I should know, I'd been beaten up by some of the best punch-up artists around. That was why I decided to speak as little as possible to Mr Benjamin, assuming that as soon as I opened my mouth he would immediately put me in a certain, unflattering pigeonhole.

So I just looked down and waited, but to my surprise Mr Benjamin's complaints never came. I momentarily flicked a glance up towards him. My attitude was softening – Mr Benjamin had a gentle way about him. He was a Jesus lookalike, with a very relaxed manner. He sat there cross-legged, caressing his well-trimmed, greying beard with his thin, delicate fingers, gazing intently with no particular hurry about him, contemplating the pictures spread out across the table. Slowly he raised his head to speak. Because he had looked so deep in thought, it made what he was about to say all the more important. I bent forward to listen.

He spoke in a calm, almost whispering voice. 'This one here . . .' He leaned over to point at a portrait I'd painted of my mum. It was one of my favourites but, of course, I assumed he wouldn't like it – that's why he'd picked it out. Whenever I painted, I always approached it with energy and excitement. I would set about the canvas with a real verve, constantly changing brushes and colours over the whole piece. For the particular work Mr Benjamin had chosen, I remembered I'd used a whole range of different hues, emphasizing my mum's beautiful, warm green eyes with blues, pinks, aquamarines, purples and turquoises. Mr Benjamin continued, 'Your use of colour . . .'

'Oh?' I shrugged. 'Everybody always says that about my paintings. There's too much colour and that's why it doesn't look how it's meant to.' I thought he was about to say the same.

'Yes, but only an idiot would think that, right?' Mr Benjamin interjected.

'What do you mean?'

'Well, I can see that with your use of colour, you're painting what you see. That's important. Who cares what others think? I don't. It's about risk, right? I can see what you're doing, I can see it, Lee.'

My jaw dropped. I was astonished. Blimey, I thought, either this bloke gets it, or any moment now he's going to burst out laughing, say he was joking and send me packing. But he didn't. He just stood there, helped me pack up my paintings and said simply: 'I'll let you know formally in a couple of days. The clock-watchers who run this place force us to do all this paperwork lark to make it official. But I can tell you now, I love your work, Lee, and really hope you'll come and study with us.'

I couldn't believe what I was hearing. I was glued to the

seat – no one ever got my paintings! 'What?' I asked, trying hard to suppress my incredulity. 'You don't think it's a bit mental?'

'Yep!' he chuckled. 'That's why I like it!'

From that day on, I was bowled over by the openness and impartiality Mr Benjamin showed towards me. He seemed not to care at all about how I looked or the way I sounded – to him, none of that mattered. I got the impression the only thing that really mattered to him was what I had to give as an artist. He looked at it simply as a contribution, another idea, a way to reach a path to somewhere else. I could have entered the room on a space hopper in a Kojak cap, blowing 'Who loves ya baby?' on the bombardon and he wouldn't have given a rat's arse. How you actually don't give a rat's arse is something I have never really understood, but that's a discussion for another day: 'Hello, here is a rat, but the bit you ain't getting is right there at the back.' Anyway, what Mr Benjamin cared about much more was what I was trying to say through my art.

I began attending art college full-time. I hated the early mornings – still half-asleep, I'd crawl on to the bus at the stop in Billericay with my humungously large art folder. That was always a pain: whenever it was windy, you'd see me in the street looking like a man who was trying to parasail on dry land without a board. I'd shoot up the road, desperately trying to control the huge, flat, black case that threatened at any moment to whisk me into the air and away.

If it wasn't that, I'd be struggling to manoeuvre it up

the aisle of the packed, steamy, morning bus. It always had an atmosphere of heavy drudgery. Its oh-no-another-day-at-work passengers all had zero patience, especially when nudged or poked by a passing duffel coat with fuzzy hair holding an oversized briefcase.

As I heaved and huffed – with great physical effort – up the aisle of the bus to the nearest vacant seat, my art folder would usually attract attention from some of the different crowds of workers. At that moment, I would inevitably become the morning's entertainment for some lunkhead at the back. 'Someone run over your briefcase with a steamroller, mate?' some weasel face would cry out. That was a real crowd-pleaser, eliciting great gales of laughter from the packed sardine-like top deck of desperately grey passengers. 'Here he comes, the incredible shrinking man.' Funny! Yeah, but not every freaking day.

As the two-hour journey went on and the bus got closer to the college, the early-bird passengers would all eventually get off, gradually to be replaced by the second crowd of morning travellers. They were the art students who eventually filled the bus and turned it into what could only be described as a freak show. They were the complete opposite of those who had been on the bus earlier. It would now became an entirely different journey, as the vehicle filled with punks with huge spiky hair, Mods and young girls dressed up as their idol, Adam Ant, a massive hit with students at the time. There were others sporting wedge cuts and wearing jodhpurs like the pop group Haircut One Hundred, and the couple who got on every morning all done up like Dave Sylvian from the band Japan. I wondered how this lot ever got out of the door in the morning, with the amount of garb and make-up they were all wearing. It must have been like getting ready for panto season, but every single day.

The bus would arrive outside the college and offload its morning menagerie of oddballs and misfits. An exotically dressed crowd, it looked like the circus had hit town. We would all enter the college, walking down the long corridor to the art department. This would lead us past the various other departments. First up, our parade would trigger the usual morning barrage of catcalls from all the testosterone-fuelled lads in the engineering department. Dressed in oily, these-prove-I'm-not-a-poof dungarees, they stood around next to their huge manly lathes, sniggering at us. 'Look at them!' they would sneer at us as we went by. 'Lazy bastards!'

Then we would pass the catering department where a few of the students would inevitably stand on the other side of the glass in aprons and white trilbies, pointing and hurling taunts at us. 'Benders! Bleeding weirdos!'

I kept my head down and carried on walking. Sporting only a duffel coat, Hush Puppies and bushy hair, I was able to blend in and not draw too much attention to myself. The abuse was aimed at the ones who were wearing make-up and decidedly different clothing.

I had a deep sense of admiration for the way they would stick passionately to their beliefs, always adhering to an unyielding and non-conformist dress sense. When they received the attention of the more macho students, these alternative types would shout back, thumbing their noses and barking back in return, like some mad gang who had just jumped out of a *Mad Max* movie. 'Piss off, you boring, conventional tosspots.' I saw it as a badge of honour to be associated with these defiantly individualistic art students. I liked the fact that they viewed it as their duty to stand out from the crowd.

All the same, there were times at first when I may also have been guilty of thinking that perhaps art wasn't a 'proper job'. That idea stemmed from Dad, my brother and lots of the lads I hung around with at the time. It wasn't their fault, of course – it was just born out of ignorance. They quite rightly considered art, drawing and painting an easier choice because it wasn't traditional manual labour. It didn't involve the honest sweat of a working man's brow.

Of course, now I know that you have to reject the sort of closed-thinking crap they want to force-feed you at school, the narrow idea that you should keep your head down, never speak up and get a proper job. Now I understand that art *is* a proper job; for example, some of the students who were at art school with me went on to St Martin's and later into the fashion industry. Spencer, my friend from art school, is now a great artist. Mark, another friend of mine, works at Warner Brothers' animation department. I've also met other former art students working on film sets. I ended up as a comic. OK, so I let the side down, but at least it's creative.

Yep! Now I was at art school, I was turning into a different person. I had changed my mind about the direction I wanted to take in life. I adopted the ideology that I would no longer be a slave to other people's ignorance. I had reviewed everything and was now going to be a famous artist. It became obvious it was time for me to stop denying myself. Above all, I was convinced that I could no longer deprive the masses, who undoubtedly would have been enthralled if they hadn't been totally unaware of my true artistic genius. I reflected upon the fact that I might even throw them the odd painting here and there, perhaps one I had whacked out on a napkin while sitting in the Wimpy, as a sort of titbit. I would while away the days delving into my more important, meaningful work. I wasn't yet sure of what that work would be, of course. But I would ponder and, in good time, perhaps after a blue period or a lemon one, either way after a right good muse, dive into Little Lake Me at some later stage. But, for now, I shall conclude that all that's –

'Bollocks.'

That's what Dad called it. 'Are you all right in the head, son?' he asked as I held aloft one of my paintings to show him what I had been working on. Dad got up and turned the sound down to '*3 – 2 – 1 –Dusty Bin*'. Mr Benjamin always said that our work should provoke a reaction and a discussion, and it certainly did in our house. My art had changed the whole mood in our lounge. I had meaning-fully introduced this piece to everybody as 'The Crying Tree'.

'A bloody crying tree? How can you have a crying tree?'

I'd hardly pulled the painting out of my folder when Dad's sunny face changed to thunder, and I could hear Wayne chuckling from somewhere behind him. Wayne was revelling in my discomfort, as Dad ranted and raved: 'Call that art? I could do better than that with my eyes closed!'

Dad moved across the lounge to get another angle on it and to think up a new way of abusing my painting. As he did so, he revealed Wayne sitting in the armchair opposite, still wearing his work clothes. My brother Wayne had acquired a job steel-fixing on a building site. The heavy lifting and working outside had made him look solid and fit. His youthful, tanned face complementing his blue eyes, he was a good-looking young man earning good money. He smirked over at me as he scoffed another mouthful of food from a piled-high tray on his lap. He had what was considered in our house a 'proper job'. He was also paying Mum housekeeping and so suddenly had a say in what went on around the place. I, on the other hand, was an art student and earning nothing and so had bugger-all say. It was never vocalized, but because Wayne had a 'proper job' I felt as though I was seen in the house as some sort of slacker.

The views of others around me only helped to feed my sense of rebellion and so, influenced by college, I began wearing odd, if not rather radical, bits of clothing. Trying to break away from the person I had been and fit in with the other students, I started changing my appearance – at first only slightly, nothing too outrageous. I mean it wasn't even Trinny or Tranny, or that other bloke – Cok Wank? By today's out-there standards, it was boring pipe-and-slippers stuff.

But to my family, I was becoming uncontrollably out-rageous. I would wear mismatched socks or decide to cut one sleeve off my jacket. This made me look like a one-armed bandit, especially since my eyes rolled around all the time as I was constantly on the lookout for a good scene to draw. People stared at me as if the five bells were about to come up.

One morning, I might try trimming one side of my hair with Dad's old nail clippers, before realizing my fringe was at a certain angle across my forehead that made me look like someone who had just woken from major brain surgery. Whatever, it didn't look right. So I would trim the other side, and then I looked like all Three Stooges.

Because of my new-found dress sense, Dad became suspicious that I might be a little too happy or even gay. 'Well,' I would reply, 'I was smiling.'

I soon guessed he was concerned about my sexuality. After all, I'd taken to wearing odd clothing and had never brought a bird back home. This was in stark contrast to Wayne, who was always boasting about his sexual conquests at the weekends. The way Dad looked at me, I could sense his suspicion, and that suspicion rubbed – if I can say rubbed right now . . . anyway, rubbed – his working-class roots up the wrong way. It went against what he saw as the norm.

He seemed consumed by the idea and would keep making oblique comments or slip something randomly into a conversation. 'It's good to keep yourself fit,' he would announce, rising up from his armchair and jogging on the spot to demonstrate in a very manly fashion. 'But it's not so good to hang around the gym, is it, Lee?'

Later, he would be sitting there listening to his record player and suddenly declare, apropos of nothing: 'I like all sorts of music, but I don't like musicals at all. Right, Lee?'

I'm sure he just wanted me to say it, simply to confirm his fears. He would even say jokingly: 'What, are you gay or something?' But instead of it being friendly banter, I got the feeling he was deadly serious, as there was always a pregnant pause afterwards before I answered: 'Nooooo, Dad.' Then the conversation moved on for another day.

It didn't turn out to be that much of a rib-tickler in the end, but I tried something just for a joke one Christmas. I was sixteen, and this particular Yuletide was a little more important than others as Dad, who was hardly ever with us over the festive period because it was one of the busiest times of the year for him, was actually at home. Having him at the table for Christmas dinner was rare and very exciting for all of us, so maybe I didn't think it through properly, but I decided to wait until the main course to make 'An important announcement'.

Timing is everything in comedy, of course, so once I'd hushed everyone round the festive table, I thought I'd selected the right moment to declare, with great pomp and circumstance: 'Mum, Dad, I'm gay.' I really wish I hadn't because all hell broke loose.

'Get out of this house!' Dad shouted.

'But I was only mucking about,' I whimpered.

Mum got up and left the room, sobbing. 'You don't muck about with that sort of thing in this house, young man.'

Ooops.

20. Power to the People

There are not many moments in your life – perhaps one or two maybe – when you feel the inclination to jump out of bed in the morning with a keen sense of purpose, excitement and enthusiasm and a desire to burst forth out of the front door as quickly as possible in order to go and do something you really love. But I felt that way about art college.

When I arrived there in the mornings, I even liked the smell of the art department, its heady scents of resins, paint thinners, clay or the thick white dust of plaster of Paris that hung in the air. If I was lucky, I would get Mr Benjamin, head of the department, for a lesson, and usually when that happened, any chance of doing any art was quickly forgotten. As soon as I got him talking about my favourite subject, John Lennon, I would sit for ages, completely engrossed, listening to him recollect his days in the 1960s attending Liverpool art school with the great musician. Lennon was my hero. He was then and has been ever since. Always will be.

Why? I think most probably because I could at that time relate to him as a working-class hero. I also loved the way he always seemed to stick two fingers up at the Establishment. For someone like me, so introverted, and always at odds with people in authority, Lennon's example in a

strange way gave me hope and inspiration. Having idol-
ized him all through art school, I felt he'd become part of
my life. So a number of years later, when I heard that he'd
been shot, it was as if the killer had taken a piece of my
life away. Kids like me need someone like John Lennon,
heroes who are from where you're from. His murderer
deprived people like me of a role model, a benchmark, a
standard to go by.

Yep, I loved every minute of art college. I kept myself
to myself as I was still agonizingly shy. But, for the first
time in my life, I felt I fitted in some place. No longer
would I be pulled up for being a bufflehead; in fact, whatever I did or said was – quite amazingly – considered an
idea of some sort. This, I felt, was the place for me. I had,
as they say, found my promised land at last. My thoughts
and feelings – which out in the real world had been seen as
ridiculous – were allowed to run amok at art school. What
the tutors were teaching us never for one moment felt
staid or boring, but seemed open-ended and interesting.
They were keen for you to contribute, and even though
every other student was in their own strange artistic bubble, it felt as though they were of the same mind as me.

At least, that's how it was at first. It slowly emerged
that we were as different as the myriad pebbles on a beach.
As the year rolled on I started noticing how the students'
different characters came through. I discovered that one
in particular was very different from me.

I was sitting quietly sketching in a corner when suddenly,
out of nowhere, a girl appeared next to me. Another student from another part of the art department. I recognized
her from the canteen at lunchtime. She always sat up one

end of the hall at some tables that had been pulled together, surrounded by a whole bunch of students from other departments. From where I was sitting, it looked like they were having some heated discussions; this girl in particular would get very irate about things, and begin slamming her hand down hard on the table to make a point while shouting something or other. I couldn't tell what it was, as I was too far across the canteen to hear, but her vehemence made all the others do the same in agreement.

As she spoke to me, she was breathing heavily as if she was in a hurry about something. She had unconventional looks, but was nonetheless mesmerizing. I was instantly smitten and particularly struck by the way she dressed. She was a bit punky-looking, with spiky white and blue hair and frightening eyes so heavily made up she must have spent the whole morning unblocking her eyeliner-pencil sharpener with a compass. She looked like Johnny Rotten dressed up as Zorro returning from a happy-hour booze-up down at Pepe's Bar and Tapas in Santa Ursula, Tenerife. It was not a look that you could ignore. But back then I was lured by bright objects, and she was definitely bright; it was like having a conversation with the sun's inner atmosphere.

'Hi, I'm Sarah. Are you going to the demo over the weekend?' she asked in a forceful, excitable, upper-class accent.

I was confused. I was desperate to fit in with all these arty types. Also, I was seventeen, I was keen to find myself a girlfriend and I thought that maybe she might be asking me out. I reckoned I could easily get used to all the make-up. After all, I thought, girls never talk to me and here's one actually chatting to me unprompted. There again, I was so desperate, she could have asked me to eat my duffel coat and I would have started munching away at the hood right there and then.

I answered like I knew what she was talking about. Eager to match hers, I also put on a very bad posh accent. 'The demo? Yah. Are you gooowing?' I said, crossing my legs and swaying back and forth in my chair to look more intellectual.

'Oh, yah,' Sarah replied. 'We really have to wipe out nuclear weapons, right? If the bloody Yanks think they can just pitch their pipes of evil death over here, then, like, they've got another thing coming, right?'

She shouted the word 'right', which made me jump. It also simultaneously startled a few of the very sensitive neurons in my brain, making them vault around a bit, which for some unknown reason forced my lips uncontrollably to shout back in her face very loudly indeed: 'Too fucking right, Johnny Rotten, my son!'

Sarah then turned to leave. I couldn't really tell because her Coco the Clown make-up rendered her featureless, but I think she had a confused expression on her face thanks to what my mouth had involuntarily blurted out. 'Outside the college gates, Saturday morning,' she barked. 'Coach leaves at nine o'clock.' And, with that, she was gone.

'Blimey,' I thought, 'I'm going on a demo. Wait a minute – who cares? I'm going on a date!'

If it was a date, then it was a funny one. I imagined it to be something different, perhaps a bit of fun, a meal and a chat. I knew we were going up to London on a demo, but at least a couple of moments alone wouldn't go amiss. To be fair, I'm not one for conversations, especially with a girl. I get too nervous – which was handy on this occasion because I hardly spoke to her.

Having built up the date with Sarah throughout the week, adding bit by bit another vignette to the already epic scenario, I was under the false illusion that Saturday would be spent shagging. I had deluded myself that somehow, as she was such a confident person, she would just make me have it away with her instead of going on the demo.

So you can imagine my complete and utter disappointment when I hardly saw Sarah at all that day. As soon as we got off the coach at Trafalgar Square, she was gone – instantly disappearing into the heaving crowd. Left there like a lemon, I just stood and waited for her to come back. I gave her the benefit of the doubt, thinking maybe she would make her way back to me at some point. As I twiddled my thumbs, I watched the massive crowd start chanting about a bomb.

I wondered, as I waited in vain for my posh 'date' to return, looking up at one of the four lions that guarded Nelson's Column, what we were all doing there. Then I found out. There was some bloke at the front of the crowd who looked like he was geeing them all up. He was holding one of those loudhailers and shouting into it. At first, it seemed as though he – like me – had no idea why he was there, because all he kept shouting was: 'What do we want?'

And then everybody appeared to remind him by shouting back at him: 'No more nukes!'

But again he had to be reminded, because he then shouted: 'When don't we want them?'

And everybody once more jogged his memory: 'Right now!'

I thought to myself, 'You would have imagined they'd have put someone up the front who knows what we're doing here. Either that or the poor fella has the memory of a goldfish.' Because at that moment, he started asking everyone again: 'What do we want?'

As the ever-expanding crowd squeezed, heaved and pushed further into Trafalgar Square, I managed to lift myself above the masses and peer across the sea of heads towards the front – appropriately enough, just beneath the National Portrait Gallery, another place filled with a bunch of odd-looking heads, funny how it works isn't it? – to see if I could spot my date.

Yes, as luck would have it, I saw her! She was up there next to the big temporary stage on the shoulders of a very tall, leather-clad, well-built bloke who actually looked a little like her, if I'm honest, with a shock of white spiky hair. Between them, they were wearing more make-up than a Yardley's counter. Sarah was frantically goading the crowd around her, before breaking into manic laughter – I think she was really hepped-up by the occasion or perhaps something else as I could see her eyes rolling around her spiny head like bingo balls.

I definitely got the impression she was having a great time. She kept joking with that man between her legs. I was glad it was him, as I'm not sure I could have sustained someone sitting on my puny shoulders and riding me like a Blackpool donkey for three hours. She would periodically swoop over, kiss the bloke's forehead, then sway back up straight and start ranting again at the people around her. Well, at least one of us was enjoying the 'date'.

I was cautious not to draw any conclusions from Sarah's behaviour towards the man between her legs. After all, I told myself, he was only assisting her in seeing over the crowd. But I was, I must now admit, delusional in thinking I still had a chance with Sarah. She had barely said two words to me all day.

Just then a loud screeching noise pumped out from the massive speaker system, filling the square and echoing around the walls of the surrounding buildings. The crowd fell attentively silent, and all eyes trained on the front as a man in a long grey coat and grey hair to match entered the stage. He was introduced very enthusiastically by some mad woman with a headful of springy hair, shouting his name so loudly that the people in Russia might have thought we had sent a few missiles their way: 'EVERYBODY . . . BRUCE KENT!'

The crowd went wild.

They only settled when he tapped lightly on the microphone, testing to see if it was working. Referring now and again to his notes, he began to speak, slowly but with great authority. Before my trip to Trafalgar Square, I hadn't known who Bruce Kent was – I don't know why, but I kept thinking he was Superman.

Anyway, I have to say, standing there listening to his words echo and bounce around all those buildings that day, it certainly made a lot of sense to me. I mean, before then, I wasn't really aware of how bad things were in the world. There was I, happy in my own abyss of naivety – the world hadn't really paid me any attention so, I thought, why should I bother to pay it any? That way, I could just keep my head down and get along without any trouble.

I knew that there were big rockets directed at our country and that some madman was ready to press what I imagined was a small red button if he got angry with us. Wayne had informed me when we were kids, 'Rockets that can destroy the whole world are pointing right at us.' He went on to tell me what happens when one of those rockets explodes. He loved to watch my reaction when explaining in gruesome detail how you would be vaporized on the spot and all your skin would fall off and your hair drop out.

It'd had a profound effect on me. I remember after he told me, that night when I went to bed, I lay there in the darkness unable to believe it was true. I was nine and it frightened me so much, I just lay there, body locked, staring at the ceiling, my hands clasped firmly together, praying so hard to God that He never let it happen. I literally begged Him for weeks and weeks. Why, I asked, could you allow anyone to build such a cruel thing that could destroy everything in such a wicked and horrible way? I don't know if He heard me, but it hasn't happened yet.

Anyway, there I stood, listening to Mr Kent. But I also had half an eye out for my so-called date, the one who said I had to come to the demo if I wanted a shag. She didn't say that, but that's how I heard it.

'The British people,' declared Mr Kent, 'are not pre-pared to be blown into dust and accept the destruction of the entire world.' Quite stark words, you'll agree. How-ever, Sarah didn't seem to be taking much notice of them; she was too consumed with riding that bloke's head like it was the dressage, arching over again and kissing him between her legs and laughing at something he'd said to her. Here I am at a peace march, and all I want to do is go and smack them both well and truly up the bracket.

I watched the girl who, just days earlier, had ranted and raved to a rapt audience in the canteen and demanded that I come along to today's protest. She had ordered me to listen to Mr Kent, explaining how we all lived in mental castles facing potential enemies in other castles, cannon balls at the ready. Mine were ready, too, but sadly they were never called into action.

As Mr Kent's rhetoric began to draw me in, I found myself gradually forgetting about the hypocrisy of posh Sarah. I may not have copped off with the upper-crust crumpet, but I was still – quite unexpectedly – getting a heck of a lot out of the day.

I dropped my head and listened to his words. I stood there staring at the ground beneath Nelson's Column – he himself a victim of war – and began to cry.

'Why?' Mr Kent pleaded. 'Why wasn't there a better link between military spending and poverty? Couldn't a more realistic distribution of the world's resources ease global conflict?'

I wiped the tears from my eyes. 'A-friggin-men to that,' I thought. 'I could do with a few quid myself, as I'm well and truly skint.' But, joking apart, the message had struck a chord with me. It illuminated a light bulb in my mind. And, from that day, I started to ask myself the age-old question: What's so funny 'bout peace, love and understanding?

Now all that reminds me of my Granddad Evans. He was a staunch and very proud Welshman, right down to the bone marrow, which was made up mostly from crushed

leeks and coal dust. He would wolf down a vatful of
sherry during Nan's massive Christmas dinner. It consisted of a large plate of lard with generous amounts of
lard topping, and if you ate all that, you were allowed a
piece of flan made mostly of lard, sprinkled with CPR
flakes for your blocked arteries and a heart attack to finish.

But after dinner, Granddad Evans would suddenly
stand bolt upright, as if on parade in the middle of his
small, frayed lounge. Such was the speed of his rise, his
trousers had to catch up with him afterwards. He would
stand there, white shirt sleeves rolled up, tidying his hair
in the mirror above the fireplace. From there, he would
proceed to do his annual Christmas speech about the ter-
rors of fighting in the war. His stories of his time in the
army were so heart-wrenching and sad, they would always
make us cry. And his melodic Welsh accent somehow
gave what he was saying more resonance.

He would tell what it was like to see your friends die.
He would talk about the heroism and the ultimate sense-
lessness of it all. Then he would turn, his mood becoming
even darker. Growing ever more angry, he would recount
how he and all his mates hated the toffee-nosed buggers
who were in charge and who always seemed miles away
from any of the actual fighting.

But mostly he liked to vent his rage at his Japanese
foes. He would shout: 'And thaaaat is whiiiieee Ieee reff-
fuuwwse . . .' Real venom now infused his voice, as if it
were from the very depths of his soul, as if it seethed and
bubbled inside him like some vengeful toxic mixture.
Building to a crescendo, spit would fly from his mouth.
Then, having used the last remnants of oxygen left in his

lungs, he would slump back down into his well-worn armchair. 'And that's whyee Ieee reffuwse to buy any-thin maide buyee the Japaneeese.'

It was a good job he made that announcement about the Japanese then, as in the future they would start making just about everything on the planet. If Granddad were still alive today, I'm not sure his speech would have the same significance, as he and Nanny Evans would pretty much be sitting in the dark with no telly, no radio and probably no heating, as I'm betting the Japanese make the computer chips that go in our boilers too.

Mr Kent's speech made me think of my Granddad Evans standing by the fireplace, raging in his castle. Granddad was probably no different to some German or Japanese bloke who, after a few jugs of beer or some bottles of saki, would no doubt have a rant about us from the safety of his own castle.

Anyway, all the way home, I didn't speak to the posh girl once. I had sat uncomfortably on the coach, looking out of the window at her kiss the tall bloke goodbye before climbing aboard. I wanted to keep out of her way. I was content to sit some way up the coach, staring out at nothing much, content to take in and contemplate what I'd heard that day. All the same, I couldn't help overhearing what that posh bird made of it as she, along with a large group at the front, vented their anger at the government.

The coach dropped us all off back at the car park in front of the gates to the college. By now it was late, about one in the morning, and very dark, with only the nearby street lamps giving a little illumination. I watched the shadowy outlines of the last few students getting off before the coach slowly pulled away.

Only then did it cross my mind that it might be a bit of a struggle to get home as the buses probably wouldn't be running at that time of night. Cars began arriving with parents picking their sons and daughters up. I don't know why, it just sounded strange hearing all these slightly posh accents from the parents say stuff like, 'Was it a good rally, darling?' or 'You didn't get into any trouble, did you?' It got quite busy at one point with cars coming and going, filling up the car park with their headlights. The air rang with the sound of car doors opening, then slamming shut again.

Sarah, the posh punk girl, came over and spoke to me for the first time in many, many hours. 'Well done for coming, Lee. It was great, wasn't it? One day they'll get our message, right? And we'll bring down this corrupt Tory government, won't we?'

I shrugged my shoulders with indifference. I wasn't too pleased with the way it had gone on the bird front, but I didn't want to offend her. I'd learned an awful lot from Mr Kent, but bollock-all from Sarah.

'Where do you live?' she asked.

'Billericay,' I answered, hoping that might mean she would give me a lift home.

But she just rolled her eyes and turned to go, saying, 'Oh, God. Good luck with that one!' Dumbstruck, I stood and watched as she trotted over to open the door of a waiting Rolls-Royce. She gave me a small wave, uttered a couple of words of excitement to whoever was driving, closed the door and was gone.

Suddenly the car park was dark and empty. I looked

around. Everybody had gone. Silence. I looked at my watch. One o'clock. I shook my head disconsolately: what's the point? I started walking. I had a long walk home in which to contemplate how this situation was not right.

This, I thought, is bullshit!

And that's when everything got confusing for me. I was sucked into these bewildering thoughts. That posh girl had ordered me to go on the demo and had then abandoned me in the car park. She had glided off without a care in the world in her Rolls-Royce, which to me, then a scruffy art student with no money, was a giant symbol of wealth and privilege. I know I probably looked way too deeply into the significance of it all, but I *was* seventeen, and that's what you do when you're seventeen.

Sarah's appallingly arrogant behaviour unfortunately implanted a huge chip the size of a country estate firmly on my shoulder. It was so big, it would take me until I was forty years of age to rid myself of such negative thoughts. At the moment Sarah ran off in her Roller, a chip was born. It may have been irrational but, boy, it certainly added to the feeling of inadequacy that was already my constant companion.

Mind you, even now, I think I had a point. It really is quite odd to be picked up from a CND demo in a Rolls-Royce, isn't it?

21. Teenage Wasteland

From that day on, art college lost a little of its romanticism and profundity for me. Now, instead of searching for a meaning in everything, I would instantly look for the cynicism and triviality of it all – not just in the art but the people who created it. It was a blow, but the reality was I suddenly realized there was quite a lot of bullshit in the world of Art (with a capital A).

I'm sure most people knew that already, but I didn't. It was a shock to discover that, in most cases, art is made up of ten per cent effort and ninety per cent eyewash. That realization hit me like a truck delivering sledgehammers.

From then on, I began to get all my wires crossed. I was too young to understand what was going on in my head. Just when I thought I'd found the place I belonged, just when everything seemed to be falling into place, I'd suddenly lost my direction in life. I was now confused as to where I stood in the great scheme of things. Were the art students my kind of people . . . or were they chicken turd?

It eventually became clear to me that I was caught in the middle of a culture clash. On the one hand, there was art college and all its enticing middle-class ideals about freedom; and on the other, there was my dad's constant rant about what it is to be working class and know your place. Dad's attitude clashed with all these middle-class studenty types urging me to: 'Break free, man, stop watching the clock, be your own person, you don't have to be a part of the system.' Well, that was great and everything, but they didn't have to worry about money.

On top of this, there were the old friends from school I still hung around with at weekends. It was as if I had a kind of split personality. During the week, I was attending art college, a place that encouraged calm, studious free-thinking and individuality, that urged you gently to take convention by the hand and lead it to the land of creativity. Then, at the weekend, I was out with the lads cruising the streets, looking for trouble. In some ways, the two apparently contrasting groups had similar outlooks: they both wanted to challenge the status quo – but with very different levels of violence! My old school friends had found that merely pondering the boundaries of what might be considered acceptable wasn't enough. They became so angry, they wanted to grab the normal rules by the throat, throw them to the floor and kick the crap out of them. We were at that age. Rebellion was in the air.

And I was getting dragged into it. Having previously only shown a slight tendency towards unruly behaviour, I was beginning more and more to be surrounded by gangs of furious, discontented youths who seemed hell-bent on getting things off their chest.

The cult film *Quadrophenia* had exploded on to the screens of Britain's cinemas. A huge hit with the young kids all over the country with its graphic scenes of violence, it had touched a nerve with our disenchanted teen population. We were a frustrated generation of Punk safety-pin-and-bondage-trouser-clad aficionados that had set the country on a path towards anarchy in the UK. But a new tribe had also rolled into town on their Vespas and Lambrettas, wearing smarter, crisper clothes. By the late 1970s, Mods were all the rage – and they were certainly raging. Every teen's urge then, it seemed, was to let off some steam in the name of their new-found tribe.

Following in the footsteps of their predecessors from the 1960s, these new-model Mods were just as anxious to get at their arch-rivals, the Rockers or Bikers. While the Mods liked to dress in natty clothes with clean-cut lines and neat haircuts, the Rockers by contrast favoured oily leathers and long, greasy hair. It was a discord made in heaven – or should that be hell?

It all cried out for an expression of violence. To add fuel to the fire, it was also the time of the menacing-looking skinhead, whose job was not just to look hard, but also to possess an insatiable desire for disorder. Your common or garden skinhead – more common than garden, to be honest – was willing to take on all-comers. On occasions, skinheads and Mods could be drawn together by a shared love of Two-Tone fashion and music – a ska-influenced genre played by bands such as The Specials, Selector and Madness.

But, above all, being part of a tight-knit gang meant belonging to a select group, whose rules demanded courage, a sense of duty to others and a strict obligation of loyalty. I, of course, fitted perfectly into the role every gang has: the funny, stupid kid.

In the late 1970s and early 1980s, Britain was suffering

from grinding mass unemployment. The UK was seen as the poor man of Europe and had undergone years of recession that had left its mark on our landscape. Housing estates were wastelands, shops in the local high street were boarded up and there was nothing but greyness and depression all around. Most of all, however, young kids had absolutely nothing to do. Having been so long in the doldrums, we teenagers were by this stage really pissed off and itching to express our frustration.

There were, naturally enough, stark disadvantages in belonging to such a gang. Once a card-carrying member, you were called upon to fulfil certain obligations – and they were chiefly of the violent kind. The gang's sole purpose was to release its pent-up aggression. We were intent on causing nothing less than unholy commotion wherever possible. Our teenage explosive temperaments demanded delinquent, rebellious behaviour. If trouble didn't find us, we would go out and find it. It wasn't a decent weekend if we didn't get blind drunk and have at least one punch-up. If we couldn't get into a punch-up with strangers, we would simply start punching up each other.

The overriding law of our gang was that if there was any sign of trouble, you were expected to stand your ground and not even think about running away.

'Do Not Run.'

That was always our mantra. It didn't matter if you flailed around like a demented idiot when the action started – just so long as you never ran or left your post. If you were to turn and run, you would instantly be ostracized by the rest of the group, considered unreliable. So you were conditioned to stand there, head down, and fight your way out, whatever the situation.

It was all about loyalty now, it was always the sticking together that counted. That was something that had been drummed into all of us, having grown up together. It was something we just did.

It helped enormously, of course, if you could actually fight. Despite all my years in the boxing ring, when it came to a real fight, I still didn't really know one end of a fist from the other, and I was at an immediate disadvantage in a ruck. At the first sign of trouble, my motto would be: stand and get beaten up.

There was always one small consolation. It appeared it was true what they say, that you don't actually feel the pain while it's happening to you, while you're in the thick of it. It's only afterwards that it hurts. It's the adrenaline, I suspect; you feel the kicks going in, but somehow you're numb to them.

Whenever there was trouble, I would more likely than not be curled up on the floor in my little ball of protection while my mates fought gallantly around me using their fists. When it all went off, as they say, I would try to fight, of course. But inevitably it was only a matter of time before I was peering out through a mass of shuffling feet that clattered around the ground where I lay, as the kicks rained down from whatever gang we had picked a fight with that week.

Let me tell you a bit more about the ethos of our gang. At that age, you believe you're indestructible. You truly think there is all the time in the world. In those days, for us bunch of mates, something risky would always present itself as a test, to see how far you could push the boundaries in a world of authority, rules and regulations. All boys do it to some extent, it's a rite of passage, and hopefully always great fun.

We were no exception. For some insane reason, we always either had an ear to the ground or were on the lookout for the most pin-headed, pea-brained, high-risk scheme that would nudge us a couple of notches up the pecking order. Depending on the amount of risk you took, you could be hailed by all your mates as 'A friggin' nut-case' – that was as good as a knighthood – or, better still, 'You're mental, you are!' – that's a military cross right there.

For example, I partook in any number of ridiculous, chicken-headed, dim-witted, clodpoll activities, that only a vegetable called stupid would think of doing, just so I could wring perhaps a laugh out of my mates. It would either be hitting myself full on in the face with a frying pan or any other object that might get a good twang, or a demonstration of how I could light my own farts without snapping my spine in the process.

Oh yeah, you name it, we tried it: sticking ferrets down our pants, eating live insects, learning to puke on cue (which always created an interesting chain reaction), keeping a stern face while one of your mates kicked you full in the testicles.

I was very proud to be proclaimed 'a gourmet solid top bloke' for daring, on one of our many night-time exploits, to crawl into a tomb for the night at a remote churchyard just outside Billericay. The graveyard was voted by everybody as the scariest and most haunted place in the area. I spent the entire night there while everybody else sat in awe on the other side of the stone wall in the pitch black, admiring the way I shat my pants. Yep, there wasn't anything we wouldn't do.

For some odd reason, our gang of boys had the notion that climbing out of a perfectly comfortable bed, sneaking from our houses in the middle of a freezing cold night on any given weekend and meeting up to traipse down to the local industrial estate and find a rough place to sleep was good fun. Probably just because it was there and unexplored, we found it particularly hilarious to climb over a wall and down into the back of various factories at all hours of the night. There we would stumble around like fools in all sorts of chemicals, plastics and God-only-knows-what-that-was pools of hazardous crap in the pitch black as we rummaged amongst the loading pallets, containers and skips.

Giggling with excitement at the chance of being caught, we would clamber over boxes and through piles of various off-cuts, searching for a place to sleep for the night. We would much rather freeze our tabs off than sleep in something that was specifically built for sleep, called a bed. We would be woken by the factory as it heaved slowly to life with men wearing overalls in the early hours of the morning.

On the industrial estate, we thought it was a real bonus one night to stumble across what we all thought was a cotton factory. It was difficult to tell in such darkness, but the consensus among all of us as we descended the wall into the factory yard on the other side was that it was a real stroke of luck. We were delighted by the prospect of a decent night's sleep tucked like tiny mice in various little cracks and spaces found between the massive industrial rolls of cotton that were piled up as tall as a house waiting for dispatch.

So you can imagine our surprise when we were abruptly woken in a fit of absolute torture half an hour later. 'Run! Run! Get out of here quick!' Up went the cries, as the massive rolls of stacked cotton began popping out boys like popcorn from all sections of its mountainous honeycomb structure. We landed on the floor in a heap, jumping to our feet and running towards the wall and our escape.

We quickly realized there was definitely something wrong. Each of us suddenly broke into a sort of crazed-t'ai-chi-karate-kid-on-a-bucket-full-of-E-numbers jig. All our bodies were racked with some kind of furious plague of torment and itching. It seemed no amount of scratching or rubbing would ease the fire that buzzed right through to the bone. It felt as if someone had crawled inside my body wearing a suit of feathers and begun dancing the Macarena, such was the mass of tickling that afflicted the insides of the skin.

After frantically stumbling back over the wall and into the yellow street lights on the other side, we were even more alarmed. It was swiftly becoming clear that our faces were visibly changing to the colour of beetroot. Our features were sinking behind rapidly growing lumps the size of sprouts. We were like a bunch of extras who had burst out of the make-up truck on an episode of *Dr Who*.

We were so tormented from head to toe, all we could

think of was to run off slapping and scratching as if in some sort of imaginary wasp attack. We headed off in a random direction, thought to be somewhere, anywhere, less itchy, if such a place existed. This affliction would plague us all for a full week and a half. Even then, it took another week for our faces to go back to normal instead of looking like a yam pushed into a baboon's arse.

How were we to know, without night-vision goggles, that we had in fact crawled into a giant, extra-itchy, skin-shredding pile of industrial-sized rolls of fibreglass? Before running away, I took a quick glance up at the huge illuminated hoarding on the side of the factory. It bore the name of a fibreglass company and a picture of a woman in a swimsuit waving at me as a boat swished past behind her at speed. But if she'd been where we'd just been, she would not be wearing that swimming costume because, like us, her entire body would be covered in angry welts.

Once the swelling had gone down, everything was for-gotten and, of course, we resumed our night-time factory excursions – right up until the time we climbed into the back of a nail-varnish factory. Sitting amongst the barrels of varnish, we found that the waft of the fumes was highly intoxicating, drawing us in, making us see far more pleasant images than mere lumps, I can tell you.

My friend Don, for example, before falling over in a fit of giggling, mumbled that I looked like a giant rabbit with big goofy teeth and pointy ears. Out of my tiny mind, I slowly lurched around in the dark, much to the amuse-ment of all the others. I'm told people laugh at anything when they're well and truly varnished. I felt as though I was walking on air, but they informed me three days later when we all finally snapped out of it that I was traipsing around imitating a spaceman, arms akimbo, taking giant steps for mankind and making lots of bleeping noises. As far as I was concerned, I was on the moon. But I think we all went on a little journey that night, a much longer trip than we'd anticipated.

We were all still there, as if sat round Pete Docherty's house on a Sunday morning, when the factory clunked to life the next day. Someone with half a wit about him did shout 'Run!' But it sort of sounded like, 'Rrru-uuuuuuuuuuuuuuuuuuuuuuunnnnnnnnn!'

Of course, it was those incidents that brought us together. Just as an army unit must be first broken before they can be put back together, bonding them even closer, the same could be said of our group. We just looked out for each other.

Take the notorious Battle of Basildon. It had started out as a simple night out for a group of kids attending a well-known nightclub in Basildon. But that night would eventually lay the foundations of my personality – in solid, reinforced concrete. It was an occasion that I was made not only to pay for, but never allowed to forget. I truly believe it has been a major psychological driving force throughout my life and my career (if you call what I do any sort of career).

Even today, and probably for evermore, the events of that evening are burnt into my memory – because, when it came to it, I ran. I ran away, leaving my friends to endure a pasting so bad that one of them suffered a brain injury and was hospitalized for months afterwards. Others were beaten so bad they looked like one of Jackson Pollock's paintings during his Blue Period, or Mike Tyson's sparring partner after telling him in a clinch that he had done his wife big time.

Running for it cut against everything that had been engrained in me by Granddad Evans, my dad and the kids I hung around with. It was instilled in me from an early age: you never run, you stand and fight, face up to whatever it is.

But I ran.

Not only was I racked with guilt, but I was made to suffer for it. I swore to myself after that incident that I would never run from anything ever again, and I haven't – since then I've never ducked from any risk, any challenge, any fight, anybody or anything. There are always major lessons in life, and that was one of mine.

Anyway, back to the beginning of the story. It was ridiculous really to want to go to that disco, but when you're a teenager, you yearn to be an adult. One of us got the news that a popular Basildon nightclub for adults was now holding a teenage night. Lots of clubs were having them. Thinking we might pull a few birds, the whole group of us dressed in our best stuff, which was then high-waistband trousers and DMs. We were bathed in so much Brut, the fumes could have peeled paint at fifty paces.

In addition, we poured gallons of talc into our underpants, hoping that if a bird put her hand anywhere near it, she would have the sweet smell of Johnson's. However, it only resulted in a huge white patch that showed through your trousers in the ball area. If you patted it, it would send a plume of refined talc into the air, creating a dust cloud so massive it could have blocked out the sun's rays and triggered a new ice age.

We caught the bus and went on to the top deck. After all, we were teenagers and that's what they do. There was the usual loud bantering between excited lads, and you could already feel the tension on the bus as we were venturing into hostile territory: Basildon.

Long before Wayne and I had arrived as kids in Essex, there had always been a rivalry between Basildon and Billericay. I found it odd at first that any time Basildon was even mentioned, kids you were having a perfectly normal conversation with about, say, marbles, would suddenly lose theirs. Boys as young as twelve would start snarling, 'I fucking hate Basildon.' As they vented their spleen on the neighbouring town, their fists would be clenched at their sides, all the while staring spaced-out and wide-eyed into nothingness, like those weird ankle-munchers from *Village of the Damned*. Then they'd just as quickly calm down and snap out of it, acting as if nothing had happened. 'Sorry? What did you just say?'

No one knows what really started it, but apparently there has always been a history of fights and trouble between the two towns, both of which are made up from the London overspill. If you were in their high street and the kids in Basildon found out you were from the next town along, you were mincemeat. And if you happened to stumble into a pub in the middle of Billericay and one of the locals got even a sniff you were from Basildon, it would be only a matter of seconds before you were dismembered and your body parts sold off for spares at one of the many local car-boot fairs.

Whenever the two towns came together, there was always trouble, so we lads were in no doubt that if anyone found out we were from Billericay, there was going to be mayhem. It was the equivalent of being dropped behind enemy lines. It would be even more galling for the boys of Basildon that our mission was to disrupt the supply of girls – in other words, to see if we could pull any. Basildon being a much bigger town than Billericay, they would have a lot more birds than we had. The trouble was, they had a lot harder boys there, too.

The bus journey only took half an hour, and although I had butterflies, I dared not let them show. As usual when nervous, I was playing the idiot and doing something stupid like making faces into that square hole with the mirrors in that the driver uses to keep an eye on the top deck.

We had a great night at the club. It felt so good to act all grown-up – although we knew we weren't. We acted like men, hanging out, drinking the only thing they served, cherryade and Coke. We held our drinks as if they were gin and tonics in a plastic beaker and leaned against the bar, posing for the teenage girls who milled around the dance floor. Now and again we thought one of them might be looking up at one of us boys from under her heavily hair-sprayed fringe that was flapping up and down to the rhythm like a piece of corrugated panelling on a windy day. 'She just looked at me . . . I think.'

What is it with girls and their fringes? They spray enough lacquer on their fringe to fill a skip, so that it becomes a reinforced, hardened wing, a fashionable shield that hangs rigid down and across the spotty forehead, a rock-solid mix of frozen-in-time strands of stunned hair and chemical spray. It always looks like they've spent the morning in the prosthetics department of *Star Trek*, turning into a Klingon.

Girls couldn't care less about any other part of their body or even the world. But the fringe – prepare to meet thy doom if you so much as go within a light year of it. And God help them if it rains. Even in a light shower, you always see girls make a sort of awning by cupping their hands and holding them just above the fringe over their forehead, protecting the all-important front bit of their heads, just before making the frantic, death-defying run from one shop to the other.

At closing time, we filed out from the club in amongst the crowd of teenagers, out into the street. We never pulled any girls – surprise, surprise – but we were still grinning from ear to ear, so happy that we'd had our first night out at a real club. It was just us, friends, all by ourselves; this, we felt, was going to be our gang for the rest of our lives. The mood was high as we skipped along the pavement, making our way to the stop just around the corner from the club to catch the bus back to Billericay.

But then everything started to go wrong.

After reaching the bus stop just off the main drag of Basildon High Street, we looked around and noticed that the street was strangely quiet. Somehow you could feel the menace in the air. Standing at the bus stop, we must have looked like a bunch of chickens waiting for slaughter.

It's a strange feeling when all your survival instincts kick in; it shoots right up your spine to the back of your head, your legs go all wobbly and your face turns white as the blood drains away and mans the muscles like soldiers to the turrets at the ready.

I think it was Don who whipped his hands out of his pockets and looked up. He was a small, skinny kid and always reminded me of Jack Wild, who played the Artful Dodger in *Oliver!* He was the one who saw it first. 'Watch out, you lot. Look!' He nodded up the road and took up a kind of fight or flight position, leaning on the furthest point of the bus stop away from what was coming towards us. His head was darting in all directions, searching perhaps for somewhere we could run. The laughing and joking stopped, and we all looked at him. We could hear it in his voice, but we could also see it in his face – it was definitely something bad.

I spun around and couldn't believe my eyes. A massive bolt of fear ripped through my body. I was frozen to the spot as we all watched a parade of what must have been the whole of Basildon's teenage population gradually begin to fill the entire street. I thought for a moment that maybe we'd just missed a carnival. But no one was smiling.

They were big, small, wide, long, all shapes and sizes, their numbers at least four or five thick. Streaming around the building, the Bad Lads' Army of Basildon just kept on coming. They were led, I noticed, by this one huge lump of a kid who marched out front like someone had just taken his toys away. His face was red with fury, but I couldn't work out why he looked so angry. He walked with such determination. Eyebrows narrowed to a point, it looked like he had just used a pencil sharpener in the middle of his forehead. This lad's face had the appearance of a well-used claw hammer; in fact, I thought that young fella hardly had a head at all, just a huge fat neck with a couple of eyes pitched on the front of it.

The marauding Basildon street fighters filed around the corner towards us. The cool summer night air that had felt so fresh after leaving the club earlier had now became thick and hard to breath. I realized that there was no carnival, that this lot were here to make us the entertainment tonight. My heart jammed itself into my throat. Maybe it was doing what I was doing: looking for a way out.

If that wasn't enough to get the bowels rumbling, from around the opposite corner of the building appeared another lot, easily thirty strong, maybe forty. The two crowds of kids marched onwards, merging into one big bustling group like some Chinese Olympic display team.

Now as one mass, they drummed a beat towards us at the bus stop. Then, as they got to a couple of feet away, they suddenly stopped. We stood there rooted to the ground, stunned at the long line of kids packing the whole width of the street. They were now so close to us, we could hear them breathing. All this lot just for us? It was as if the town had a special bell or a big horn someplace, like you see in the films, perched high on a tower made of bamboo that someone had run off and sounded, making a call to arms and bringing out anyone who was able to fight. It was as if every kid born in the last seventeen years had turned up for a reunion punching party,

'For the good old days.' I wasn't sure, but I think I spotted a young Uncle Tom Cobley and all.

Their ranks contained kids of all different sizes, large, small, young and old. They'd even brought a few girls along as spectators. They stood at the back or out on the edges, chewing down on gum like cows grazing. Others were puffing away on smokes, cheer-leading and egging on some of the hard nuts to get stuck in.

'Go on, Darr, hit that one there! Go on, Darren!' When the boys in the group started edging forward, it prompted more goading. Various voices here and there in the crowd began picking out targets amongst us. 'Hit that little bastard over there, Kev,' said a voice. 'Let's 'ave 'em,' shouted another.

One of the girls pointed at me: 'You!' I looked at her. 'What you staring at, eh?'

I tried to answer. 'You just said "you". I thought you meant me.'

But she jumped back at me. 'He's staring at me again. Stop staring at me. Get that weirdo, Barry, get him!'

'But you keep talking to me . . .'

Then hammer-head-flat-face fella stepped out in front of the crowd and bowled over to my mate Colin, a short, stocky kid with lively fuzzy hair combed into submission down each side of his head. His boyish face had a lovely button nose. Colin wasn't considered much of a fighter at school, but this night would propel him into folklore because he was just about to launch himself at claw-hammer kid. It was hammer time.

It was a ridiculous conversation that started the whole thing off.

'You 'it mow brovver last week, dincha, mate?' the Hammer Head – the boy with the brain of a tool – ground out menacingly through his teeth. After listening intently, Colin breathed a huge sigh of relief – we all did. It was obvious this was just a simple misunderstanding.

Colin turned to look back at us. He smiled and flapped his hands around as if to assure us we had all worried unnecessarily and he would explain everything. So he turned confidently back to the hammer-head fella. I have to admit, I thought Colin did a pretty good job explaining: 'I wasn't 'ere last week, mate, none of us were.'

We all thought that might do it, but then Colin was asked a question that probably the top negotiators at the UN would have struggled to answer. Hammer Guy stared Colin right in the eye and growled: 'Yeah, bu' if you was 'ere, you wood-a-itt-im, wun't cha, eh?' There was simply no way out of that one. How can you guarantee something that never even happened?

It was inevitable. Colin looked briefly over his shoulder again at us and raised both hands in disbelief. 'I don't believe this,' he whispered to himself. He looked terrified but was resigned, as we all were, to the impending pummelling. So Colin simply shrugged his shoulders and did something I'd never seen him do before. Without warning, he shouted, probably to rally his strength, then lashed out. Before you could cry 'Bundle!', Colin was flinging punches everywhere. Oblivious to his own safety, he sank into the heaving mass of flying fists, the kicks just swallowing him in. And then he was gone.

This was it. The inevitable had happened. FIGHT!

As Colin was enveloped in the ocean of aggro, I was

unable to rally anything. My arse had got in first, already rallying everything in my body to the back door. It all turned to slow motion. Just like that, a giant wave of kids rose up and swept over my head, accompanied by shouts of 'Let's 'ave 'em!'

The immense tide of bodies cut out the street light in an instant. Suddenly, I couldn't see anything at all.

Just darkness.

22. The Running Man

After the Basildon Brigade had route-marched all over me, I staggered to my feet. There seemed no point in lying in the middle of the road waiting for them all to come back. Now I was up, I was able to gather my thoughts, my equilibrium. I looked around and realized that this had merely been the first wave of attackers. We were still completely surrounded. An unbelievable number of people were sucked into the fever of it all, joining in the beating and being urged on by the roar and excitement of the massed crowd.

It had very quickly descended into unrestrained anger. No one was in control of their feelings – it was clear someone was going to get badly hurt here and, knowing my luck, it was going to be me. No two ways about it, this was a really awful situation. I straightened up and felt a sudden excruciating pain in my back and the top of my legs. I looked up and saw one of my best mates, Pete. He was indefatigable, Pete, and was still going strong. Then the heaving mass of fighting kids parted slightly and out stepped the still-battling Colin, as if from an opening in some curtains made of humans. He was doing well and looked like a bull surrounded by clowns, such was his strength. Colin was still flinging punches and kicks, even though there were boys hanging off his wrists like pom-poms. He stumbled around, his legs wide apart, unable to close them as there were kids wrapped around his shins like bells on a Morris dancer's legs.

I looked around and, most worryingly, I was unable to spot any of my other friends. I panicked: where were they? Everything seemed to have happened so fast. All my mates had disappeared from view. Most likely, they had been flattened by the Basildon mob.

I clambered to my feet in the high street. Once the mob noticed I was up, they turned like a giant monster back towards me. That was when I heard the desperate cry: 'Run!' That was it, the fateful moment.

The baying Basildon lads started charging towards me at speed. I was dazed from my earlier beating, so it was taking me a while to work out was going to happen. Surely, I thought, I've had enough, haven't I? From nowhere, one of my other friends, Paul, appeared. Thank God, I'd thought he was lost. He flashed past me, clothes torn, sweat pouring, eyes wild: 'Lee, run!'

That was all I needed to spark my brain into life again. A big red warning sign flashed across the screen in the control room inside my head, an emergency lever was shunted and I was off faster than a whippet on a Kawasaki 425 strapped to the front of the space shuttle on re-entry. Or so I thought . . .

My legs wouldn't move. They were numb, useless. I watched, frustrated, as Paul sprinted off in front of me. I wanted desperately to catch up with him and began to get angry with myself at not being able to move my legs. 'What's the matter with them? Why won't they move?' The problem was, they had taken such a kicking, it was just too painful – shit, it hurt!

Thwack! I felt a sudden kick to my right thigh. The shock of the blow was excruciating. It was too late. Like a pack of wolves, they were on me. They saw me get up, and I was about to go down again. That must have injected a shot of whatever it is that first made us humans discover we could run really frigging fast when a dinosaur turned up wearing a bib, and carrying a knife and fork and a dinner voucher. I was off faster than that bloke Ben Johnson at the mere mention of a drug test.

I never gave my brain time to even think about the pain. I was cured – thank you, Lord, Hallelujah, it was a miracle! I was so hyped up on adrenaline, I thought, if my legs don't want to come, then sod them, they can stay here and take another thumping. Me, I'm off.

As I ran, I felt no pain. I was running fast, bang, bang, bang, one foot in front of the other. I never even looked back. Lungs burning with a fire hotter than a furnace, I was sucking air in, then out, in, out, like a piston. Wind rushing through my hair, I felt the refreshing relief of night air cooling the sweat on my skin. It whipped like air con around the inside of my shirt and trapped it like a sail through the gaping hole at the front, the buttons having been popped off during the violent kicking and tugging. My brand new Ben Sherman was now a dirty rag, torn open to the waist. I was the Incredible Hulk, but in reverse.

After I'd been sprinting for so long I felt like I was leaving the Earth's atmosphere, I began to slow down. I was so tired, I could have dropped right there on the ground and slept the whole night. My body had let go now. It knew, without even looking back. It could sense they had given up the chase. Exhausted and breathing like a steam train, I took a quick glance back over my shoulder and saw Peter and Colin surrounded but still fighting like lions. It was like General Custer's Last Stand all over again.

A wave of guilt swept through my battered body. I began to get angry at myself, calling myself names. I had left Pete and Colin behind. They were my friends, I had to go back. But then I thought about how I would certainly get a good kicking. I bent over, resting my hands on my knees, desperately trying to force some oxygen into my lungs. I just didn't know what to do. Everything that Dad, my brother, my friends had rammed into me was to stand and fight, not to run.

I shouted to Paul up ahead. I'm sure he was feeling the same as me, as he was staring like a madman, his eyes wide open like a couple of portholes. I could see he was in hyper mode; his body wreathed in sweat, he was rocking from one foot to the other.

'Paul? We got to go back, mate.' I dropped to my knees in the road.

'Lee, for God's sake, there ain't nothing we can do. I mean, did you see that big bugger at the front?' He began ranting. I think he must have been in shock because he wasn't making any sense. He paced from one side of the road to the other, slapping his head, shouting and pointing back at the fighting going on in the distance. 'What the hell did we do to deserve that? Colin wasn't 'ere last week, was he?' Next to Paul was a road sign that read 'Billericay 5 miles'. 'We can't go back there,' Paul continued. 'Look at it! We're just going to get beaten up again.'

I lifted my head, took a look back at Basildon and the

illuminated bus stop in the distance, the massive crowd of boys. You could still hear the shouts and cries that always seem to echo through the night air but never the day. I climbed to my feet and looked at Paul. I gazed up and down the road. I didn't know. That's the thing with life; whenever there's a real, proper decision to be made, there's never anybody around but you. All these people give you loads of bullshit advice about how you should do this and 'If it was me, I would do that.' But at the end of the day, it always ends up with just you.

I couldn't think straight. My head was racing. I was mumbling, 'I think we'll have to go back, Paul. We got to go back, mate. Where's everybody else gone? There's only Pete and Colin left.' I started to cry. 'They ain't going to make it, if we don't go back.'

We looked at each other for a moment. I wiped my torn sleeve across my face and sniffed. We both stood up straight, raised our heads and began walking slowly back towards the fight.

But, unfortunately, our heroism wasn't going to be recognized that evening. After only a few steps, we were spotted by the Basildon Massive. A shout went out across the swirling mass – 'Get 'em!' It stopped us in our tracks. We watched as another crowd of boys peeled off and formed a shape like the one you see under a microscope of a cell duplicating itself. Then a separate mass of lads, a few at first but then all of them, was running like a giant tank full pelt up the road towards Paul and me.

That was it.

That was all that was needed to trigger our self-doubt. 'Run!' Up went the shout. Again.

We whipped round and ran for home. As we legged it, I looked across at Paul. His face was all creased up, not from the pain of running so hard, but from guilt. I'm sure I had exactly the same look. We knew we had failed, not just our friends, but ourselves. We had run away, I had run away, I had run away when it counted. My head went down and I ran for home.

That incident, that night, is something that will haunt me for the rest of my life, not just because I had to live with the disgrace of it when I faced my friends, but also at home. Even to this day, the guilt from that night sits smugly at the back of my mind, always ready to remind me whenever I feel fear or doubt.

Just recently, I was standing backstage at the Wembley Arena. The crowd were in, the lights were down, the music already playing my intro. It had been billed as a record-breaking show, 10,000 people, the biggest-ever comedy gig by one person. No one in history had ever done it before, they said.

As I stood silently in the middle of the dressing room, as I do before every show, having a quiet little word with the man upstairs, the door was flung open and a member of the stage crew popped his head in. ''Ere, you sure you want to do this?' he asked. 'It's massive out there and there's a heck of a lot of people.'

A tear formed in my eye as I was reminded of that evening when I ran away. I lifted my head and said firmly: 'Well, I ain't running away, that's for sure . . .' I passed the confused crew member in the doorway and walked out on to the stage.

There's no doubt about it, you should always face your

fear. Running away is much, much worse, not just for other people, but for you too. And as for poor old Pete and Colin, they ended up tasting nothing but hospital food for the next few weeks.

Not too long after the Battle of Basildon, I did get the chance to redeem myself at the now-notorious Battle of Brighton. We were attacked by a gang of crazed skin-heads on the seafront. It was like *Quadrophenia* all over again. But, I'm very proud to say, this time I stood my ground. I took an absolute pasting, but I didn't run. I'd learned my lesson.

In the aftermath of the Battle of Brighton, on the way home, I started to think about where I was. I wondered whether I indeed had a contribution to make, not just in my group of mates, but in this life at all. Did I have a role to play, apart from being a fool whom people laughed at?

There was no doubt about it: I was changing. It had altered my perception of what was significant and, most importantly, what wasn't. I wasn't interested in the macho campaign to determine who might become the next dominant leader of our group. That wasn't going to be me, that's not what I wanted. No, I now knew where I stood all right. I looked around the car at my friends; in the gang, they were all such heroes and I was such a fool. Despite my newfound, street-fighting bravery, I felt I just didn't fit in with the group any longer. I wondered where I would end up.

I discovered the answer sooner than I'd expected.

23. The Girl on the Bus

Just a week later, I met someone who would change my life forever. But our first meeting did not go well, to be honest.

As a gang, we had gate-crashed a party at the flat of two girls we barely knew. What I did to their new apartment summed up what an aimless cretin I was. Oh, everyone laughed at my antics, yes, it got great laughs, went down a storm, but it made the person I most wanted to impress really angry at me. I did what I did because I liked playing to the crowd, and I was too embarrassed to tell her what I thought of her. What an idiot you are, Lee Evans.

Why wasn't I able to sit there peacefully and at ease with myself? Why did I find it necessary to disrupt a conventional event? It seemed that the more orthodox a situation was, the more – for some ridiculous, exasperating reason – I'd screw it up. Maybe I have a deep-seated desire to do something daft because of my insecurities, to cover up my lack of confidence. Freud might explain it in that way, although scientifically I may just be a pea brain. I still play the fool – it's just that they pay me for it these days.

Anyway, back to this girl. She was so beautiful. As soon as she entered the room, I was awestruck, immediately frozen to the spot, unable to move even a muscle. It was as if Cupid himself had struck me with a right-hander across my spot-festooned chops.

She stood in front of me, waving her arms wildly, shouting something. What she was shouting, I couldn't say; my mind was a complete blank, my whole body numb. I stared as her huge red lips opened and closed. Everything was in slow motion. There was no doubt she was furious with me, and yet her face looked even more beautiful all scrunched up like that. Her perfect eyebrows were crumpled in the middle of her forehead like two caterpillars making love. Her massive brown eyes, the size of saucepan lids, raged at me – it was as if someone had thrown a stone into a calm, dark pond and instantly agitated it. She had a gorgeous figure, easily the match of any of the girls in Mum's Green Shield Stamp catalogue – well, that was my only reference point at that age.

She stood in the bedroom doorway, insisting that I would not leave. It was nothing to do with her being attracted to me, of course – quite the reverse. 'You ain't going nowhere!' she shrieked. 'You are not leaving this friggin' flat until you clear up all this mess, you utter, utter berk!'

Those were the first words she ever spoke to me. It was not the most auspicious first exchange with the girl who was to become my partner for life. Yes, this adorable, insanely attractive young woman standing there yelling was none other than my beloved future wife, Heather.

Somewhat teary-eyed and shaking with rage, she carried on screaming at me. I can't tell you here all the other stuff that she shouted at me, in case our daughter reads

A charity cricket match during Blackpool's summer season with Dick Hills, Tom O'Connor, Dick Richardson, my dad, Los Zaffiros, me and the dancers from the show.

Dad on stage playing one of the many instruments at which he excels. A mean sax player – as a boy, I loved to watch him on stage.

Me on guitar!

Behind the bar, aged eighteen, at the Bell pub, in Scarborough.

Celebrating with Heather after winning my first fight in the
East End of London at one of the many boxing shows.

Me revving up for the big one!

PROGRAMME OF BOUTS

JUNIOR

SENIOR CONTESTS

1.	S. FLYN Garden City	10.70	V	J. BATES Shell	4.7			
2.	C. DENNING Berry	5.71	V	D. MATTHEWS Garden City	7.7			
3.	M. YOUNG Sheerness	10.68	V	A. BUSH Alma	5.6			
4.	J. GARRITY Berry	11.70	V	S. SAUNDERS Shell	8.7			
5.	A. FLETCHER Berry	8.69	V	S. O'MALLEY Canvey	6.69			
6.	T. STEVENS Berry	5.69	V	R. O'CONNER Cambridge	3.69			
7.	R. EFFENEY Canvey	4.69	V	L. WILSON Alma	9.68			
8.	P. DOYLE Berry	7.71	V	D. WEEDON Alma	9.71			
9.	A. GEORGE Berry	4.69	V	D. HINCH Belhus P.	5.68			
10.	J. KINGSLEY Garden City	12.67	V	D. ROSE Belhus	7.6			
11.	D. ROLLINS Sheerness	11.66	V	J. KNIGHT Belhus P.	7.6			
12.	K. BAYNE Berry	12.66	V	A. CROWE Cambridge	11.66			

13.	R. ESTABROOK Berry	V	P. BAKER Col
14.	M. ALLSOP Berry	V	M. KANE Camb
15.	L. EVENS Berry	V	J. WOOD Gard
16.	R. TURP Berry	V	R. FRASER Tc
17.	G. MAKIM Berry	V	W. BROWNE Cc
18.	S. BOHEA Berry	V	S. ANDREWS N
19.	C. SMITH Norwood	V	A. LEWIS Cal
20.	D. HUMBLE Chelmsford	V	W. SIMPSON C
21.	SPECIAL CONTEST 3 x 3		
	S. Gale Berry	V	A. DAVIDSON

Recorder: Mrs. D. Jefford

PLEASE SPONSOR A BOUT

A.B.A. Offical in Charge: R. SAUNDERS Esq.
Referree: D. Rulton Esq. Judges: Essex A.B.A.

Berry Boys boxing programme – Fight No. 15
– they spelt my name wrong!

A night out in Scarborough for Heather's twenty-first birthday.

Me and Heather after getting engaged.
We were the happiest people on the planet –
although she's smiling, you can't see the
gleaming Ratner's ring in the picture!

Strumming away in our donated chair during the first Christmas in our flat in Westcliff-on-Sea.

Eastbourne, 1984, during the summer season, watching my dad rehearsing the trumpet. I would sit for hours and listen while he practised.

The kitchen cum bathroom in our Westcliff flat!

My and Heather's wedding day – 22 September 1984.
Have you noticed the bouquet covering the ring!

Talent contest finalists with Oakland Hotel bar and restaurant proprietor Mr John Green (front left) and his wife Joy (back right).

Talent contest

THE search for a star in South Woodham Ferrers has proved a winner for madcap comedian Lee Evans.

He is hoping for a glittering future in the spotlight after winning the talent contest staged by the Oakland Hotel bar and restaurant.

The comedian and instrumentalist from Southend beat eight other acts in the final to scoop the £250 first prize.

And with a panel of judges made up of people from local clubs and agencies, Lee will no doubt be keeping his fingers crossed that a few bookings will follow.

The talent contest heats have been held at the bar over the past two months.

The nine acts that won through to the final included singers, guitarists, a conjurer — and South Woodham Ferrers' own comedian Gerry Palmer.

"It was smashing. The entries were of a very high standard, beyond all expectations," said entertainments manager Mr Howard Carter, who organised the contest.

He said he hopes to repeat the competition next year and in the meantime plans are being made for a comedy showcase in the autumn.

March 1985 – my first talent show win of £250. We're all holding the giant cheque – I lost the real one on the pier!

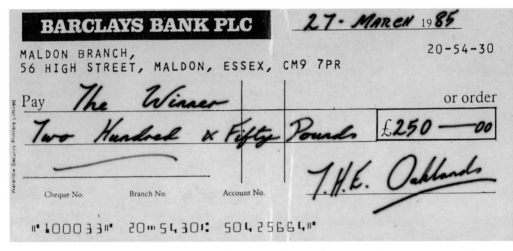

BARCLAYS BANK PLC

27. MARCH 19 85

20-54-30

MALDON BRANCH,
56 HIGH STREET, MALDON, ESSEX, CM9 7PR

Pay *The Winner* or order

Two Hundred & Fifty Pounds £250——00

T.H.E. Oaklands

Cheque No.	Branch No.	Account No.

⑈100033⑈ 20⑈5430⑈ 50425664⑈

The giant cheque, which was unfortunately too big to cash, was presented to me on 27 March 1985. Things were about to look up!

this book. She thinks her mum never swears. But I know she does – big time – especially when we're in bed at night, but our daughter doesn't know about that, either . . .

Heather didn't know me at that stage. I was certainly creating an impression in her mind – not a good one, I confess – but at least she wouldn't forget me in a hurry. I couldn't take my eyes off her as she stamped her feet in protest at my behaviour.

I couldn't blame her.

I had, as always, been an absolute wally. Let me explain. Heather's flatmate earned extra money by curtain-making from home, but she was also a dab hand at making cushions. She had in the corner of her bedroom a big polythene bag of feathers which she used to stuff her cushions. At the party we had gate-crashed, that was simply an irresistible invitation for me to display my little-known skill of aerial diving into piles of feathers. In my humble opinion, this should be an Olympic event, but no one knows about it yet. It's a simple concept and wouldn't cost much to set up. It's something Seb Coe might want to look into for the forthcoming 2012s.

Anyway, the highly trained athlete took a moment to concentrate on his warm-up. He did this by loudly boasting to his mates that he'd found a big bag of feathers in one of the bedrooms. Then, after he'd concentrated – bam – he snapped into his run across the bedroom before launching himself off the nearest bed, somersaulting into a back-dive past the Woolworths special offer ceiling light. He went into a half-gainer, jack-knifing arse first into the big bag of feathers with a loud bursting noise, a technique known as bursting the big bag of feathers. If done correctly, the bag will explode across the entire room and probably into nearby France. Middle podium, here I come.

So there was Heather, glaring at me as I sat in a pile of feathers and what was left of the bag. She had come running into the bedroom, alerted by the lads' whoops of encouragement to the superbly conditioned athlete. Now she was standing over me, white feathers floating all around her as if she was in one of those Christmas snow balls you shake. Mind you, the way she was shouting and bawling at me, she looked more like an employee at one of the sheds on a turkey-plucking farm at Christmas time.

Everything seemed to be in slow motion. She stood there, her outstretched hand stabbing the air and pointing over at her moody flatmate who was out cold in bed. Having earlier complained of drunkenness, the flatmate had stumbled off to bed, and here she was, dead to the world. Did I mention that she was sporting a pair of circular glasses and a Hitler moustache that I had helpfully drawn on her face with a tube of toothpaste while she slumbered?

Pure fluke, I thought at the time. If I hadn't been in there drawing the glasses and Hitler moustache on her face, then I wouldn't have fortuitously spotted the big bag of feathers or have met Heather. What I find fascinating is that at that moment she didn't realize the idiot on the floor in front of her would one day be her husband. Strange world, eh?

I obviously wasn't creating a very good first impression. Well, she didn't appear too happy to see me, let's put it that way. After she had stopped shouting, she whipped round and stormed out of the room, slamming the door behind her.

I snapped out of my reverie and, with the enthusiasm of a research monkey pressing a button that would send a banana down a chute, I instantly began tidying up, making sure every single feather was back in the bag. I even removed the toothpaste from her flatmate's face before she woke up. I was that committed to wowing Heather.

The party continued throughout the night but, unable to find Heather, who seemed to have completely disappeared, I sat around while my mates copped off with a couple of birds. When I asked another party-goer about the girl I'd seen earlier, he told me that she'd had to leave suddenly as her mum had been taken ill.

So my first encounter with the girl who was eventually to become my wife wasn't exactly impressive. From that first time Heather and I came into contact with each other, I have always had the feeling that I somehow took her by surprise, that I came out of the sun at her in a sort of kamikaze, unexpected attack. I was on her case straight away, a buzzing fly, you might say, who got on her nerves. I feel as if I've been something of an irritant ever since. She's forever saying to me, 'Go away – you're annoying me now!'

Seriously, Heather does at times accuse me of behaving in a challenging, irrational, off-the-wall manner. But I get the impression she's always found that quite exciting for some reason.

I constantly have to defy convention and now when we're together, if I do something out of the ordinary, like I will, in a public place, she'll give me the evil look of daggers. Her demeanour will resemble one of those blokes you see on the news holding a club above his head ready to bring it down between the eyes of a baby seal. But at the same time, I can spot a little smile and a sparkle in Heather's eyes which tell me that, deep down, she finds what I'm doing amusing. It indicates that she would like to be doing it too, but can't as she's far too self-conscious, too scared and, unlike me, was brought up in a way too respectable to let go.

That's how our relationship works on one level. Just as I challenge her shy, rigid, conventional upbringing with my free thinking and take-it-as-it-comes attitude, by contrast she represents the voice of reason in our partnership. She has – and will gloat about it – a far superior, academically gifted brain. I often imagine she's the equivalent of a laboratory scientist observing a chimp after giving him a colourful toy to play with.

Oh, I almost forgot the most important part. Did I mention that I also find her the sexiest woman on two legs? Admittedly, I've never met a woman with three legs, which in my opinion is a little more sexy, but would cost a fortune in Odour Eaters.

Heather's first, brief encounter with me confirmed that evidently I was a witless thick-wit who always seemed to foul everything up. But then I hadn't introduced myself properly. She hadn't seen the other side of me yet. That was a lot worse.

To Heather's white-linen, cosy, 'normal', lower-middle-class household where everything was well ordered, I would be considered far down the food chain. A beautiful, well-behaved, sensible, smart girl like Heather was way out of my league. Even armed with a ten-foot barge pole with another barge pole taped on the end, she wouldn't have usually gone near me. I wouldn't have fitted the 'nice-boy' mould that a pretty girl like her would traditionally go for. Anyway, fate intervened, and our paths would cross again the following week . . .

Once more by sheer, utter chance, it appeared something was pulling us together. It had been a week of intense mental turmoil for me. My mind was not fully on matters at hand. Let's be honest, while most people use both sides of their brain, I only use one, so you can imagine how little brain I was operating on.

I carried on as usual, attending art college and seeing my mates at the weekend, but I was only going through the motions. What really occupied me was the beautiful girl I'd seen at the party. Girls weren't interested in me as a rule, but I had become obsessed. The whole week at college, all I kept either drawing, sketching or painting was feathers, feathers and more feathers, then perhaps a bird, or even some eggs. I wonder what was preoccupying me.

'What's-a matter with you, Lee? Everything I ask you to do somehow reverts to birds,' my perplexed tutor said.

'Really? I don't see that at all, Mr Jefferies.'

'Lee, you sculpted a papier-mâché chicken this morning, and now you're sticking feathers on that canvas. And you're also wearing a cardboard beak on your head.'

'Yes, I see your point. Oh no, I had some eggs at the cafeteria earlier. Blimey, do you think I may have a problem?'

I took my usual bus journey home from college that evening, which allowed me some thinking time. I concluded that I would probably never see her again. Even if

I did, I wouldn't blame her if she didn't want to talk to a fool like me – not after the impression I'd left her with, anyway. In fact, if I were her, I'd run and hide.

As I stepped off the bus and into the cold early winter wind that swept through the town centre, it was dark. The bus pulled away and I quickly buttoned up my duffel coat, shoved my hands deep into my pockets and headed towards the alleyway at the side of the Chequers pub. Behind that was the hill that would take me to our house. Just then, I heard somebody shout my name.

'Lee!'

I turned round. It was my friend Spencer from art college. He must have got the earlier bus. I thought about throwing him a casual wave and going on my way. It can't be urgent, I thought, I'll see him tomorrow and if there's anything needs saying, he can say it then. It was cold, and I knew Mum would have a bit of hot tea on the go at our house.

But, alas, I can't rush away – it's just not the way I am. If you call my name, I will come. I sometimes hate being like that. So I shuffled towards Spencer, shifting around in my thick coat to try and get warm.

'All right, Lee, how –' Just as he began to speak, another bus pulled up at the stop, and annoyingly I found it a struggle to hear what Spencer was going on about over its engine noise. I shouted to him from under my hood.

'No, wait, Spen. The bus. I can't hear!'

I gestured, pointing in frustration towards the bus and . . .

It was Heather! I couldn't believe my eyes. I wasn't sure at first, as she had her face covered with her hands.

But perhaps I just knew. Plus, it also may have helped that I hadn't been able to get her face out of my mind all week. Her features had appeared on other people, as I optimistically imagined every girl I set my eyes on would be her.

Just then the girl on the bus took her hands away from her face, revealing that it really was her, the girl from the party with all the feathers. My heart began pumping so fast and so loud, it drowned out the sound of the bus in my ears. I couldn't feel the cold any more. It really was her. I watched as she pulled a handkerchief from her sleeve and wiped a smudge of mascara from under her eye. She was crying! Why?

Spencer carried on talking, as I started running towards the bus. 'Lee, where you going, mate?'

It was too late. The bus had just pulled away.

I don't know what I would have done if I'd got there anyway. If I'd started banging on the window, it would only have further cemented the psychotic image she already had of me. I quickly ran over to Spencer, urgently pointing, desperate to know.

'Listen, Spen. Do you know that girl there on the bus?'

'What? Blimey, what's-a matter with you? You look a bit off, mate.' As he talked, he casually looked over his shoulder towards the bus as it rolled past us.

'That girl there, Spen, the one on the bus. Who is she?'

'Oh yeah, that's Heather. Heather Nudds.' He turned back to me, getting annoyed with himself. 'Bollocks, I've forgotten what I was going to say now.'

'Never mind. Listen, do you know her, Spen?' By now, I was a bit frantic. 'Please, mate, help me out here.'

'All right,' he huffed. Affronted perhaps by my insistent pleading, he moaned away to himself, 'I mean all I wanted was to say hello.'

I stopped and stared at the tearful girl on the bus. My heart went out to her. 'Why would she be crying?' I asked.

'What?' Spencer said. 'Oh.' His mood changed and his voice lowered. 'I think her mum is ill.' Then something seemed to have occurred to him. He whipped his head round quickly towards me. Tilting it, he narrowed his eyes. It felt like he was scrutinizing me. He seemed curious as to why I wanted to know about the beautiful girl on the bus. He suddenly clicked into talking rapidly like a machine gun.

'You don't stand a chance,' he sneered. 'She's way too beautiful for you. Everybody knows she doesn't go out with anyone. There's no way she'd give you a second glance. I asked her out once, and she didn't want to know. You won't get anything out of her.'

As the bus eventually disappeared, I gave Spencer a friendly tap on the shoulder, telling him I would see him tomorrow, and skipped off down the hill towards home. As I bowled down our street, it felt as if a heavy weight had been lifted from my mind. I was now wearing trampoline shoes and had suddenly grown wings. I could have sworn I floated down our road.

I knew who the girl was now. Heather!

Then, just as quickly, my wings fell off, and I dropped like a stone. It no longer felt like I had trampoline shoes on, and I slowed to a stop outside our house. I was suddenly wearing lead boots.

I felt ashamed. How could I think of my own feelings while that poor girl was in such pain? How could I be so selfish? I raised my head to look at the sky. I watched a low grey cloud drift elegantly over our roof and thought of her on the bus. I mumbled to myself: 'I'm sorry. Blimey, I don't half love you.'

'Thank you, and I love you as well,' I imagined her replying.

I suddenly jumped, snapping back into the real world. 'What?'

It was Enid, our next-door neighbour. She gave me a little look, as she waddled past me struggling with a bunch of shopping bags in each hand. She must have heard me.

'I don't care,' I muttered. I rallied myself, pumping up my chest, lifting my shoulders. I straightened my back and said quite loudly: 'I love that girl, and if I ever see her again, I will tell her so!'

Then, of course, I realized I was kidding myself. 'Actually, I know I won't do that, because I'm Lee Evans, and I'm a fool.'

'You are!' Enid shouted before disappearing inside and slamming her front door. 'Who else would talk to themselves like that in the middle of the street?'

She had a point.

24. Fairground Attraction

It would be another few agonizing weeks before I would quite literally smack into Heather again – with such force that I knocked her to the ground. I might have said that landing on top of her would be a very fortunate place to end up, but as we lay there in a crumpled heap on the grass, our faces just inches apart, it was embarrassing rather than erotic. The only thing between us was a crushed see-through plastic cup she'd been holding. Just before the fall, it had held a full half pint of coke, which was now taking the form of a massive patch down the front of her white dress.

After a few seconds on the ground, Heather's eyes must have focused. I watched as her huge, ebony, saucer-like pupils shrank down into two pinholes as she realized who I was. 'What the bloody . . . ? Oh no, I know you, don't I?'

So how did we wind up on the ground, with Heather furious with me once more?

In the early eighties, the economic crisis was affecting most of the country. The local council in Billericay thought it a good idea to promote local business by staging a concert in a huge field at the end of the town called Sun Corner. There was a fair there, with side stalls and a disco that would start up later in the evening.

I'd made up my mind not to go, even though it was the talk of the town. Nothing like this had ever happened in Billericay before and everyone was really excited, but I needed to finish some college work. My mates had been calling, asking me to come out, but I was in no mood to go anywhere.

I'd endured months with no money. It didn't make it any easier that my brother Wayne, who was now working as a hod-carrier, would every Friday sneak up behind me and taunt me by waving in my face the wad of money he had earned that week. He thought I would find it funny, but I was just feeling sorry for myself.

I had to make art college work, as I'd failed at everything else. If I flunked art school, there were few other prospects for me. It was at a time when if you went for any interview, there would a line of at least a hundred people also wanting the job. Perhaps they should have advertised for crowd-control operatives.

If I didn't have a piece of paper with at least some semblance of a qualification on it, then I might as well have found the nearest scrap heap and jumped on top of it. Plus, at home I was made to feel as though I was lucky being able to do something that I loved.

Dad didn't add to my confidence as he thought I was a bit of a drop-out. I think, if he'd had his way, I would have been working down the pit at the coalface like Granddad, who shortly after retiring coughed his way full pelt into an early grave, God rest his soul. I think Gran only buried him because she couldn't stand the noise. I had to prove to Dad that I could make something of myself, even if it might be with a pencil rather than a pick-axe.

Despite all that, I'd managed to get a summer job in Scarborough, the North Yorkshire seaside town. After days of pacing our hallway looking at the phone, I'd plucked up enough courage to call Scott, who owned the Bell pub. I'd helped him by doing odd jobs around his pub a few years back when Dad was doing a summer season there, and he told me if I ever needed a job, there would be one at his pub.

So I'd called him up and he'd said, like a jolly game show host, 'Come on down!' Now it would be only a matter of days before I was in Scarborough. I was very glad. I was seventeen, and my loans had already grown so big, they had me round the neck and in a very nasty armlock, frog-marching me towards the debtors' prison.

In spite of having less money than a Robert Maxwell pension fund, I was persuaded to go to the fair by a couple of my mates. Their tactic was simple: they refused to leave our front step unless I came out. I'd been working hard, so perhaps I did need a couple of hours off. Plus, they told me there was the prospect of winning a goldfish, and that was a challenge I couldn't refuse.

It was my last dart. If I got this one in, I would win untold riches – well, the aforementioned goldfish, anyway. I was shaking and the dart was slippery from the sweat between my fingers as I took aim at the dartboard. It's not easy to concentrate while being egged on by two mates and about sixty goldfish, all of them peering out from clear plastic bags full of water hanging up around the stand like baubles on a Christmas tree. You could see the poor things crossing their fins, urging me to save them from their little watery penitentiary. If I could save one poor limbless aquatic creature from this polythene Abu Ghraib Prison, I would.

I threw the dart and we all watched its flight through the air: me, my two mates and all the fish, wide-eyed with optimism, mouths agape. I think I even saw a fish take a large gulp of water to calm its nerves.

Thump! In it went, right in the red. Yes! I would now be the proud father of a goldfish. I was going to be a dad! I decided on the smallest one, as I took that to be the youngest. That way, I would save more of the fish's life. As the stall owner handed over the fish with a look of disdain, I announced to the world that, 'Thou, o gold fish, shall from this day forth be known as . . . Torpedo. Or Torp, for short.' Well, I wasn't going it call it 'Pedo', was I?

I decided on a little celebratory fish dance rather like a dolphin when it rides along on its tail out of the water. That trick always reminds me of how Mum and Dad used to look every time the cheap carpet at our Bristol flat rode up and a large speed bump would appear spanning the entire length of the lounge. To flatten it, Mum would do a sort of Michael Jackson moonwalk across the carpet but with both feet together. I don't think Jacko was in danger of losing his crown as the King of Pop.

As I held my new-found friend Torpedo aloft in his little watery bag and performed my now ever-more exuberant dolphin-carpet-dance, I quite literally fell head over heels into Heather again.

I didn't see her coming as she walked with a couple of her friends behind me. So as I moon-danced, I thumped into her. The force of the collision knocked us both down on to the grass. There we were lying together, her lovely white dress now sporting its attractive new Coke stain.

I said the first thing that came into my head. 'Did you know your eyebrows look like two furry caterpillars kissing when you get all angry?' I'm afraid that's all I could think of.

'Yeah?' she snarled in reply. 'Hang around and you might see what they do when I punch someone.' I took that as a sign that she was still angry.

I looked up at Torpedo. Luckily, he hadn't sustained any injuries in the fall. As the string from the bag was wrapped firmly around my fingers, he hung there looking embarrassed between our faces.

I looked at the fish, then back at Heather. 'You're not going to let a fish come between us, are you?'

'Is he with you?' Heather asked, spitting out grass and rolling her huge eyes.

'Who are you talking to, me or the fish?' I tried joking with her.

'It doesn't matter.' Heather tried to get up – she wasn't having any of my nonsense.

'I've just won him,' I blurted out.

'What are you talking about? Get off me, you idiot!' Fuming by now, she looked down at the Coke stain, which only made her more livid.

'I called him Torpedo. What do you reckon?' I was desperate to keep her attention.

'I reckon you're a bit weird.' Her face began to soften a little. She even gave a little smile. I couldn't take my eyes off her. I was completely hypnotized.

But she soon snapped me out of it. 'So!' Heather

shunted me off her quite firmly. I rolled across the grass, still holding Torpedo in the air. I quickly jumped to my feet and tried joining her two friends as they bustled around her, brushing her off, but they gave me a look that told me maybe I should step away and perhaps jam my fuzzy head in the Waltzer for a while.

I didn't actually join in this activity, of course – that would have felt wrong. Plus, I got the impression that if I'd tried to brush Heather's dress, one of her friends would have seriously smashed my face in. So I contented myself with jumping around like a cat on a hot plate making all kinds of hand gestures and pointing frantically at bits of grass and dirt.

I was panicking. I knew I was out of my depth completely, but somehow I felt compelled to stay near her. Usually on such occasions, if I was within a five-mile radius of a girl, I would break out in a sweat, my acne would swell roughly to the size of the Pyrenees and I would begin stammering faster than a stuck DVD.

But this time I felt calm. I just stood there with my tongue hanging out to one side like a recently tranquilized chimp, staring at her. Blimey, she looked good. I'd never seen such a figure – her long legs seemed to go right up to just above her head some place . . .

I was interrupted.

'Lee, come on, mate. We're over by the shooting gallery.' One of my friends had come over to get me, but I wasn't going anywhere. I just had to stay with her.

'Yeah, I'll see you there in a minute – as soon as my brain starts working again.' I spoke to him in a trance-like state. He just shrugged his shoulders and walked off.

My immediate concern was that I had messed up my chances with Heather. After all, I had been dreaming of this very moment for a month. Here she was right in front of me and, like a fool, I had made her angry. I was annoyed, frustrated at myself; I kept going over and over it in my head.

'Can I buy you another Coke?' I asked, without thinking, just for something to say.

'Why? Do you want to throw another one over me?' She held up the Coke stain on the front of her white dress.

I immediately went the colour of a ripe beetroot. 'If I buy you another one then you do know, there's a lot of sugar in Coke . . .'

'So what?'

'Well, look on the bright side . . .' I had no idea what I was going on about. I was flailing badly, on fire and going down. *Mayday, Mayday!* But I did what I always do when I'm nervous – I just kept talking. 'When your mum puts the dress in the wash, she'll have free candy floss in her tumble dryer for a week.'

Her face changed, like I had touched a nerve. 'Goodbye.'

She began to walk away. One of her friends hissed at me, 'You dick-head!' She spat out the words, shaking her head with derision and disbelief that I could have said such a thing. Then I remembered my friend Spencer telling me about her mum being ill and thought it must be that.

'How's your mum?' I blurted it out with urgency, just desperate to keep her there.

Heather stopped and turned round.

Her two friends looked as if they wanted to slice and dice me, shave my head and drag me through the streets of Billericay as an example. 'What have I said?' I wondered what could be so bad.

'She died,' Heather said quietly, then turned back and went to join her friends.

I felt all the blood in my body sink to my feet and begin packing a case to leave me through sheer shame. I thought of collapsing into a heap, curling up into a ball and blubbering like an idiot. But now I felt I needed to redeem myself quickly. I couldn't leave it like that. I reckoned by then I had nothing to lose and went for it.

'Look, I really . . . I really like you – like, a lot, loads. I haven't been able to stop thinking about you for a month, not since I first saw you with all those feathers floating around your angry head.'

Heather stopped in her tracks and spun round. 'I know who you are now! It's been bugging me since I saw you.' She began to scrutinize my face as I stuttered and stammered my way into a dark hole of shame. I could see the tell-tale signs of the dreaded caterpillars begin to rise up again in the middle of her smooth forehead. You could tell her mind was slotting me into place.

'You're that idiot, aren't you?'

I carried on regardless. 'I think you're amazing – no, not just amazing, more than that, oh, bollocks . . . I'm really sorry, all right, about the bag of feathers. If it's any consolation, I sneezed for a week afterwards – I had a terrible allergic reaction.' I began to go into a mock sneeze.

But my words ground to a horrible halt . . .

LEE, EMERGENCY! EMERGENCY! MUST . . . DO . . . SOMETHING . . . NOW!

'I came out in errrrgh, lumps, eerrrgh, the size of space hoppers. My eyes looked like Alan Minter after a title fight. Look, my ears haven't gone down yet. Just thinking about it makes me snee-snee-sneezeeeergh!' I stopped fooling around and looked serious for a moment. 'I didn't know about your mum. I'm sorry.'

She pondered for a second. It looked like she was reappraising her attitude towards me and spoke softly. 'Look, don't worry about it. My mates are a bit on the defensive – that's why I'm out tonight. I don't really want to be, but they just thought I might need to get out of the house for a bit. They said it would help take my mind off things, you know.'

'Well, I know a really good joke that's guaranteed to take your mind off things,' I said, changing tack.

'Guaranteed?' She smiled again. I noticed that when she smiled a tiny dimple appeared in her cheek. I instantly, directly and without passing go, fell in love – not just with her, but with that dimple. I could have quite happily run off to Benidorm with that dimple there and then.

'Parts and labour guaranteed for three years. If the joke doesn't make you laugh within three years or if any bit falls off it, you can ask for it to be replaced by another one.'

She laughed. 'Go on then. And I hope no bits fall off it.'

She came a little closer. Her friends stayed where they were, but Torpedo looked interested, so I had a crowd.

I told her my joke, there in the middle of the field surrounded by hundreds of people, side stalls, generators, fairground rides and the noise of the giant disco in the field next door. But it wouldn't have mattered if we'd been standing in the speaker at a Led Zeppelin gig in a breakers' yard next to a panel beater with physical Tourette's. I couldn't hear any of what was going on around me – all that seemed to be filtered out somehow. All I could see was her beautiful face, so innocently staring at me in anticipation of the joke that I hadn't even thought of yet. So I did what I always do: said the first thing that came into my head.

'So, there are these two women in a field picking carrots,' I began, really laying it on thick, adding some texture and colour by acting out the entire joke complete with characters, using my full range of hand movements and body coordination. Basically I fell back upon my natural skill as a professional buffoon.

'And so one of them pulls this carrot out of the ground, turns to her mate and says, "Do you know, this carrot reminds me of my Fred." The other woman looks at the carrot and asks, "What? That carrot? Your Fred?"'

I was encouraged at this juncture, as I could see Heather start to giggle at my antics. The same couldn't be said of her two friends, who stood behind her, arms folded, staring at me with real contempt and looking like they were chewing down on a mouthful of nails soaked in nettle juice.

I kept going. "'Yeah," says the woman, "my Fred." "What?" asks her mate, "the colour of it?" "No," replies the woman, "not the colour of it." "What then? The length of it?" "No, not the length of it." "Well, what then?" The woman looks her mate right in the eye, holds the carrot up and says, "The dirt on it!'"

Heather laughed, hard. Then, turning round, she laughed even harder when she saw her two friends, who hadn't even flinched but just stood there locked into a deadpan stony stare as if still waiting for the punchline.

'The dirt on it,' I repeated to her friends, trying to make them crack a smile, but their nonplussed glares were still fixed on me. Heather found this hilarious. Great, my joke had worked! It'd had the desired effect: she was laughing.

'Do you know?' she exclaimed, taking in a huge gulp of air and wiping the tears from her eyes. 'I haven't laughed like that for such a long time.'

That was it.

25. Are You Going to Scarborough Fair?

The rest of the evening, Heather and I spent strolling around together, hardly paying any attention to the bustling crowds that had now packed the fairground and the disco in the field beyond. We were just content to be in each other's company, able to talk to one another with such ease. It was suddenly as if we'd known each other for years. We never stopped talking – somehow it just felt natural that we wanted to tell each other everything.

When we left the fair, Heather let me walk her home. Although we nattered all the way, I noticed she'd forgotten to mention one important detail. She lived so far away that if I'd known, I'd have taken some survival supplies, a good camel and a couple of Sherpa guides, or at the very least dropped bread to find my way back home again.

But the time seemed to fly by as she told me about her mum's illness. She said she'd had to leave the newly rented flat (need I be reminded – the one where I'd burst the big bag of feathers) to move back home in order to help her dad and look after her little brother while her father was busy organizing the funeral. We talked a lot – well, she talked a whole lot more than I did. She talked loads, actually. In fact, between you and me, and I've never mentioned this to her, ever, she didn't friggin' shut up!

That was OK, though, as I got the impression she hadn't been able to just chat to someone, get it off her chest. So I was glad to be there. It also meant I didn't have to tell her about my family, as I was always – not exactly embarrassed – but aware that people from more conventional backgrounds might not fully understand the eccentricity of the way our house worked.

Whenever anyone asked me to tell them about my family, I'd always revert to my little diversion routine. 'I was adopted. Then one day my dad gave me some sad news: "Son, I'm afraid we are your real parents."'

That sort of thing covered my tracks. If I ever had to introduce Heather to my parents . . . well, I just figured I'd cross that bridge when I came to it, but thought it best to leave it blank for the moment. I don't want you, the reader, to think I am in any way ashamed of my parents. They've changed over the years. After doing better for us all and moving to Billericay, they've mellowed.

I've also always hated trying to explain the whole thing about what my dad does, finding it much easier just to say he works in public relations – well, he does in a way. Then if anyone asked what that was, I would say it was the opposite of private relations. Then, I would add, of course there are all the relations he doesn't even know at all. Usually, by then, they'd be so confused they would just wander away in a trance to smash their head against the nearest solid object.

As Heather and I walked, then walked some more, my feet began to swell up to the size of two giant lilos you might find being towed behind a boat by a bloke called José. I felt sad as Heather explained to me that her family home – once a sunny place filled with her mother's effervescent, breezy personality – had become so depressing since her mother had passed away.

'Mum always had flour up to her elbows, cooked all the time,' Heather reminisced. 'She had queues of local people at the front door willing to wait ages for the curtains or clothes she would make for them.' Then her mood changed. Dropping her head towards the floor, she added sadly, 'Now our house is a dark, cold place.'

Her father, she went on, was only going through the motions and, however much he tried not to show it, he was very down. Her two brothers were just walking around like robots, not having accepted it at all. Most of the household chores were now left to her.

As we arrived outside her house, she told me how much she'd enjoyed our chat. I told her I'd also enjoyed it. I said, 'Perhaps we could meet up again soon so that next time I can get a word in edgeways!' She laughed, thanked me for listening and wondered if we could really meet up next week.

I couldn't believe my luck! She actually wanted to see me again. But before I could get excited, I suddenly remembered that I was leaving for Scarborough in a few days. I had to go; I desperately needed the money for college. I'd failed at everything else, and there was no way I could fail this time. I'd also told Scott, the pub landlord, that I was coming to work for him.

Then it struck me, so I just said it without really thinking about it. After all, it was an outrageous idea – she had only just met me. It was ridiculous, but it just exploded out of my mouth without really giving my brain the chance to catch up. I asked Heather if she fancied going with me to Scarborough.

As I said it, I already knew the answer would be 'No'. I am a dreamer. I always think things are so simple, but of course they're not. How could I ever have imagined that a beautiful girl like Heather would even consider –

'Scarborough, you say?'

'What?'

'Scarborough? I've never been to Scarborough. I've never been anywhere.' She looked up at her house, and I could see her come back to reality. 'What about my dad and my brothers? What would they do?'

'Look, I shouldn't have interfered, I'm a dreamer. I have these big ideas, but I don't really think them through properly. I shouldn't have mentioned it. I'm sorry.'

But I could see in her eyes that she liked my idea. I don't know if that was because her mum had just passed away – they do say these sorts of things make us more aware of our own mortality and eager to grab opportunities before it's too late.

She asked if I could come over tomorrow, a Saturday, and meet her dad. I told her that would be great, but first I'd have to adjust my sleep pattern as the journey to her house from mine would probably take me through at least five time zones, three different language barriers and take at least a light year to get there. She laughed again, and I set off home.

As I walked away, Heather called after me and asked me pleasantly enough if, before meeting her dad, I could make a small detour to the nearest barber's for a haircut. She was obviously not familiar with the art student standard-issue attire of really long hair and baggy, cheap clothes. But I agreed anyway because, basically, if she'd told me to bend over and bite my own bum, I would have done it for her there and then.

Once home, I got a really good night of no sleep what-so-frigging-ever. I was far too worried about meeting Heather's father to drop off. The next morning, I was out the door and up the hairdresser's begging for a short back and scrape. Then I went straight back to our house and did the best I could to hide my art-college, scruffbag image. I was desperate to create a good impression with Heather's old man.

So there I was, nervously tapping on the door of Heather's small semi in the middle of nice-wife-2.4-kids-and-a-Ford-Mondeo-on-the-drive territory. I was all done up like a doughnut, plimmies, some old Mod drainpipe trousers that looked as if the bottoms had had a right barney with my feet and retreated halfway up my shins, a bespoke, off-the-peg jacket from Oxfam and enough Brylcreem on my head to grease up the Chippendales for a fortnight.

Luckily, I needn't have worried. Mr Nudds was great, and my training from Mum and Dad always to call people 'sir' and remember the pleases and thank yous went down a treat. I found him a really nice bloke. In fact, he made me feel so relaxed, it was the very first time I'd visited a girl's house to meet her parents without creating may-hem, being thrown out on my ear or being sick in their kitchen.

I admit I really laid it on thick, calling him 'Mr Nudds' or 'sir' at all times. I also don't mind confessing that I did my best-ever creeping routine. Immediately after arriving, I noticed he was out cutting the grass at the back of the house. I quickly saw my chance to get on the right side of him by offering to cut it for him. Of course, as soon as he left it to me, I made a really good job of slicing clean through his orange extension cable, rendering the Fly-mo a Fly-no. Good start, I thought. That'll convince him I am the right bloke for his daughter. I can't even cut the grass.

I stayed for the day, getting well acquainted with Heather's dad and her little brother. I had dinner and explained I was off to Scarborough and would love it if Heather could come with me. I added, 'I know you've only known me for a day, and I've broken your mower but, I can assure you, I only have the best intentions for your daughter.'

Mr Nudds told me he needed to talk to Heather about it, but right now he needed to take the dog for a walk. Well, naturally, I said I'd take out the dog – that would give Mr Nudds a chance to talk to Heather. He agreed, but told me in no uncertain terms that I should not let the dog off its lead as he was a little blind and senile and would get disorientated and lose his bearings.

By the look of it, the dog had already lost his bearings. He was a grey, mangy thing who barely stood a foot off the ground and was definitely getting on in years. I don't know what he was in dog years, but he looked older than a Lassie film. With his head bowed, he wobbled about the house with the right ache. He had a real chip on his furry shoulder, I'd say. He moved more slowly than an antique footstool and blew off vile, trumpeting wind louder than the horn section of the James Last Orchestra.

When Mr Nudds uttered the words 'Dog' and 'Out', something must have clicked in the section of the pooch's brain that wasn't dead yet and reminded him he was once part of a long line of vicious, ancient, hunting, wolf-type creatures that roamed the outlands killing anything with fur on it. He hobbled over to the front door as fast as his wobbly legs would carry him and stood there without even lifting his spiky head, resembling a pensioner waiting for the home help to arrive to take him up the shops.

I showed the dog the lead – nothing! His bloodshot eyes were deader than a stuffed toy in the bargain bucket. It was getting dark outside, so I didn't want to be out long – just long enough for Heather and her dad to have a little chat.

My elderly new pal and I eventually made it down the road and into the park at a pace so slow that snails were overtaking us and laughing as they went by. However, by that point, I felt as though I'd got to know the sad old dog. Feeling a bit sorry for him, I decided that maybe what was needed was a bit of freedom. It could be that he wasn't getting much of that from Heather's rather conventional family. So, I thought, let's give the poor mutt a bit of the old Evans anarchy. I unclipped the lead and he slowly raised his head, took what looked like a little sarcastic glance up at me out of the corner of his eye and then, quite unexpectedly, he was gone.

I hadn't seen anything shoot off that fast since visiting the greyhound racing once with my brother Wayne. That old codger of an animal who, moments earlier, looked minutes from death, was now, it appeared, hours away from me. He just shot off into the darkness like an Exocet missile. He was like a gazelle on rocket fuel fired from a cannon. As I stood there in the middle of the park, still crouching and holding the end of the smoking lead, it dawned on me – I hadn't actually asked anyone what the damn dog's name was.

Even if I was to try searching for him across the park, there were no lights so it was well-nigh impossible to see anything further than your own eyelashes. And if I saw the wretched dog, what name should I call out to bring him to me? I eventually decided on a whistle.

Three hours later, my inner-body core now a solid block of ice, my mouth frozen into the pursed whistling position, I looked like Percy Thrower caught in a snap freeze. Completely exhausted and a near-nervous wreck, I returned to Heather's with the dog. I say returned – in fact, I found him quietly waiting for me at the front door. I hadn't a clue how long he'd been standing there. After trawling the park relentlessly and by now covered in mud and sticks, I'd staggered back to the Nudds' house, all the way acting out various scenarios of how to tell them their dog had gone. All of them involved lots of crying on my knees and begging for forgiveness.

After only a day, Mr Nudds had already been introduced to the real Lee. An idiot.

26. It's Not Grim Up North At All

One week later, Heather and I were on a train going north to Scarborough. I had my job working for Scott at the Bell pub as a barman, and the expectation was that Heather would find something when we got there. We went on the assumption that, as it was summer season in a seaside town, she would easily pick up a job. Heather is a very clever woman and she'd had a job as a secretary in London, but had taken leave to sort things out at home.

For the life of me, to this day I have never fathomed why a beautiful, perfectly sane woman like Heather took a chance with me. But, like she always says to me, she fell in love with me on that day we landed in each other's arms at the fairground. I am her fella and will be till the day we die.

To us, Scarborough was the best place on the planet. I worked hard at the pub, stocking up, lifting, carrying, cleaning and serving drinks to mostly Scots, Geordies and Mackems, a cross section of people who made the atmosphere in the pub electric. They'd arrive by the coachload, packing the town throughout the summer on day trips. They transformed Scarborough into a bustling, loud, exciting place with every pub, café and amusement arcade jammed full of families and groups of men and women hell-bent on having a good time.

Heather had managed to find a job working at the John Bull Rock Shop around the corner from the pub. To top it all, the amazing landlady who ran the place had a small room free above the shop, and Heather I rented it from her. Life, we thought, just could not get any better than this. It wasn't much, but we were together and we were able to eat and we had a roof over our heads. Scott at the pub was also very nice, giving me overtime to make my money up.

The only drawback was that the rock shop would close around eight o'clock, when I'd just be starting my evening shift, so we never really saw a lot of each other. But we did have one day off a week and would always spend it getting the train up the coast to Whitby or down the coast to Bridlington for the day. They were both beautiful Victorian seaside towns. Sometimes we'd even make the slightly longer journey inland over to the ancient town of York. That became a place we would visit time and time again. It turned into our 'just between us' town. Our days out always felt so special because we knew we only had the one day together.

I'd decided to ask Heather if she would like to get engaged. I loved her from her head to her toes – not her feet, mind you, just the toes – and couldn't ever see myself with anyone else. I hoped against hope she felt the same, so I set about putting a small amount to one side each week in order to afford a ring. I knew it would be difficult as Heather did all our finances and if there was even one penny missing she would spot it quicker than a tightwad. It would be hard as we had to pay the rent and buy food each week. Plus, the whole reason for going to Scarborough in the first place was so that I could save enough money to get me through the last year of college and show my parents I was capable of something.

I'd been eyeing up a beautiful ring in a jeweller's window just around the corner from the rock shop. I'd stand for ages on my way to work imagining myself handing it to Heather. I'd picture her wearing it with a tear in her eye, not because it was too tight or because she'd had a terrible reaction to the metal that made her hand swell up to the size of Pat Jennings's, but because she loved it.

If I'm honest, it looked the most substantial ring in the window for its price. All the others looked cheap, but this one appeared expensive. If I could get enough money together, that would be the ring I would get for Heather – a difficult task as it was a lot of money to us at the time, £13.99. It may not sound a lot now, but to us then it was a fortune. To me it looked like something Richard Burton might give to Elizabeth Taylor. Liz would throw it directly in the bin, but he still might give it to her.

After weeks of painstaking, covert money-hiding operations to keep it a secret from Heather, I managed to siphon off enough to buy the ring. So while I knew she was busy at the rock shop, I made a trip to the jeweller's. Once there, I did have second thoughts; I felt guilty as the money I was about to blow would in fact have come in very handy, but there you go. There was no stopping me now.

Back then, the best-known jewellery chain was probably Ratners. The Scarborough branch of Ratners was always busy, packed full of customers all gagging for its range of affordable-to-the-masses bling. And, today, I was one of them. I had £13.99 exactly burning a large hole in my bar-staff-issue trousers.

I purchased the ring. My plan was to present it to her on our day off in York. We caught the train as usual. The whole journey was a torment for me; I found it so difficult to restrain my anxiety about what might happen when I handed her the ring. She might say no, I thought. My nerves will show through and surely any moment now Heather will realize there's something wrong and confront me. I won't be able to hold back. I'm a terrible liar.

We arrived to a beautiful summer's day, and the streets of York were packed with day trippers and tourists. We did our usual thing of strolling around the town, chatting and fantasizing about what we might do if one day we ever had the chance to walk into one of the many lovely old-fashioned shops that sold all kinds of luxurious food and ornaments, and actually buy something. Then we made our way through the many lanes and dreamed about having our own house and what it might look like. Finally, we ended up at a pub, shared a lunch and treated ourselves to a pint of John Smith's bitter and a glass of wine.

All I needed to do now was manipulate it so as to get Heather into York Minster, the massive Gothic cathedral that dominates the town. Persuading her that there was something inside that she might find interesting was difficult as Heather has never been interested in history, but I managed it.

I knew about the great stained-glass window at one end of the Minster, having done a project about it at art college, but I never imagined it would be as amazing and beautiful as it was. We sat quietly on a stone bench beneath the massive window that depicts the journey through life until death. As Heather looked up in awe, I tried my best to explain the window's incredible illustrations. Then I did a little scoot around with my eyes and noticed the tourists had thinned out. At last, we were alone – this was my chance. I fumbled about and produced the ring. Shaking, I opened the small fake-suede box and asked Heather to be my wife.

I wasn't fully prepared for her reaction. She just seemed to stare at me for a long time. Then tears began forming in her huge eyes and running slowly down her blushing rosy cheeks. Interestingly, she was not actually saying much, apart from the odd murmur. She would go to say something, then stop, pause and wave her hand in the air like she'd just put a hot potato in her mouth.

I looked on with keen anticipation, waiting for some sort of answer, even a sign that things were going well. But it was a bit like the process of watching a fax machine trying to receive a message that had got stuck in the system. She suddenly pointed up at the window and let out a little squeak, pulling a face of terror. Then she snapped her hand over her mouth to stop the noise, frantically began shaking her head and burst into tears again, fanning her face in an attempt to cool herself down. I remember thinking, 'Blimey, hot, cold, then loads of moisture. It's like sharing a seat with a Russell Hobbs kettle.'

But then she threw her arms around me and began crying into my shoulder. So I wrapped my arms around her, held her tight and spoke quietly into her ear.

'I'll take that as a yes then, shall I?'

Thinking about it afterwards, perhaps I shouldn't have said that, because that's when the floodgates really opened and I got the full Niagara Falls. It's just an expression of emotion, you might say, and I'd agree. But this was accompanied by a lot of quite loud and – to anyone who didn't know what was going on – very disturbing wailing and sobbing noises.

I'm sure you're aware of the acoustic ability of the inside of a large church to amplify even a light whisper into a ZZ Top farewell concert with extra speakers. That's fine and hunky-dory if you have your face buried in someone's shoulder and out the way, as Heather did. But it's not so brilliant if, like me, you have your face on full show. The place was frigging teeming with tourists who were giving me some very accusing looks. They must have thought that I'd just given Heather some terrible news.

'You bastard,' 'Son of a . . .', 'Nice one, pal.' Those were just a few of the sarcastic remarks from some of the passing visitors I had to put up with. In a cathedral, no less!

That evening we huddled together on the couch in the tiny living room of the flat before I had to drag myself away to do the evening shift at the pub. The trip to York and the presentation of the ring had added something a little extra to our relationship. Every time I looked at Heather, she would already be staring back at me, smiling and fluttering her eyelashes, and in turn I would be proudly smiling back with a grin that a Cheshire Cat would be jealous of. We were nuts for each other.

Heather appeared very proud of her ring. Later, I couldn't help noticing that whenever she was in the company of other people, she would make sure the hand with the ring on was always visible, so as to invite enquiries about the new shiny object on her finger. Then, as soon as anyone took the bait and asked, 'Oh, what's that on your finger, Heather?' she'd immediately dismiss it as if she had no idea what they could possibly be referring to.

'Sorry? Where? What do you mean? What ring?' she'd say with surprise, looking everywhere around the room but the direction of her hand. At the same time, she made sure she kept the hand with the ring in full view of the onlooker.

'I didn't mention anything about a ring,' they would protest.

'Oh really, I could have sworn you said something about a ring,' Heather would answer.

Whenever she was working in the rock shop, for example, she'd always volunteer to reach up and get something off the shelves for someone. 'Half a pound of bonbons, please.'

'Let me get those for you.' Up went the hand with the ring on it.

'What's that you're wearing?'

'Sorry? What? Ring? Oh! That old thing! Bonbons, you say?'

Some years later, we were watching the TV news when the newsreader started to talk about Ratners, the high-street jeweller's. I nudged Heather in recognition.

'Remember? That's us, that is.'

'Yeah.' Heather stared proudly down at her ring. But then the expression on both our faces began to change, as the newsman went on with the story. We were dumbfounded to hear that Gerald Ratner, the head of Ratners, had given some speech in which he joked to the crowd that the company sold crap and that he couldn't believe people actually bought it. The news footage showed that the whole room fell about in fits of laughter, as people cheered and whooped. We looked at each other, stunned, then slowly down at the ring on Heather's finger.

By my reckoning, that bloke from Ratners may have joked that he sold crap, but so what? It gave lots of people like us with not much money a chance to buy a little bit of the dream. In my opinion, people shouldn't have slagged him off. He was a great bloke – without him, perhaps millions could never have afforded the chance to fulfil their desires.

Heather still wears that ring to this day. It may have only cost £13.99, but to us it's completely priceless.

27. The Lady is a Vamp

A couple of months later, we had settled into life in Scarborough. Heather worked days in the rock shop, while I did the lunchtime sessions at the pub for Scott, did a bit of extra work in the cellars or the back yard, then skipped off back to our flat we had now made really cosy. I always made sure I was just in time to meet Heather closing up the shop. We would then sit and have something to eat together before I'd give her a big romantic kiss and scoot off to do the evening shift back at the pub. Then there was the odd half-hour here or there during the day when we could sneak off and grab a cup of tea together in one of the many cafés that stretched along the seafront next to the amusement arcades.

It never takes me long to get to know people. I'll have a chat with anyone, and by now we had both got to know quite a few locals. We'd made many friends who, just like us, were working throughout the summer. So nine times out of ten we'd get our tea free of charge; sometimes we'd even get a full free meal at the pub. The Bell was a real hub for the locals, so the advantage of working for Scott was that I got to know everybody from the boss of the arcades and the owners of the restaurants to the local mayor, who came in for a pint of Bass. I know it's a bit of a cliché, but I'm going to say it anyway: we had nothing, but for Heather and me life couldn't have got any better. The sun just seemed to shine every day.

Only on one occasion would our precious bubble of bliss be popped by the harsh realities of the world outside. Mr Nudds, Heather's father, unexpectedly arrived in Scarborough one day, checking into the best hotel in town, on what he said was a short visit. He explained to Heather over the phone from his suite that it was time for her to meet the new woman in his life and the one he had arranged to marry.

Heather was taken aback – not just about meeting the woman but about the fact that her father suddenly had all this money and could afford to be staying in hotels and hiring suites. 'He's never had money like that,' she said. I felt slightly awkward. I didn't really want to get involved; after all, it was Heather's family and I thought it wasn't for me to give an opinion on the odd behaviour of her father. I barely knew him and didn't want to make a judgement. 'He seems like he's been possessed by this woman. He's acting like a teenager,' Heather reflected after putting the phone down.

Still, her dad was desperate for Heather to meet the new woman and had taken the liberty of booking a restaurant so we could join them for dinner. I remember thinking at the time, 'It sounds like an audience with the Pope. Why can't they just come over to the flat?' But I suppose he wanted to give her the big introduction, do her a bit of justice. Also, I knew the restaurant he was talking about and was aware how nice the food was. We hadn't been able to afford to go out anywhere posh and – not wanting to be disrespectful – I fancied a right go at the menu.

The dinner was a disaster from start to finish.

I took the night off from the pub in the expectation of really filling up on the food at the restaurant. I was going to make sure I reminded Mr Nudds as I tucked into dessert that it was he who had asked us, so I took it that he was paying.

We had no decent clothes, as we couldn't afford any. So I went in my work clothes, hoping they wouldn't get too close to me as I smelled of pub beer and pork scratchings. And Heather? Well, whatever she wore, she looked amazing.

We made sure we arrived at the restaurant at the arranged time, but found we had to sit at the bar waiting for quite a while. Things got tense as Heather was extremely nervous, and we felt out of place hanging around for that long. We certainly couldn't get a drink as we had no money. So we had to sit there pointing at the optics for an hour. There are only so many times you can make a joke about optics. I did it to stave off Heather's mounting anxiety and then I started on the beer mats.

At last, the door swung open. It was a very excited Ted, Heather's father. He quickly urged the waiter to gather us up and hurry us to the table. 'Here we go!' I thought. Ted made sure we were all sat down and ready when she arrived. I was quite fired up about it all, as it seemed quite exciting. But then I glanced over at Heather and could see she looked very anxious. After all, it was only recently that she'd lost her mum. For her, perhaps, the dust hadn't quite settled yet, and here was her father introducing her to his future wife, a woman she'd known nothing of until the day before.

'Stay there. I'll go and get her,' Ted said, fussing around the table to make sure everything was just right for what had now been built up into the big arrival. I smiled at him, but even I was turning into a bundle of nerves as he ran out of the restaurant again. There was a long pause, as Heather and I, beside ourselves with expectation now, fixed our eyes on the door.

Suddenly Ted burst in, waving his hands in the air. He stood there, holding the door to create the maximum effect for her entrance. Bam! In she strutted, a cross between Danny DeVito and Bette Midler. She was a strumpet and a Rottweiler rolled into one. Three feet off the ground, she was a little ball of hard-as-nails hellcat. You could tell straight away that this woman had been there and done that.

'Heather, Lee,' Ted said proudly. 'Meet Denise!'

If I'm honest, I wanted to laugh, but I managed to keep it inside for Heather's sake. She just sat there, completely confounded that her father, who had previously only ever behaved in a relatively sane and conservative manner, could suddenly become so besotted with someone who could clearly eat him for breakfast.

Denise played the part to perfection. She stood there, taking in the moment. Then, flicking her leopard-skin fur coat back over her shoulder, she gave a mock display of searching the room for someone she might know. But all the time it was quite clear it must be us she'd come to meet as we were the only ones in the frigging place!

I was keen for us all to get started as I was starving and desperately wanted to dig into the decent-looking nose-bag on offer. After all, a chance like this wouldn't come along for perhaps many years. But, unfortunately, despite the good food, the evening went rapidly downhill.

The whole meal was taken up with this strange women – who we'd never met in our lives – filling us in on the most intimate details of her and Ted's sex life: he likes it like this, I like it like that – you get the picture. This, I decided, was a family affair, so I tried hiding my head in the menu, but Denise was a relentless piece of work. It kept coming thick and fast, some of it quite sordid. By the time we were halfway through the dinner, even I was finding it difficult to swallow any of the cock and bull stories emanating from her overly crimson glossy lips, so I can't imagine how Heather was taking it. I watched her as she ventured little disbelieving glances at her father, hardly touching any of her food.

Ted, on the other hand, seemed in raptures, laughing boyishly and suggestively nudging the rattling big hairdo on legs next to him. Their hands were all over each other as she ramped up the vamp. It was perfectly obvious she was playing a game with Heather, so that right there and then she would know who she was dealing with.

Looking at it objectively, I felt sorry for Denise as she appeared very insecure. She was straight on the attack from the beginning and really needn't have been. Heather was just a young girl, inexperienced in the games people play, only wanting her dad to be happy. But, alas, from that first meeting, there would never be a chance of a relationship between poor Heather and that woman. Even an idiot like me could see that would be impossible.

We all left the restaurant on apparently friendly-enough

terms. Ted and Denise seemed happy, which only empha-
sized their lack of understanding for Heather's feelings.
From that moment on, a cloud hung over Heather's head.
Me? I did what I always do: tried to make light of it.

Having hardly eaten a cocking thing all night, as soon
as we got back to our flat I made Heather and me some
toast. But as we sat down on the couch to eat it, she burst
into floods of tears. I put my arms around her – this, let
me remind you, was before even taking a bite out of the
toast, so I still hadn't had anything to frigging eat. I held
her tight as she gradually and quietly fell asleep. As we sat
there in the small, dark room, Heather lightly breathing in
my arms, I thought, 'What a shame! Why do some folk
want to break other people's hearts? It could all be so
much better.'

I looked around the room. It was just the two of us, all
still, no sounds. Then I caught sight of my plate of toast
on the opposite arm of the couch. It was lying there,
taunting me.

I harrumphed to myself. 'I won't be getting that
tonight.'

28. The Stork

Scarborough was now a whole lot different. The mood in the flat had changed. The clouds seemed to gather, blocking out the rays of the sun. The work at the pub seemed to get longer, harder. I didn't mind – it was extra money and I was enjoying it. But Heather had made up her mind: she wanted to return home.

I could see she had begun to worry, probably about her father and what might be happening back home – after all, her younger brother was still there. But there was something else playing on her mind, something deeper. I took it that it was down to her father's recent mad visit. I watched patiently as she went about her business, working in the rock shop, coming home, making dinner. She was doing things around the flat, but not with her usual busy, rushed-off-her-feet attitude. It was more like she was going through the motions. She looked vacant, like her mind was fighting something else.

We used to chat loads over dinner, but now we sat in silence with just the sound of the clock ticking. So quiet was it, in fact, that we could hear each other's eating noises. I initially decided I'd let it go on as long as I could and wait until she was ready to tell me whatever it was that was troubling her. But it had hung over our flat for a week now, so I confronted her at the dinner table. 'Right, that's it, Heather. I can't take this any more. You have to tell me what –'

'I'm pregnant.'

'What?' My mouth dropped open.

'I'm sorry.' She lowered her head and began crying.

I sat in stunned silence. I mean, what do you say to that? As per usual, I just said the first thing that came into my head. 'If you keep crying like that, you're going to run out of liquid. How much more can you have? You must be nearly empty by now –'

'Lee!' she interrupted. I was rambling and she knew I hadn't quite taken it in. 'This is very serious. I'm pregnant.'

I didn't know what to think. This was all new to me. 'What? Actually, like, really, I mean, you're –? Honestly?'

'Yessss!' she insisted.

'Well, how did that happen?'

Heather started laughing across the table. 'Oh, the stork came last night, you fool.'

'Stork? What stork? I'll kill him.' I knew what she meant, of course, but I wanted to make light of it. It was my defence mechanism kicking in. If in doubt, muck about.

I jumped up from the small table, sending the plates flying. I reached over, grabbed her face and gave her a massive kiss. She smiled broadly and began whipping the tears away. 'So that's all right then?' she sniffed.

'All right?' I shouted. I was ecstatic. I paced the tiny room, frantic, one hand behind my back like some sort of statesman, the other pointing, jabbing towards the floor. I rattled out my plans like a machine-gun. 'Well, we'll have to get started right now. I don't want my son growing up –'

'It could be a daughter,' Heather interjected with a laugh.

'Exactly. I don't want my son growing up being no daughter of mine. Oh no, he'll need proper stuff – like shoes. Actually, I don't know why, we'll be carrying him about for two years. Well, that'll save us a few bob any-way. Wait. I'll have to sort myself out, get a proper job, somewhere to live.'

'Not just you! Us, all of us,' Heather protested.

Then the magnitude of what she had just told me sank in. I stopped dead like a plank in the middle of the room. I could not believe it. I slumped back into the chair, my eyes glazed over, and fixed a stare straight ahead of me. I was void of any thought and only managed to mumble a few words. 'I'm going to be a bloke. I'm actually having a baby, Heather . . .'

She rose from her seat and calmly came and stood next to me. She took my hollow, silly head gently in her hands, pulled it to her tummy and held it there. 'I can hear it,' I whispered.

'Lee! It's only just happened.'

I looked up at her, as her huge, watery eyes scanned my face. 'Then what are you panicking about?' I asked.

She spoke very firmly. 'We need to go home.'

I noticed the clock from the corner of my eye. 'I'm late for work.' I sprang from the chair, grabbed my jacket and gave Heather a big kiss. Just before running out the door, I looked back at her; she was crying and laughing at the same time. I was so happy, I shouted, punching the air: 'We're going to have a baby!' And I was gone.

A couple of weeks later, we arrived back at Heather's house in Essex in the early hours of the morning. It was pouring with rain, but luckily we managed to jump in a cab at the station. After dropping Heather off first, I was intending then to ride it on back to mine. But the moment the cab came to a stop, Heather peered out of the rain-splashed window and instinctively knew there was something wrong about her house.

Because of the rain, we hurriedly climbed from the back of the car. Grabbing the suitcase from the boot, we quickly ran to the front door. Heather slammed in the key and swung the door open. As soon as we entered, it was obvious: her dad had done a runner.

Empty houses always have that same cold echo when there's nothing to soak up the sound. Heather groped around for the hall light-switch, but it didn't work. As we stumbled through the dark into the kitchen, we could tell the full extent of what had happened. The house was stripped bare; there was nothing left, not even carpets.

Although it was pretty dark, fortunately a street lamp directly outside the house dimly illuminated the room. I spotted an envelope that lay on the kitchen cabinet with Heather's name on it. I picked it up and handed it to her. It was from her father. He had gone and, unbelievably, the house had already been sold. That was it.

The note didn't really offer much in the way of an explanation, only that he had gone off with Denise and that Heather's belongings were in the garage. Her brothers had flown the nest, too. That ghastly night in Scarborough would be the last time we ever saw him. I mean, I know I'm funny-looking, but I didn't know I was that bad – sorry, I was just trying to lighten it up a little.

As you can imagine, Heather not only was distraught then, but has been completely devastated ever since. As people always do in those situations, she blamed herself for her father's apparent Reginald Perrin disappearing act. I was mystified by the whole thing. He had just vanished; it was like a magician's trick, but for real.

I was only eighteen years of age and was hardly capable of peeling a banana. So I was nowhere near able to comprehend what Heather was going through emotionally. She cried lots for weeks and weeks. Most nights, we simply lay in the darkness of our back room on two separate camp beds pushed together, and I held her as she cried herself to sleep.

But Heather is a very strong woman – she comes from a long line of beautiful but tough women. I don't know if it's anything to do with the fact that all her relations come from the East End of London, smiling through the Blitz and all that, but she has never once spoken about how she really felt about her dad just taking off like that so soon after her mum's death. Perhaps one day, when she's ready, she will.

Luckily, though, what Heather and I have in common is an intrinsic belief that once you're down, the only thing is to get up and, not only get on with it, but fight harder than you did before. I don't think it's a choice one has. When you're up, there's only one way you can go, and that's down, down. But it's also true that when you're down, there's only one way to go, and that's up.

I've always said that if we have enough money to eat and pay the rent, then everything else is a bonus. I truly believe that, because growing up I witnessed it every day as Mum and Dad struggled.

There was no other answer but to get on with it. We had a baby on the way, and we had to find somewhere to live.

For the next few weeks, Heather set up camp in the back room at my parents' house in Billericay while we both looked for work and somewhere to live. Art college, let alone a career in art, would have to be put on hold for now as it was all hands to the pumps. There were more pressing problems at hand than trying to contemplate my navel. We desperately needed to get our act together immediately.

The great news was, Heather was an all-round brain box and was GCSE'd up to her big brown eyeballs. Plus, she had already worked as a secretary in London. She landed the first job handed to her by the Job Centre, working for an import–export company near Southend-on-Sea. It wasn't highly paid and she hated it because her boss was one of those bullies who liked to shout at the staff. But it was a job, after all, and we needed it right now.

I, on the other hand, had no qualifications whatsoever, apart from a first-class honours degree in being a halfwit. It was pretty obvious that I had devoted my whole life to studying how to be a full-wit, but as Heather explained, 'That doesn't get you anywhere in this world, Lee, wandering about with your head in the clouds being everybody's mate.'

'Well,' I argued, 'it didn't do Gandhi any harm.'

We had a bit of money saved from working in Scarborough, so we could get by for a couple of weeks, but after that we would be reliant on what Heather was bringing in. I was willing to do anything as long as it paid, so I set about finding work anywhere I could. I registered at the Job Centre and would trawl through the local papers' back pages looking for vacancies. I didn't care what it was – I just went for it.

Increasingly desperate, I went for a turkey-plucking job after a fella sidled up to me outside the Job Centre in Basildon and surreptitiously told me about it. 'Twenty-five pence per bird,' he whispered in my ear. 'The more birds you pluck, the more money you earn.'

I immediately jumped at the chance. These sorts of offers don't come along every day, I thought. I couldn't believe the idiot was just throwing his money around like that. I said to him, 'So it's up to me how much money I earn?'

'Yep,' he replied, 'your future is in your hands.' I didn't tell him, of course, but this was ticking all the right boxes for me. My small brain was already planning how to make a fortune. The way this fool is talking, I reasoned, well, I will surely be a millionaire in a couple of days. With the number of those simple, bollock-chinned, floppy-washing-up-glove-headed birds I get through, I'll be strolling around the Ferrari showroom by lunchtime. I mean, how hard can it be to pluck a turkey?

The answer is: bloody hard.

I took up my allotted position beside a large hook hanging from the shed roof by some old rope, alongside twenty to thirty other pluckers. We all stood in front of our own 'money hook', as I liked to refer to it before I had even got going. We had a couple of minutes before it started, and most people went out for a fag. But I used that time to have a go at getting friendly with the goofy kid at the next hook to me. His teeth protruded from under his top lip at such an angle, you could hang your coat on them.

Amazingly, he said he was married with three kids, but he looked no older than sixteen. That was about all I figured he had going for him, as if you saw him, you'd think he'd just climbed off the porch in *Deliverance*. He kept looking around the shed at everyone else, sharing a bit of a crafty chuckle with them and pointing at me.

'We got a new one 'ere,' he announced. I half-expected him to take out a banjo and start strumming.

The birds arrived via a sort of waist-high wooden trap door that was lifted and tied up by our 'shed runner', George. To call him docile-looking would be an understatement – this bloke looked like a younger version of Worzel Gummidge, but with his stupid head on.

With his big walloping Wellington boots, his mad white spiky hair and his one long eyebrow, George would cheerfully lumber around the straw-strewn shed, checking that we were all plucking the birds in the correct manner. The birds were hung upside down from the hook in front of us and we would have to tear the feathers away from them as fast as possible. I stood there at my hook, frantically plucking. I ripped away handful after handful of feathers, revealing the white goosepimply skin beneath that reminded me of my legs when in swimming trunks. It was truly gruesome work.

I found George's little quality-control visits difficult and unsettling, as his eyes weren't exactly in tune with one another. When he stopped to talk to you, they would dart independently around in their sockets, as if a fly was constantly buzzing about the inside of his head.

I tore at my bird, the pound signs popping up in my head. But, after about a minute, it became blatantly obvious it was going to be more difficult than I'd first thought. I took a quick look around the shed. Everyone else was going great guns. I realized I was amongst professional pluckers here and I was way out of my depth. The people around me were tearing the feathers off these creatures as if the birds had flown through a jumbo jet's engine on take-off. The woman across from me was already on her third bird, and I hadn't even finished the intricate bit around the bird's arse.

It reeked enough in that shed to melt nasal hair, and I couldn't get the smell out of my head for weeks. I still can't eat turkey. I even got queasy when Sir Bernard Matthews used to come on the telly and coo, 'Bootiful!'

It was the end of the day and, if I'm honest, things hadn't gone well for me. I'd only managed to pluck two turkeys, and so I was taken off into a quiet corner of the shed and informed by George that my services would no longer be required. I had to face it, the money-making world of turkey-plucking wasn't for me.

I was left with something, though. For days afterwards, the smell of turkey was still on me, and everyone I met

either started sneezing or began to have breathing diffi-
culties right in front of me. At night time, I would lie
alongside a puffed-up, sneezing, wheezing Heather. Her
allergies going nuts, she would banish me to sleep in the
bath in a sort of isolation block. Although she was angry
at me because we had no money, I think she was willing
to let it go because she couldn't suffer this turkey-induced
allergy any more.

As George told me, eyes rolling around like lottery
balls, I just wasn't fast enough. He was right – I wasn't cut
out for it. The others? They were just amazingly quick.
One hefty woman in the shed could get a petrified turkey
to practically undress in front of her just by looking at it.
I, by contrast, was still on my first bird when George rattled his big triangle for lunch. So, on average, I would
have been earning roughly fifty pence a day. That, by my
reckoning, would make me a millionaire turkey-plucker
by the time I was . . . dead. And my bus fare to the farm
was sixty pence, so I would actually be paying to turkey
pluck.

Interestingly, during lunch as we all sat around on
bales of hay in the shed next door, I noticed that all of
the other pluckers had brought in turkey sandwiches. I
mean, not only would you think they might have had
enough of turkey, but also they were eating turkey in
front of turkeys.

Now that just ain't right.

29. Kilburn's Answer to Gordon Gekko

Every evening after returning from the Job Centre, I'd pick up a copy of the *Evening Standard* at the train station. The back pages always had an extensive job section. Most of the jobs required highly skilled personnel, but there were always one or two where they wanted someone to make the tea. That's all right, I thought, that's how it works; you make the tea for a couple of years, prove yourself and they might give you a proper job.

Even though I knew by the time I'd paid out for the train fare for the interview in London, it wouldn't be worth my while, I was determined not to sign on the dole. I saw that as just wrong and I would always make the effort to go to the interviews. I knew Heather was working her arse off, and we were very anxious to move out of Mum and Dad's back room into some place where we could not only be properly together but also make room for the baby.

So I wanted to show her I was doing all I could, even though it was soul-destroying going for job after job after job and getting nowhere. The trouble was, at every interview I would go for, there were twenty, sometimes thirty others all way more qualified than me. It was like you had to be Picasso just to make the tea at an art shop, and you can imagine what sort of weird shit that would be.

After being rejected by yet another interviewer in London, with the morale well and truly sucked out of me, I was determined to return home to Heather with at least something. So I took the Tube over to Kilburn in North London after reading a small ad in the *Evening Standard*'s 'No Qualifications Needed' section that had caught my eye earlier. After all, I was already wearing my faithful Oxfam suit that I'd had since college. I'd got quite a bit of wear out of the poor thing, and it was starting to beg for mercy.

I was also sporting a pair of shoes I'd bought as part of my bar uniform in Scarborough. After a whole season's worth of mileage hiking around the back of the bar and now all the traipsing about London looking for a job, the soles of both shoes had sprouted holes. I had temporarily managed to mend them using a puncture-repair kit and, to my artistic credit, that was working very well, for now.

I am an eternal optimist, a dreamer and, as you will know by now, a bit gullible. That can be mistaken for stupid – all right, I accept it, I'm eternally stupid.

Which is my excuse for why I got involved in such an obvious scam. After walking for miles from the Tube station, the soles of my shoes feeling a bit thinner with every step, I eventually found the door I was searching for in a parade of pretty grim shops. It didn't look like what I was expecting. It was squeezed between a laundrette and a betting shop, but the discoloured notice taped to the inside of the grubby glass panel did tally up with the advert in the paper. I held it up to compare the two: 'Financial advisers urgently required. Apply within. No qualifications.'

'That's me,' I said to myself. For a moment, I caught my reflection in the dirty glass door. With the suit I was wearing, I looked like Poncho the Clown, not a financial adviser. However, I was determined to give it a go. I entered the door and climbed the steep steps. The thick nylon red and yellow stair carpet was all lumpy, with bits missing so it showed the wooden floor beneath. The air was thick with the eye-watering, tangy burn of cigarette smoke from the bookies downstairs. That hung with me all the way up the wonky, narrow stairwell, which was decked out in the finest woodchip wallpaper. This, I thought, is like walking into Lompa Lompa Land.

As I got closer to the top of the stairs, I could hear the muffled sound of what appeared to be chanting of some sort. There was a moment when I wondered if I had the right place because as I reached the top it was like a scene from *Alice in Wonderland*, as the walls and ceiling suddenly closed in on me. I was now standing on a landing in a small sort of box at the top of the stairs that was so tiny I was unable to even lift my arm with the piece of news-paper to check where I was. My nose was pressed up against a single purple door with a sign taped on it that was very difficult to read. There wasn't enough room to pull my head back and focus on the lettering without banging the back of my bonce. However, I was just able to make out the words: 'Sales conference in progress.'

The chanting was a lot louder now and was definitely emanating from the other side of the door. I thought about waiting where I was, not wishing to disturb a sales conference. I didn't know what that meant, but I realized it sounded very important. No one I knew had ever been to a conference. That was something you only saw on the telly – 'The Prime Minister is at a peace conference,' that sort of thing. But here I was just about to enter – through a somewhat battered, dirty, old purple door, granted – a sales conference. Wait till Heather finds out what I'm up to, I thought.

I rolled the scenario over in my head. I'm loosening my tie and a butler hands me a gin and tonic. 'Thanks, Jeeves.' Heather is standing in a negligee next to a live leopard. I raise an eyebrow and strike a pose. 'Sorry I'm late, darling. I've been at a very important sales conference.' Nice.

Then it occurred to me that I couldn't knock anyway, as I couldn't lift my arm. In fact, the only thing I could do was slide my hand on to the door handle and enter. It was tight, but I managed to squeeze my hand along in front of me. By now the noise was really getting up some speed. The chanting was a lot louder – it sounded like some kind of religious cult carrying out a spiritual exorcism. 'Out with the old, in with the new!' they chanted. 'Out with the old, in with the new!'

I turned the handle and the door swung open. I stumbled into the room and found myself standing in front of a smartly dressed crowd of about fifty or sixty people. They were all sizes, shapes and colours. They all had their arms reaching up to the heavens, as a tall, boyish man with blond wavy hair, blue eyes and the sharpest pinstripe three-piece suit I have ever seen paced up and down encouraging them. His shiny Italian shoes gliding along the thin grey office carpet, he was prancing around in front of a white board that stretched along the entire wall. On it, Pinstripe Boy had written slogans such as,

'Screw the fuckers into the ground,' and 'Don't even let them breathe.' He kept hitting the air in front of him like there was an imaginary punchbag and shouting angrily at the crowd: 'Out with the old, in with the new! Come on, you bastards, let's hear it.'

The man in the pinstripe suit – clearly, the leader of this sales cult – suddenly noticed me and shouted over as the crowd in front of him carried on their chanting. 'Why are you here?'

I couldn't quite hear him at first because of the racket in the room. 'Sorry?' I asked, volunteering my ear.

He shouted at me again, more forcefully this time. 'I said, why the fuck are you here?' I held up the paper and was just about to tell him it was about the advert when he cut me off. 'Are you here to make some money?' I was confused. I was there for the job, but I was now thinking I might have the wrong place. He came closer and bellowed in my face. 'You don't like yourself!'

'What?' It was difficult to know what was going on. Maybe, I thought, I have the right place and this is part of what it's all about. After all, everyone else in the room was a bit lively, so I decided to play along. I shouted back in my best Kirk-Douglas-we've-got-to-build-a-long-boat-right-now rallying cry. 'Yes, I don't like myself!'

I thought that would do it. I smiled at the crowd who, noticing that the man in the pinstripe was shouting at an odd-looking scruffbag in a clown's suit with out-of-control fuzzy hair, suddenly become less enthusiastic about their chanting. It began to fade out until eventually they stood staring at me with bemusement.

I was also bewildered by Pinstripe Guy, who was now

circling me as if he were a lion just about to pounce on a vulnerable antelope, which just happened to be wearing a comedy suit. He started shouting at me again. Fuck me, I thought. What the fuck have I done to this bloke? 'You hate yourself, don't you?' he shrieked. 'And you're here to make some money. Am I right?'

Now I felt uncomfortable. 'You fucking hate yourself, don't you, fuzzy boy?'

That made me jump, and I reacted by shouting back angrily, 'Yes, I do.'

He smiled. He knew he had me. In his mind, he had cracked me, and so he went in for the kill. 'You are a pile of dog's shit, a useless piece of human waste. What are you?' He waited for my answer, and the crowd watched this rather one-sided game of verbal tennis with interest.

I shouted back, 'Dog shit!' This time I slapped my forehead hard with the palms of my hands for effect, hoping if I showed a bit more anguish he would stop shouting at me, but he kept going.

'What are you?' he roared again.

I thought perhaps I'd got the last one wrong, so I tried another one. 'Human waste?' I stared at him to see if I'd got it right, then realized I hadn't done the slapping of my forehead bit, so I smacked my brow again, harder this time. But it was too late now and must have appeared out of context. Mr Pinstripe simply shook his head.

His ritual humiliation of me now over, he grabbed a plastic folder from the top of a cabinet, held it in front of my face and tapped on it with his finger as he spoke. 'This is your sales kit. Look after it, it is your friend.'

The king of the pinstripes, who, I later discovered, was

called Dan, handed it to me. 'It will earn you a lot of money, fuzzy head.' Then he shouted at me again. 'Go and sit down. Join the winners, you loser.' Then he began rallying the crowd again by pointing randomly at various people and shouting at them, 'Darryl, how much did you earn this week?'

'Five hundred pounds.'

'Five hundred pounds? You're a winner, Darryl. Calvin, how much?'

From there on in, I was paired off with a mentor. He was a black lad named Joe. He took one look at me and burst out laughing. He did that a lot; he laughed at everything and everyone. He led me away from the rest of the group into an adjoining room. There we sat at a small desk for the rest of the day until it got dark as Joe took me through the plastic folder's pages of illustrations, diagrams, graphs and newspaper cuttings highlighting the benefits of unit trusts. The folder underlined how unit trusts performed compared with other similar offerings. It also explained interest rates, APR figures and a load of other financial jargon that made my head spin.

It contained all that was needed to make you sound just like a proper financial adviser. Then there was a dummy form that Joe took me through as if I were a customer. He showed me his trick of how to get the punters, as he called them, to sign it just by offering them the pen, looking them right in the eye and just waiting, not saying a word. Joe demonstrated that, but then he started laughing again, saying he couldn't look me in the eye as I made him crack up. All the same, he assured me that the tactic worked every time.

I couldn't make head nor tail of it all, but Joe kept drilling me. 'Learn it, geez,' he said, clicking his fingers. Then he would bounce around the room laughing. 'You're gonna make a mint, right, geez?'

I liked Joe a lot. He had patience with me. He knew I was an idiot, and he knew I wasn't a salesman, but he could tell just by looking at me that I was desperate. He himself had gone through the same process. This was the only job going, and I really needed it. Heather and I had no money.

Joe just wanted to try and help – plus, it was in his interest, as whatever I made, he would get a cut of it. I worked for him now so he was very keen to get me to sell. 'The unit-trusts financial package, unlike other insurance policies, is diversified across the entire stock market. So all your money isn't in the same basket, but is spread by our expert teams across only the most successful companies.' That was the sort of sales jargon I had to learn parrot -fashion from the plastic pages of my sales kit.

Joe told me to go home and learn it off by heart, as tomorrow we would be going out selling. 'I need you, bruv,' he said as I left for home, shutting the purple door behind me. I could hear his loud laugh as, by now completely exhausted, I walked down the stairs. But I would find out I needed Joe a lot more than he needed me where we were going.

I got back to our house very late in the evening, and Heather quickly forgot her anger about my tardiness as I explained that I'd actually managed to find a job. However, her enthusiasm quickly waned when I told her what it was. But if there's one thing she always falls for, it is my perpetual positivity, and so I soon had her back on my side.

She sat on the camp bed giggling at me, as I strutted around our tiny cramped bedroom pretending I was Gordon Gekko. I must have looked such an idiot in my Oxfam Poncho the Clown suit with extra large lapels and strategically missing trouser turn-ups.

Heather said she had some good news herself. She had been looking in the *Southend Evening Echo* and had found a flat that she thought just right for us. 'We have to act fast,' she buzzed away, 'as it was the cheapest one there and could easily be snapped up if we don't show interest very soon.' That brought me crashing back to reality. Heather always does that. I'm forever doing my 'I have a dream' speech, and she will be the voice of reason, of authority and of reality in our relationship.

It's a good job she wasn't married to Martin Luther King or any of those other people who do great things. 'I have a dream –'

'Oh blimey, 'ere he goes with his "I have a dream" malarkey again. Sit down, you great walloping buffoon.'

'Ask not what your country can do for you –'

'You can do something for me – you can put that shelf up in the back bedroom.'

'One giant step for man, one –'

'You can stop leaping all over the place, for a start. What's the matter with you?'

I knew she was right, of course. We needed to get somewhere proper to live as we had a baby on the way. So not wanting to crush her hopes, I told her that we should make the effort and go to see the flat, but secretly I was concerned. I just couldn't see any way we could afford it, but Heather was adamant that she wanted somewhere other than just one room to live in with a baby. She eagerly explained she could just about do it on her wages, and if it meant going without, then that's what we'd have to do.

I did what I always do when I have to face the real world: I either make a joke of it or let it go over my head and carry on in the hope that it will eventually go away. I took the path of least resistance. I went along with Heather's plan, adopting my customary I'll-deal-with-it-when-it-happens attitude.

'Blimey,' I began sarcastically, 'you give a woman everything she wants –' I stood up and showed off the small cramped room with two camp beds squeezed into it – 'and still she moans!'

I sat back down on the camp bed. 'Right now, can I please be left alone for a minute as I need to learn what I've got to say tomorrow when I'm out with Joe?' I stabbed my finger down on the bed as if to make a point. 'A tycoon financial adviser's work is never done.' I then busied myself flicking through the pages of the plastic folder.

'But, Lee, we need to talk about this flat!' Heather protested. At that moment, she unexpectedly stood up. As soon as she did so, the other end of the camp bed flipped up and suddenly I was trapped between the camp bed and the wall.

From this awkward position, I said what I thought she wanted to hear. 'Heath, you want that flat, right? Then I need to memorize all this stuff, so we can perhaps earn some money.' She burst out laughing at my predicament, which lightened the mood a little. But I could see that as far as she was concerned, I'd agreed.

Then I tried to read the folder, I really did, but it was damn hard when I was still wedged against the wall and in great discomfort.

Clearly, Poncho the Clown was going to struggle to sell financial services.

30. The Death of a Salesman

By the morning, I'd put all the distractions about flats firmly to the back of my small, but on this particular day, Getty-like brain. I had much more important things to worry about. After all, I mused, the world of finance waits for no man – money never sleeps. Today I was up'n'at'em, jumping out of bed and executing my usual early-morning fitness regime of one and a half press-ups, done mostly by looking for one of my shoes that had been lost underneath the camp beds.

When I did find it, the shoe was a right mess. The three-hour journey on the train and the Tube to get to North London, followed by the long walk through Kilburn, had now worn out one of the puncture-repair-kit patches. The sole of my right shoe had begun to flap, so not only did I look like a clown, I was also starting to sound like one: SLAP, STEP, SLAP, STEP, SLAP.

But I was soon in the traps at the shabby Kilburn office, waiting for the off, sitting with all the salesmen I had seen the previous day. I have to say, they all looked a shadow of how they'd appeared the day before when they'd all been chanting like maniacs. Yesterday, it was like a religious meeting; today, it felt like I had stumbled into a funeral. They flopped around like deflated balloons.

By contrast, I was really up for it, believing that this

was my chance to shine. You only get one, maybe two at the most, so when an opportunity comes knocking, you have to grab it with both hands. By the look of this sorry lot, I thought, in a couple of hours I was going to be running rings round them. I was already pumping myself, telling myself, 'I was born ready!'

At that moment, 'Dynamic Dan', the pinstripe guy from the day before, bounded into the room. He was followed by a smiling Joe and about five other sales managers, all of whom seemed to be buzzing with enthusiasm, whistling and clapping. Programmed to please, I clapped like mad back at them, stamping my feet and whooping a lot.

I suppose I got a bit carried away with it all. As I was cheering so much, I didn't notice that the entire room had fallen silent. Everyone was now staring at me with a nonplussed expression on their faces. I gradually realized and began to taper it off a bit.

'All right, Lee, for fuck's sake!' Dan barked at me. I was embarrassed, but still beaming away; too much, to be honest. I looked like I'd had a massive dose of an earlier version of Botox. But I didn't want him to think I'd suddenly lost my vocal devotion to the cause.

Dan waved his hand at me to calm down. Then he stood on the spot and shook all his limbs out, like a triple jumper just about to start his run-up. He took a deep breath and concentrated on the rest of the class. 'Right, you fucking losers, it's too quiet in here. Let's hear you,' he shouted, as he began writing with a flurry on the whiteboard in big red lettering.

'Screw them into the ground.' That was met with a

resounding silence from everyone but me. I was right up there with Dan and Joe, clapping, shouting and repeating their mantra over and over: 'Out with the old, in with the new!' I'd got the sales bug big time.

It wouldn't be long now until I would be out on the streets, banging on doors and selling my financial services. Just thinking about it was getting me so hyped up I could have sold an ice-maker to Eskimo Eric right there and then.

Every team had been given a couple of streets of a certain area by Dan. For Joe and me, it was a huge housing estate in Brixton, or 'A large pot of gold', as Joe called it. He was being sadly optimistic.

If anyone answered their front door, it offered us the chance to give them our sales patter: 'Our team are in your area, and we just wondered if we could offer you a life-changing opportunity. It would benefit you and your family, earning you substantial amounts of easy money at no risk to yourself. Would you be interested?' How could anyone refuse that?

Those were the opening lines Joe had coached me into saying. By the time we got there, it was evening, and I worried a little about disturbing people at that hour. But as Joe explained, this was the time when everyone was in – anyway, it would only be a matter of seconds before I had them in the palm of my hand.

I certainly looked the part now, I thought. I'd paid Dynamic Dan five pounds – which was all I had – for a briefcase that had been abandoned at the sales office by some idiot who had made an early exit. He probably couldn't take the pressure, I sneered. Still, his loss, I concluded, as it gave me somewhere to put my plastic sales kit. Plus, Dan said I had to have it, as he reckoned I looked a prize twat and a half, and the briefcase might go some way towards making me at least appear competent and something resembling professional.

As we began our door-stepping, it started to rain, which made me thank my lucky stars even more that I had bought that briefcase – it could double up as an umbrella. I chuckled at my own cleverness as we entered a block of flats and made our way upstairs to the first-floor landing. I approached my first door. Everything just keeps going right for me at the moment, I thought. As soon as the door opens, I will knock this one out and –

Suddenly the door swung open and before I could even say 'Unit trust', the biggest Rastafarian gentleman I had ever seen had me by my huge lapels and was demanding to know why I had disturbed him. He also informed me of another use for my new briefcase, which I considered ridiculous as the size and shape of it would make sticking it up there utterly impossible.

Joe quickly jumped in between us, trying to calm the man down. 'It's cool, guy. It's all right, bruv, he's with me.'

The man began getting very animated, complaining loudly to Joe out on the landing about people in suits who kept knocking on his door. This started to draw attention from other flats in the block. Doors began opening and people were coming out to see what all the noise was about. Then I started to notice a crowd of youths who seemed to spill out from the flats and gather downstairs at the exit. There was an uneasy atmosphere; all of a sudden, out of nothing, I could feel tension in the air.

Joe seemed to calm the situation down, and we were on our way back down the landing that led to the staircase. Joe had hold of my arm as we passed various people along the landing who stared at us as we slid by. There was a definite atmosphere of menace but, as always, I tried making light of it, desperate not to let it show that in fact my pants were well and truly full.

But as Joe and I reached the bottom of the stairs, the tension rose a few notches more on the bowel scaredy-o-meter when our exit was blocked by a gang of lads, one of whom wanted to know what I had in my case. Heaven knows why – it was obvious it wasn't going to be much. I didn't exactly resemble Donald Trump; a Poncho the Clown-style chump more like. But after a little look from Joe, I handed the case over and said goodbye to my five pounds' worth of makeshift umbrella and the plastic sales folder within. I did mention to the bloke as I gave it to him, 'Be careful with what's in this case, as it has the potential to change your life forever.'

Then I turned to Joe for confirmation. 'Right, Joe?' But Joe only looked at me in confusion, as if I'd lost my tiny mind. Well, I thought, some people handle fear in different ways.

If Joe hadn't been there, I would have been stripped down to my bare monkey-like frame and sold at a local market. But with some smooth talking from him, we managed to slip away from the gang. They seemed satisfied with the offering of the briefcase. I suppose they thought that five-pound case was the most expensive object we had between us. They thought right.

On the advice of Joe, we tried another, less lively, section of the estate. I followed him as we made our way, sprinting as fast as we could through the cold and by now torrential downpour, across to another block of flats.

'Never give up, guy, never give in.' Joe's voice echoed as it bounced off the towering blocks of ominous-looking flats. While we raced across the huge square in the middle, I cursed the uneven pavement that had created unpredictable, large puddles. I desperately tried to avoid them, as every time I inadvertently stepped in one, the water shot up through the hole in my sole and filled my shoe.

We made it across the square and quickly into the entrance hall of another block. But as we made our way up the steps, my shoes began to make a loud squelching, farting noise, so not only did my shoes flap, now they squelched and farted as well. STEP. FLAP. SQUELCH. FART. STEP. FLAP. SQUELCH. FART.

It reverberated right up through the stairwell, much to Joe's irritation. It was freezing now, and Joe and I were drenched right through. Even my bones felt spongy.

The door-knocking was scarcely more fun. Joe would thump loudly on the door then stand to one side, pinned against the wall, leaving me to get on with it. If he saw I was doing anything wrong, he would immediately point it out to me. Despite my obvious nervousness at the door, a lot of people would ask me in. I would then disappear for half an hour, getting the benefit of warming up a little. Then I'd re-emerge, shrugging my shoulders and shaking my head to the rigid-with-cold Joe, who eagerly waited outside for the smallest indication of a sale. But there was never anything.

At one flat, it was not difficult to come up with an excuse for Joe. There was no way I could have even begun to talk about unit trusts as the young woman in question had a pet python. When I sat down and began my big pitch, she sat quietly in a canvas chair on the other side of the room and glared at me with fascination. She wanted to gauge my reactions as the snake slowly wrapped itself first around my legs then up to the top half of my body. I was aware that with every tightening of the snake around me, my voice went an octave higher.

It was getting late now, and I could see Joe was getting more and more frustrated by my failure to sell anything. So he informed me at the next flat that he would step inside with me as he wanted to know what was going wrong.

In the next flat we entered, there was an elderly but very cheerful Jamaican woman who introduced herself as Marie. You could tell by the look of the place that she lived alone. I felt the only reason she'd let two strangers in was that she probably hadn't seen anyone for days and just needed someone to talk to. But that was of no interest to Joe, who was keen to get going with the sales pitch.

We entered her kitchen and sat at the small Formica table. Marie fussed around and was kind enough to offer Joe and me a cup of tea. He nudged me in the side – he wanted to get on with things. I kept thinking there was no way an elderly woman like Marie would buy unit trusts from two very wet-looking strange men who had just strolled into her house. And, anyway, she was at an age where she would be unable to see any benefit from it – even with my tiny brain, I realized that.

After she had made the tea, Marie sat and got comfortable with us at the kitchen table. 'Right, what is it you two lovely boys want to talk to Marie about then?' she asked, with a huge beaming smile.

Apprehensively, I went through the sales banter that Joe had taught me as he looked on. Then, at the end, I got to the bit where I had to hold the pen out and make full eye contact, pausing, as Joe had instructed me to. And as he had also so brilliantly demonstrated back at the office, I did not say a word. I just stared at my punter.

But, truth be told, the idea of making the sale never even crossed my mind. All I kept thinking as I held the pen out and stared at Marie's jolly, friendly-looking face was, 'Would I sign that form? What is it anyway? This is not me. I don't want this, this is bullshit. I don't want to screw anyone into the ground, especially someone as lovely as poor old Marie. It just feels wrong.'

I peered out of the corner of my eye and saw Joe, his gaze fixed on poor Marie like a laser beam. All night, I'd been dreading this point. I'd never wanted to make a sale in the first place. I just needed a job. I was trying to earn some money, but not like this. In a way, I was in the same predicament as Marie. I looked at her on the other side of the table, sitting like a rabbit trapped in headlights. I could see she was all confused, desperately trying to fathom out what the form I was asking her to sign was all about. I believe the only reason she was considering signing it was because she thought Joe and I were nice boys, and to her that would have been enough.

'Anyway, thank you for listening, Marie,' I concluded. 'If you ever change your mind, don't hesitate to call us. We're in the phone directory under "Pest Control".'

I quickly stood up from the table, leaving Joe staring at me, gob-smacked, as if I'd just slapped him in the face with a plastic sales folder. I knew what he was thinking: there it was, an open opportunity to make some money, and I had pulled out. I casually said my goodbyes to Marie, who also looked a bit confused by it all, but plainly relieved. I walked out of the flat, followed by the still-bemused Joe.

We got outside and in complete silence walked down the stairs. After reaching the entrance hall to the flats, it seemed suddenly to dawn on Joe what I had just done.

'What the fuck are you up to, guy?'

I tried explaining, even though I knew he would never understand. 'I'm sorry, Joe. Listen, I ain't got no money, but I just don't think I'm a salesman, mate. All that stuff about "Screw 'em into the ground" – it's not me, mate. I'm sorry.'

I turned round and standing there was Dan. He looked at Joe, who gently shook his head. Dan stepped forward, gave me a hard smile and sneered: 'You fucking loser! Go on, piss off! You're sacked.'

I walked off into the rain. 'Shit,' I thought, 'Heather's going to be really mad with me now.' I was also going to get really wet – plus, my other shoe was starting to leak. I had no idea what the time was, but I knew it was late. I wondered how I was going to get home at that time of night.

I had failed again. I'm such a fool, I thought. But then I stopped myself. I believe it's best to do what you think is right, and what Dan and Joe were doing didn't feel right to me.

I thought about the baby who was on the way.

I lifted my face up so I could feel the cold raindrops tickle my face as they hit my skin. I smiled. I shoved my hands deep into my pockets, put my head down and headed for home.

Never mind, Lee, I thought, something will turn up.

31. Life in the Arctic

I awoke the next day to the sound of Heather flying around the bedroom getting ready to go off to work. No sooner had I opened my eyes than she wanted to tell me that she had fixed up for us to go and see the flat in Southend over the weekend. I couldn't see her face – it was hidden as she stood bent over energetically brushing her hair. I could only hear her muffled voice from beneath as she chatted away into her knees. 'We can't really afford it, I know, but now you've got that job, maybe –'

I interrupted her. 'I'm sorry, Heather.' It was difficult, as she was so excited, but I felt I had to tell her. 'I got the sack again, mate.'

She stopped brushing her hair and hung there doubled over, still and silent. I waited to see what she might say, then – whoosh! – suddenly she flung her head back, her fine hair swooped up on top of her head revealing her face. She sniffed, placed the brush on the side, grabbed her bag and left the room without saying a word. I buried my head in my hands – there had to be something I could do! I was listening to Norman Tebbit's advice to get on my bike, but I kept falling off it.

Soon after, we left the back room at my parents' house and moved into the flat, and things simply went from bad to worse. It was only a matter of time before we ran out of money and found ourselves completely broke.

Matters were rapidly becoming quite desperate, and it was difficult to see any light at the end of a very long tunnel. I suppose we had held on to the naive idea that perhaps things might somehow work out even though I was just about to lose Heather her job – more of which anon.

We also may have been a bit hasty when the bloke in the suit at the housing office told us that if we wanted the flat, we would have to put a fifty-pound deposit down on it straight away. Heather duly did that, even though, as she was writing the cheque looking as if butter wouldn't melt in her mouth, we both knew that we didn't even have ten pounds, let alone fifty in any bank. We were well aware that the cheque would bounce higher than Gary Glitter's blood pressure in a computer repair shop. But we were determined to make it work together. Most importantly, we were going to have a baby.

We had decided to take the flat, and if we went overdrawn at the bank, then we'd have to think about what to do then. Heather didn't seem to care, but I was worried that our relationship would turn into a life of crime. I mean, this is how Bonnie and Clyde had started, doing banks and all.

The flat wasn't even worth the paper the fifty-quid deposit was written on. It was in a terrible state. The day Heather dragged me along to see it, I took her aside in one of the shabby rooms and whispered in her ear so the crumbling old man who was showing us around wouldn't hear us. 'You don't need to fix this place up. You need to frigging start all over again.' Not that he could have heard us; he was as deaf as a post wearing ear-muffs. How come when people get old, their ears get bigger, but they hear less?

The flat gave the impression that everything was held together with sticky tape, glue and dental fixative, and had been steadily bodged up over the years with various bits of debris from perhaps a nearby canal. It had been fashioned into serving this elderly gentleman and his even older wife's physical needs. She, by the way, couldn't make it out of the chair to greet us – it appeared it was a struggle for her even to lift her white head, hunched over as she was to such a degree that she just stared down permanently at her knees.

Her husband was no less frail. At first, we'd thought there was nobody in as we waited so long for the poor old codger to answer the door. But then we felt very guilty, as the long journey back up the stairs was so obviously a struggle for him. He looked to the heavens and made a face so pained, you'd have thought he'd just been told he would be spending another twenty years in a Siberian prison camp cracking rocks. It wasn't only torture for him, though; we had to follow up behind, silently urging his slippered feet agonizingly up and on to the next step, each seemingly more painful than the last.

But Heather was adamant that we should take the flat, even though it didn't exactly match up to the property's description we'd received. Let me put it into layman's terms: 'It was an absolute shithole.'

We never had any heating, apart from an old rusting gas cooker that sat like a keen suicide bomber waiting to go off. It was not situated in the kitchen, as you might imagine. Why not? Because there was no kitchen! No, the cooker was for some strange reason placed in the bath-room next to the lounge. But, and this is what made me do a double take, there wasn't really a bathroom, either. Yeah, good, eh? That's how it was put to us by the old fella. Oh, he was very proud of his 'all-purpose room', as he liked to call it.

'It's a bathroom-kitchen,' he beamed. 'I designed and built it myself.'

'Blimey, that's really ingenious,' I told him, my tongue firmly in my cheek. So there was the cooker sat next to a flimsy, low, rectangular wooden box. He showed us how it worked with the panache of Debbie McGee showing off one of Paul Daniels's big illusions.

'And you just lift this lid, and inside is the bath tub,' he proudly announced.

'Why has it got a lid on it?' Heather asked.

'Because, my dear, when it's closed, you have a kitchen unit to work on, but when it's open, it's a bath, see.' He demonstrated by flapping the thin plywood lid up and down.

I didn't even want to ask where the toilet was, as I couldn't see it anywhere in the room. It made me shudder to think that one day Heather might happen to stroll in to cook our tea and catch me having a quiet Marley Magoo. Or, worse still, a chieftain.

Despite all the extra fun-packed design that made the flat seem like the crooked house at a cheap fairground – roll up, roll up, for all the tedium of the fair! – we took it. In a way, we had to, as we couldn't afford anything else.

Regardless, we moved in with only a second-hand, bald-ing couch to sit on and an even more second-hand balding

TV set. It was so old, we could only receive pictures of John Logie Baird. It was given to us by one of Heather's friends, just to get us started. Some food might have been nice, but at least we could, if we got really hungry, watch Rusty Lee doing her cooking show.

Eventually I managed to find the toilet; it was in fact hiding outside along a wooden and worryingly rotten fire escape at the back of the flat. A trip to the toilet was like negotiating some ancient, flimsy footbridge.

The old Victorian houses that are the mainstay right across Southend had, over the years, gradually been bought up by builders who would turn them into flats. In order to make a profit, sometimes they might squeeze twelve dwellings into just one small Victorian house. Our building, though, only contained two, as it was so small. Ours was the first-floor flat.

When building houses for the masses, the Victorians would mostly place the toilet outside. Now you would have thought the modern-day builder might have brought the bog in from the cold and into the twentieth century when he converted it. But, alas, it remained an outsider.

If you had to go, you had to go, and that was a pretty daunting prospect in mid-winter. Southend is on the coast and can get really cold. So after risking your life going down the old balsa-wood fire escape, you would freeze your extremities off in the toilet, or the fridge as I liked to call it. I advised Heather to put on a thick coat, as I didn't want to have to come out and snap her off the bog.

The toilet was so cold – I mean, it wouldn't be exaggerating to say if you farted it froze the instant it left your arse, and then you would hear the clink, clink as the ice pop hit the solid ice at the bottom of the frozen toilet. Everything froze. After finishing, if you looked back down the toilet, it was just a bunch of brown ice. I always thought it looked like something you'd get down the ice-cream shop – don't worry, I won't go any further with this line!

Toilet roll was a luxury, so newspaper was the preferred alternative, even though it left the old hairy, rusty, fifty-pence piece a little scratched and scraped. You would always know when your partner had been for a number two because after taking their clothes off to get into bed, they would display a black inky bottom. It's not a good look, I can tell you.

The toilet was cold, but it was a sauna compared to the Arctic environment in the bedroom. In mid-winter, ice would build up on the window, but on the inside. Whipping out of bed in the morning was always a forbidding prospect. You had to try to keep moving or risk suffering exposure and certain death from the bone-chilling temperatures.

I would lie there in the morning next to the soft, warm body of Heather, who is like a radiator in bed – blimey, she's hot. We'd take it in turns to get up and make a cup of tea. Whenever it was my turn, I would shout loudly, as a way of psyching myself up: 'I'm going out for a while. I may be some time.'

Then I would throw back the covers and show Heather my black, skid-marked news-printed backside.

It was not the way she wanted to read the morning papers.

32. Getting on My Bike

Each day after attending the Job Centre, I would try to increase my chances of employment by yomping the length of the London Road, one of the main drags that leads out of Southend. I would walk into each and every shop and small business in the five-mile stretch of road, asking for work.

It became a little more difficult after suffering rejection after rejection. But then you might get the odd shop owner who would inform you that if anything came up, he'd get in touch.

Normally Heather was back from work before I got home, but on this occasion the flat was cold, dark and empty – it always was without her. After deciding to perch myself on top of the bath-cum-kitchen-unit to await her return, I began to get a little concerned as it was now getting very late. Just then, I heard the front door and Heather creeping up the stairs. I went out to meet her on the landing and immediately knew there was something wrong.

It was obvious she'd been crying. She'd been acting strangely for a couple of weeks, and I put it down to her decision to work extra hours to help pay for things. I never said anything, mostly out of my selfish guilt about not finding a job. However, after a cup of tea and a chat, it gradually emerged that she was doing the extra hours not by choice. In fact, she was being paid no more money.

She couldn't hold it back any longer, and it just spilled from her as she told me she worked for a tyrannical boss who knew of her dire need to keep her job and so played upon it, keeping her working late into the night. She had undergone weeks of abuse and humiliation. She said she didn't want to worry me with it, as it would just have made me feel worse about not having a job. We needed the small amount of money she brought in, otherwise we would go under.

I listened patiently as it became obvious Heather needed to get off her chest all the pressure that had built up over weeks of working for that monster. As her words came tumbling out, I was secretly burning with rage. We went off to bed but, while Heather slept, I was unable even to close my eyes for a second. I lay there, staring at the ceiling. I felt such shame that I'd been unable to help her.

She had endured great pain in secret. No one should have to suffer such belittlement and torment – and yet she'd never mentioned a word of it because we needed what little money she was being paid. We knew that if Heather should lose her job it would just about tip us over the edge.

But I couldn't help the nagging feeling inside that I should do something about it. That sense was embedded in my psyche, and I knew it would only burn and fester away at me until I acted upon it. I was brought up to stand up and fight, not just for me, but for the ones I love. I could imagine Granddad Evans turning in his grave if he thought for one moment I had in any way allowed my family to be humiliated. My philosophy has always been: if you're going down, go down fighting, and back out the door with your fists flying. I looked over at Heather sleeping. We needed that job, I thought, but how could I let her suffer so?

The next day Heather was first out of bed. She made cups of tea for us, as it was her turn, got ready and went off to work. I went off to the Job Centre and then did a tour around the local industrial estates to see if there were any vacancies at any of the small factories. It was on one of these estates that I bumped into an old friend from school called Gary.

He was loading up his van with double-glazing units from a factory. He was taking them to fit into a house. He told me he was doing very well for himself now, working for his father's business, undertaking general building work, painting and decorating, that sort of thing. I said I was out of work and asked if perhaps he might be able to fit me in somewhere in his dad's firm. I explained to him I would do absolutely anything.

Gary was about to drive away when he stopped his van, rolled down his window and asked if I knew how to paint. Of course, I said, but in a way that indicated he had just insulted me by even asking me such a disparaging question. I clasped my heart: 'That hurt, that did, Gary. I'm wounded 'ere, mate!'

Of course, I knew what he meant: could I paint a room or a door? I told him in no uncertain terms that I was a brilliant painter. Obviously, I didn't tell him that I meant on canvas. Well, I was sort of lying, but what would you do in that situation? I was desperate!

With that, we shook hands, and he told me I could start tomorrow. Gary gave me a piece of paper and explained I had to be at that address and report to his father, who would then tell me what he wanted me to do. 'Don't let me down now, mate, will you?' he said. He went on to warn me not to go if I wasn't serious and not to slack as his father was pretty strict. But then he added encouragingly, 'If you work hard, Dad will pay you well.' So I took a lot of positives from that. I may not be the world's greatest painter and decorator, but I've never been afraid of hard work.

I felt that my chance meeting with Gary had been a kind of divine intervention. I was feeling a little more confident about the future, owing to the fact that I was now a painter and decorator. Not as yet, obviously, but in my head I thought it would only be a matter of time before I was striding around busy building sites in yellow boots and a suit with Gary's dad pointing out various painting jobs he would like my men to do. Who knows? I imagined even Buckingham Palace needed a lick of the old magnolia satin finish to make it shine in the sun.

That newly confident note helped me make up my mind: I was going to pay a visit to Heather's work to have a chat with her boss. I didn't hang around – oh yeah, there are no flies on me, mate, when I get going. So I barrelled through the gates and up to the glass entrance doors of the offices of this import–export company. The red mist had well and truly descended, and someone was going to get it.

I didn't spot any security, so I just burst through into the office where I knew Heather worked. As soon as I stepped through the door, everyone in the long, cluttered, rectangular room fell silent. No one moved a muscle – it was like a photograph. Just the whirr of computer noise could be heard in the large, messy, open-plan room.

Piles of paper standing on filing cabinets nearly reached up to the polystyrene-tiled ceiling. Four middle-aged women who had been beavering away at their desks stopped mid-type to see what I was going to do. Towards the end of the room, I spotted Heather, head down, working away, almost hidden behind a mound of documents. She looked up and saw me. Her face dropped, her eyes widened with terror – she could tell I was raging mad. She began to turn a funny grey colour.

I noticed her eyes quickly dart towards a solid wooden door at the end of the room and then back at me. I knew what that meant – it was a giveaway. There was his name on the door: Chris Davis. That's him, the bastard! I'm having you Chris wank-features-bully-boy-bollocks Davis . . . Chris Davis! That was his name – the other stuff was just because I was angry, they weren't his middle names or anything. Just so you know.

I ploughed through the middle of the desks. Heather jumped up, but it was too late; before she could stop me, I'd charged through the door and into his office. There he was, Chris 'The Bully Boy Who Only Picks On Women' Davis.

He stood across the room, hunched over, filing a piece of paper into an open drawer. He looked up at me. He had to – he was only small, four and a half feet max. In fact, I was surprised how titchy he actually was. There was hardly anything of him or for that matter his hair.

Where does he get his clothes, I wondered, Mothercare? Fancy a little weasel like that having a go at our Heather, I thought. He probably does it because he doesn't get any attention at home and wants to take it out on other women – the bastard. I snarled at him.

I did at that juncture thank my lucky stars that he wasn't some huge muscle-head with cauliflower knuckles and forearms like pillar-boxes. If I'm honest, it gave me a bit more courage that he was small. Right, I thought, I'm going to have a right go at this tiny man. I slammed the door behind me, so he couldn't get out.

My muffled shouting must have sounded quite vicious to Heather and the others gathered outside. I went for him big time, not even giving him an inch. I just waded in and told him what I thought about him and where he could stick his company and his shit job. I made it quite clear that Heather wouldn't be returning to work and that she was coming home with me right now.

Then I called him 'Mouse boy' – it just came to me there and then. He began whimpering like a baby. He was about to say something, when I jumped straight in, leaning down close to his face. 'And the only reason I haven't smacked your miniature teeth down your throat so far you'd be eating family-sized doughnuts with your arse,' I hissed, 'is that I don't want you to have the satisfaction of getting me nicked.'

Leaving him cowering under his desk, I turned and violently swung open the door to exit. I was going to come out triumphantly and show Heather who the man was around here when I thumped my head on something very big and very solid. I stumbled back and looked up – I had to, as it was a huge, hefty man who towered over me.

His massive, planet-sized frame nearly filled the entire doorway. I mean, you could have shown a film on his crisp white shirt, wide-screen.

I could just see behind him over one shoulder and noticed the four secretaries all looking quite concerned. Who for? I wondered. I followed the curvature of the Incredible Hulk's broad shoulders to a terrified-looking Heather, with her mouth agog and her hands firmly pressed against her cheeks. I thought it strange that her mouth was open, but there was no noise coming out. She reminded me of Munch's *The Scream*.

'So? Who, like, are you, then?' I stammered. Funnily enough, it was already starting to sink in who he might be. He didn't say anything at first – he just indicated with his big fat thumb the nameplate on the door: 'Chris Davis'. Heather's boss – gulp!

'No!' I pointed back at the now feeble heap of shaking jelly on the office floor. 'So, like, that bloke . . . ?' I began to ask.

'Why are you having a pop at my accountant?' the increasingly menacing Davis growled. I could feel the hostility and anger begin to bubble in his voice. I glanced at Heather; her face said it all.

I looked him right in the eye and spoke slowly and clearly, pointing over my shoulder at the now-whimpering mess back in his office: 'He'll explain everything.' I stealthily slipped past Davis, grabbing Heather on the way out.

Then we both strolled calmly away from our only source of income.

33. Tragedy Strikes

Storming into the office – like that was the right thing to do! Afterwards, Heather told me about all the bullying of other people as well, now that was she was free to speak. Nevertheless, I wondered who the winner really was in all this.

We could survive for maybe a week at most on what Heather had earned, and with no other form of income, we faced certain ruin. There was no way we could keep up any payments on the flat. The electricity company had given us a week to settle our bill, plus our only form of heat, the gas cooker, was about to be cut off. We had no phone, so we had to make constant trips down the gas board shop to ask if we could have maybe a few more days. We had already notched up an overdraft just trying to live and were dreading the metal clang of the letterbox of doom, as that sound would hold only bad news.

To make matters worse, my job as a painter and decorator had not gone well.

'Let there be light!' I shouted. It was six in the morning, and I was eager to get started on painting my first ever window. Not that Gary's dad knew that it was the first window I'd ever painted in my entire life, but I thought naively, 'What you don't know won't hurt you.'

Gary's Dad, Kevin, believed that I was a professional painter. Oh, there was no doubt I was experienced in the classics, all right. Rembrandt, Monet, Constable – I suppose I could boast that I sat right alongside those great painters myself, as none of us four would know one end of a tin of emulsion from the other, let alone where to get a decent cup of tea and a bap in the fag break.

'What you going on about, you idiot?' Kevin sighed to me. 'Right, bollock chops, all those windows have to be painted in pronto. The stuff you need is in that lock-up over there. And don't muck about. Get it done, yeah?' Slapping a key in my hand, he got into his white van and sped off.

I looked around – still no other painters, just me. I held the rusting key in my hand. It was starting to get light, so at least I could just about see what I was doing, even though I had no idea what that was meant to be. I strolled over to the lock-up, shrugged my shoulders and said to myself, 'I'll just blag it. I mean, how hard can it be?'

When Kevin ordered me to 'Paint the windows in', that's what I did. I painted in the actual glass windows and not the frames. But the moment he saw my handiwork, Kevin erupted in fury.

As a sort of defence mechanism, I threw the rollerbrush to the floor like some great artist having a strop that his precious work had been insulted. 'Well, I didn't know, did I? I'm not a painter, am I?' I slumped to the corner of the room and crossed my arms like a school kid with the right hump. But it was too late. Kevin had found out I wasn't actually a painter at all.

He sacked me on the spot, and informed me to go

away immediately – well, in fact, his words were a bit stronger than that, if I'm honest. He then said that if he ever saw me again, he would stick the roller-brush and tray so far up somewhere that they would be surgically impossible to remove and I would suffer distemper for the rest of my life. That was just the start of it. Kevin went on to give me a really good blasting of some serious bile. He delivered it directly into my face, until my flattened features looked like they were experiencing high forces of acceleration.

But after Kevin had calmed down and I had cleaned all the windows back to how they were, I told him that I was still desperate for the work as I had a baby on the way. Kevin said he understood that – and he also understood that I was quite well known at school as an imbecile. So he found it in his heart to offer me a couple of days' work cleaning public toilets in Southend, readying them for his boys to decorate.

This time, Gary came down and showed me what to do. He was very helpful, demonstrating exactly how to prepare for the redecoration of these horribly dilapidated toilets. They were in desperate need of restoration – even the sign outside had been sprayed with a new title: 'Wank Central'.

Gary told me I had to clean them from top to bottom with hot soapy water. I also had to fill in and rub down all the woodwork and doors, including what I was told by Gary were glory holes in the cubicle walls. I thought they sounded quite exciting; I even tried explaining what a glory hole was to Heather later that night. If we ever get any money, I said, lying back on the couch, I wouldn't mind a few of those glory holes myself. She did not, it has to be said, look very impressed by my plan.

Then I had to chip out any cracked or broken tiles, so new ones could be fitted. I also had to dig out any old discoloured mastic, so it could be renewed. I didn't relish that job as mostly that was around the bottom of the toilet pan, and one could tell that there were whole new species living down there.

Making sure I was completely OK with what I was doing, Gary left me to get on with it. I got to work straight away and, making up for the window debacle, never stopped until Gary reappeared at seven o'clock that evening. We closed up the toilets and he took me home. Dropping me off, he told me he would pick me up in the morning. Then, before driving away, he told me I had done a really good job. He added that he was getting plenty of work in at the moment doing jobs for Southend Council and would soon need to take people on, which I took as a hint.

I was so happy. I was doing OK at last. I reckoned if I worked hard – and there was no doubt I was getting on really well with Gary and was making him laugh a lot – I thought that he might even take me on permanently. Things just might be looking up for us at last.

Do you ever have those dreams where everything is so vivid that you awake with a start, gasping with fear and dread and believing that the events actually happened? Well, I had one of those dreams that night. Heather had suddenly from nowhere entered my dream and screamed – something was wrong with her! I cracked open my eyes and – relief, thank God – I was just dreaming. Here was the bedroom, our bedroom. I turned over to check that Heather was next to me, but she was already up. Was it her turn to make the tea perhaps? I couldn't remember.

I lifted my head and checked the time. Four o'clock? I thought, wait a minute, that's too early, we never get up until at least 6.30. There it was again, a scream. It was muffled this time, but it was clear who was in distress: Heather!

I jumped out of bed, not even thinking about how cold it was. I didn't care, there was obviously something wrong. We have that connection, Heather and I. If she was on the other side of the world and something happened to her, I would know about it.

Seriously concerned, I ran from the bedroom and began shouting urgently. 'Heath? Heather?'

'Lee.' It was her, in the bathroom. 'Lee.' The way she said it made my stomach twist into a tight knot. I crashed through the door to find Heather sitting scrunched up in a little ball on the floor in a giant pool of blood. She looked up at me, her exhausted face begging for help. My entire body sank, my legs instantly turning to lead. Wait, I told myself, snap out of it, Lee. Come on, come on!

Suddenly all my instincts burst into action. It was as if I had just been hit with a full charge. I thought, I mustn't let Heather know I'm afraid – because I was so, so afraid. I knew what was happening and so did she. Women know as soon as it starts. Poor thing, she would have known hours ago, but had probably hoped it wasn't true. Perhaps she didn't want to worry me or tempt fate.

The most frustrating thing in situations like this is that

you can do nothing to ease the pain of the person you love so dearly. Even though you have sworn you will gladly throw yourself from a mountain for them, the only thing you can do is try to comfort them. I dropped to my knees, grabbed her, held her as tightly as I could and told her I loved her more than anything else in the world. Heather began to cry.

'We've lost it, Lee. It's gone. I'm so sorry.'

'Come on, H, you don't know that, do you? Don't worry, everything's going to be all right, I swear. You just wait and see.'

'I already know, Lee,' she cried. 'I'm so sorry.' She began to bawl uncontrollably.

When all is said and done, you're all alone. There is no one else, it's just you. That's what I concluded as we sat there, just us, huddled in a pool of Heather's blood on the hard floor of our shitty bathroom-cum-crap-kitchen, or whatever the bloody room was meant to be.

I looked up to the sky for something, anything. 'Come on, mate,' I pleaded. 'Help us out a little bit 'ere, will you? We're in a bit of a jam.' I'm not sure who I was talking to, but I was hoping someone was listening.

It was freezing, and I was worried Heather was getting cold. I lifted her up, cradling her in my arms. The blood was still pouring down – I could feel it as it got colder and began running down my legs. I carried her, her head on my shoulder, into the bedroom. I bent over and was just about to lay her down when she started worrying about the stains on the bed. It's funny, she seemed more con-cerned about that than what was happening to her. 'No! The bed! We'll ruin it, Lee.'

'Listen, I've got to put you down, love. You're ruining my back at the moment.' That made her laugh a little.

I laid Heather gently on the bed, pulling the covers over her. She instantly doubled up into a tiny ball. She was in obvious pain. I whispered in her ear that I was going to call her an ambulance. I told her I wouldn't leave her alone for long and would be straight back with the cavalry. I didn't want to leave her, but I had to.

As fast as I could, I whipped some clothes on, bolted down the stairs and out the door into the dark, wet, freezing early hours of the morning. My arms pumping like a steam train, I ran flat out along the middle of the deserted road, the white lines zipping under my feet. The dull yellow street lights, the unlit houses, everything whizzed past until I knew I was halfway between our flat, where Heather lay waiting for me to return, and the red call box that would get help.

But the phone box seemed to be getting further away with every determined stride. It was at that point that the weight of what was happening all of a sudden flashed into my mind. It was like I'd hit a wall. I burst into uncontrollable tears. My head was spinning, my whole body racked with grief. I was losing my stride, finding it difficult to run as my breathing was irregular. I put my head down and cut through the biting frost.

I felt such anger and resentment, but who do you direct it at? There's nobody. As I ran, I punched out at the air in front of me as if it were the god of fate that had just dealt us this devastating hand. I was so furious, furious at everything. 'Why us, why choose us?' I wailed. 'We have nothing, we're nobody. Why pick on us, why Heather?

She's never done anything to anybody. She's a lovely girl. Why?'

I was even cross with Heather for being so brave and taking it without herself getting angry. She always does that. If there's one thing that irritates me about Heather, it's that whenever anything bad happens, she hardly expresses any anger at all. What's that? 'I'm not very happy with you now.' That's crap! She never seeks revenge. She's always of a mind that you are innocent until proven guilty. She just takes it and gets on with it.

In Bristol, the rules were that you went over to see the bloke who had done you wrong, knocked on his door and sorted him out. Dad always said that if someone hits you, hit them back, but harder. Ever since I'd run from that one fight, I swore I would never run from anything ever again. But then you find out that's all bullshit because it doesn't work in the real world, not here, not now. There is no one to fight in a situation like this. There's just you, running along this empty street trying to help your best friend, the person you love most in the world.

Suddenly I lost my footing. I flew forward and, unable to get my hands out in time – crunch! – my face cracked into the tarmac. I lay there for a moment, face down, spread across the wet road, waiting to see what bits would start hurting first. My hands began to sting where they had slapped hard on to the unforgiving surface. Then I could feel one side of my face start to throb. I lifted my head up and examined the road where my face had hit it – no blood, good – but I'd definitely given it a good scraping. Now I was really annoyed with everything: the road, the wet, myself, the whole situation.

I gradually got to my feet, and began talking to God knows who. 'Well, then, if that's how it is, then fuck you, because we ain't beat yet!' I raised myself up and rolled back my shoulders. 'If that's what your little plan is, then you've got to do better than that.'

I lowered my head and faced into the wind. I bent over nearly double and was much more aerodynamic now. I thought of Heather lying back there on the bed, waiting. So I picked up my feet and hammered them hard into the wet black tarmac and, bang, I sliced through the sharp freezing air once more. I was flying down the street so fast, the wind couldn't even keep up. I rallied, shouting at the top of my lungs. Up from the pit of my stomach it came and roared out of my mouth.

'I'm coming, Heather. You hold on, my friend, cos we ain't beat yet. Now come on, Lee. Run, you bastard, run!'

34. Opportunity Knocks

'Sorry, it's gone. You lost it.'

That's what the tired, dishevelled-looking bloke in the white coat said, just like that, all casual. He never even batted an eyelid, nothing; it was as if he'd just put the rubbish out. He then turned, flipped the lid of a giant pedal-bin, threw in a paper towel he'd been wiping his hands with and began walking away up the long, grey, empty corridor.

It took me a moment to process what he had just told me. Lost it? What did he mean? I needed more than that. So I shouted, 'Doctor? Sorry.' I chased after him, grabbing his arm to stop him. 'Sorry, I don't understand. What?'

He looked a little irked that I'd pulled at his coat. 'She lost the baby,' he snapped. 'We're keeping her in for observation. She's asleep now. It was an ectopic, so she has lost a lot of blood. It was a good job we caught it when we did – it could have been fatal, you know. So go home now. You can come and see her tomorrow.'

He said it with such disregard that I thought he couldn't possibly be talking about that beautiful woman, my Heather. My mind was now all topsy-turvy, confused. I needed more information. I know I'm an idiot, I thought, perhaps it's me. What was he going on about, ectopic? What's that? I was only eighteen, for crying out loud!

The doctor went to walk away, but I suddenly found I'd grabbed hold of him and stared into his blood-shot eyes. Heather deserved more than that. Why was he so rude? He just stared back at me with hardly any emotion at all. There didn't seem to be anyone home – did he even care?

Wait a minute, why should he? I understood. We were just a couple of scruffbags from God knows where, brought in and dumped with him in the early hours of the morning after a long night shift. It wasn't his fault; we were just one of many he'd had to tell the same to, some even worse than us. I must also have looked like some wino with my dirty clothes and half my face swollen up.

I loosened my grip on his white coat. Letting go, I apologized. He raised an eyebrow, looked down at me with real disdain, nodded, straightened his coat and walked away down the corridor, which looked just as cold as he was. I watched him go all the way until he disappeared, flapping through some doors at the end.

I turned around, exhausted. The line of five dog-eared plastic chairs bolted to the tiled floor in front of me suddenly looked a very inviting prospect, even though they seemed to be saying they were more tired and yellow-eyed than I was. But, by then, I didn't care. I bedded down for a couple of hours, accepting that the grumpy chair in the middle was going to poke me in the back the whole time.

Almost as soon as I closed my eyes, I was gone, but not before the thought had flashed across my mind – or was it the hope? – that perhaps this time when I awoke, all this might turn out to have been just a dream.

Of course, when I didn't show up for work the next

day, my job with Gary went straight down the toilet – probably one of the ones I was meant to be cleaning – faster than a bag of the white stuff at Scarface's gaff when there was a knock on the door from the drugs squad.

Later, Gary explained that he'd lost lots of work with Southend Council to a competitor and he hoped to employ me when things picked up again. But Gary was a nice guy and did pay me for the days I'd worked for him – which, considering I only ever did infinitesimally more than an imbecile might have done, was very generous of him.

So there it was. I couldn't even manage another day cleaning a toilet. I mean, how bad had I become? I imagined Gary having a chat with his dad in some wood-panelled men's club, both of them sat in leather-backed chairs, puffing cigars and sipping cognac.

'Do you think he could actually have lasted another day cleaning toilets, Gary?'

'No, I just think he's not ready for that kind of pressure.'

I was gradually coming to the conclusion that I was one of life's losers. But, on the positive side, I was good at it.

After a few days, Heather and I returned to our flat, and I set her up with a hot-water bottle and a blanket on the couch in the lounge. She was next to the knackered old telly which, with its feeble inner illuminated tubes and dodgy wiring, would emit about as much heat as a friction burn from a gnat's wing flap. But I felt it would be even colder for her in the bedroom. It was the middle of winter now, and that bedroom was so cold, every time you opened the door, a light came on.

Heather was desperate to get well again. She wanted to find work or she knew we would now definitely go under. It was nearing Christmas, and the only good tidings we got through our letter box were a tidal wave of reminders that managed to hide the dirty great hole in the shitty carpet next to the front door.

I got straight back to looking for work again down at the Job Centre and along the London Road, proffering my services. Then, before returning home gloomily without any kind of hopeful news for Heather on the job front, I went into W. H. Smith to buy the *Southend Evening Echo*. That paper always had a decent job section in the back, which would keep me busy the next morning down at the call box ringing some of the vacancies.

I searched the news and magazine stand inside the shop for the *Echo*. Then, as I bent down to pick it up, I spotted a copy of *The Stage and Television Today*. It's a monthly newspaper aimed at all aspects of the entertainment business, a sort of trade publication. It caught my eye because I remembered when I was a kid Dad used to look in it for gigs singing in the clubs.

I smiled to myself, as I recalled those days in Bristol. Back then, I might have thought things were pretty bad, but I would have much preferred that to my current situation. I wished I was back there, maybe just for a day or two, to be a kid again, to be free, to feel protected in my mother's arms, which I always felt was the safest place in the universe, the one spot where there were no worries, no fear. I longed for just one moment of that right now.

I don't know why, I couldn't really afford it, but I picked up a copy of *The Stage*. I folded it up and slipped it in between the pages of the *Echo* in my hand. I didn't want Heather to know I'd spent extra money on buying something that was of no use to us.

Later that evening, I sat with Heather as she lay on the couch, having still not regained her full strength yet. I was attempting to cheer her up by reading aloud in some of my best funny voices and, whenever possible, getting up and physically demonstrating around the room some of the job vacancies on offer in the back pages of the *Echo*.

Then if there was anything where it sounded as if I might be qualified, which would be mostly labouring, fetching and carrying, cleaning or dogsbodying, in fact any job that needed the average brain function of a potato, I'd ring it with a pen and call the number provided in the morning. We both knew that later, when it came to Heather finding a job, it would be a lot easier as she was more than qualified as a secretary and in comparison to me had the brain power of the NASA space centre's central computer system.

After a while, Heather again became fatigued and drifted off to sleep. As I've mentioned, she was still pretty weak from her ordeal. I also put her constant tiredness down to being quite understandably depressed about losing the baby. Then she'd had to cope with the psychological strain after the hospital had had to take out one of her fallopian tubes. Obviously, after such a loss, some will feel as if they're somehow less of a woman. However, always wanting to sound positive, I constantly reminded Heather how much I loved her and let her know that we still had a chance.

As she slept next to me, I took the opportunity quietly to flick through the pages of *The Stage*. It was all very amusing. There were articles about TV shows, adverts for forthcoming tours, write-ups of touring shows, interviews with singers, comedians, stage managers and directors. I read them all and I began to smile. It brought back memories of some of the things I experienced as a kid, going around the clubs with Mum and Dad, staying in stage digs, travelling in the car, the clubs, the shows.

Then, at the back of the paper, there was the jobs section, advertisements for lighting and sound crews, promotional types, dancers and so on. The catchlines were great: 'actors needed', 'blue coats wanted for summer season, bubbly personality required'. Then another section caught my eye. It was headed 'Talent Shows'. I couldn't believe it – there were hundreds of them. 'If you have talent,' it read, shouting out of the page at me, 'then you could win £100.'

Another one announced: 'Take part in gala talent show. Are you a comedian, singer, dancer, magician even? Then call the number below to enter, and you could win £250.' I looked around me at the drab bare walls that surrounded us, then back at the advert.

Two hundred and fifty pounds!

To us right then, that would have been like winning five million now. I looked over at Heather to make sure she was still asleep. For some reason, I felt I was doing something wrong. I flicked back to the paper and allowed myself to get a little excited by the prospect. Something ignited a slow-burning fire inside me. The more I thought about it, the bigger the fire got. Thoughts began rushing into my head. I mean, I knew I could play a few instruments. There was no doubt I could definitely throw something together – a few tunes perhaps, or maybe even a song. Yeah! I could bang out a tune on the piano, then a guitar maybe: 'You hum it, mate, and I'll play it.' That sort of thing I could do blindfold.

My finger wandered, more quickly now, down the list of talent contests. Bingo! There it was, right there. Can you believe it, I thought, this is a sign. A talent show just up the road from where we lived, to be held at a pub in a place called South Woodham. You could see it was a way for a brewery to promote its pub: put some acts on and people will turn up and buy lots of beer, the winner gets in the local paper shaking hands with the head of the brewery, free publicity for the pub – everybody wins! Who cares? '£250 could be yours,' it said in big bold writing. 'If you think you've got talent, then come on down.'

Well, I'd never felt so sure about anything as I did right then. As it sunk in, a series of huge cogs seemed to click and clunk into place inside my head. I stared back down at the advert, grabbed a pen and, tearing off a corner of the newspaper, wrote down the number, walked out into the hall and stood next to my coat, which hung over the banister.

There I am, being cheered to the rafters. I have my arm around Heather, and confetti is falling all about us like thick snowflakes. There are flashbulbs exploding, and I can just about hear Heather shouting to me above the noisy crowd. 'We're not going to lose the flat now, Lee!' We both look at each other and begin laughing, something we haven't done for a long time. 'It'll get us out of debt, pay some of those bills,' she cries out, then kisses me on the cheek. I shake my head with delight and look up to the sky. 'Thank you.'

The crowd, now feverish, have climbed on to the stage, and are all around congratulating me. 'I knew I could do it, H,' I beam. 'This is what I know.' The audience parts in front of us to reveal the chairman of the brewery. He's holding a giant cheque for £250. Heather and I stare down at it with glee. Then suddenly the mood begins to change. The chairman's face becomes angry and – rip! – he tears the huge cheque in two. RIP! 'You're not worthy of this!' he shouts.

I sneaked a terrified glance at Heather. She stirred a little, but didn't wake. I looked back down at the scrap of paper I was holding and came to my senses. I began tapping my forehead with the palm of my hand to get through to my brain. 'No, stop it, Lee, you fool. You're dreaming again.' I scrunched it up in my fist, then stuffed it into my coat pocket.

I walked back into the lounge and looked at the grumpy old TV over in the corner. The dusty screen was blank, the stations off air. It was late. I rolled my eyes. 'Show business?' I mocked myself for even thinking such rubbish. 'A ridiculous idea, that is not a life for us. I know, I've lived it already.' I was sure that would never be a life for Heather and me. I was always absolutely determined one day to get a proper job with security. I sighed, shrugging my shoulders. 'Something has to turn up soon.'

I stood in the middle of the room and looked around me at the shabby walls, the lumpy, frayed carpet, the peeling woodwork, the hole in the ceiling, the dirty, bright orange, moth-eaten curtains. I thought again about travelling with Mum and Dad when I was a kid, the theatres and smoky clubs, the performers, some good, some truly awful.

All of them, it seemed, had had one thing in common: they all had the same fear and insecurity about where their careers were going or how a particular show went. It was always noticeable that the ones who were the ascending stars had a more bubbly, positive way about them. Only a few years later, if you bumped into that same person when they were no longer flavour of the month and on the way down, it would be a whole different story. They seemed consumed with anxiety about why they'd been dropped in favour of the younger guy.

I noticed how, when you met all those people who you might have seen filling the TV screens with their massive white smiles and dazzling personalities, they looked somehow odd, alien even, like their heads were too big for their bodies. They had fixed, frozen smiles and laughing eyes that, like a mask, could in an instant drop. It was like a switch being turned off – as soon as they felt they were out of the sight of the punters, their faces immediately fell.

I thought of all the wasted talent I'd seen. Then, of course, there were the ones with just a minuscule amount of talent who had still managed to become a huge success, something that only fuelled the resentment in other performers. I thought of all that. Then I began to feel a little sad as I started to recollect how it affects the families of people in show business, the kids who never see their dads, the wives who find out their husbands are having affairs while away, the constant reassurance needed from the spouses, the cleaning of the suits, the shoes, the handling of the props, the hair dye, the stitching buttons back on, the sequins and the hems.

A shiver went up my spine. No, I'd always sworn I wouldn't begin to get involved in any of that sort of stuff. I shall get a proper job, I said to myself, something I'm good at. There is something out there for me – I just haven't found it yet. But I will, and soon. I hid *The Stage* back inside the *Echo* again.

I checked on Heather; she was sound asleep. Standing in the doorway as the light from the hall rested on her peaceful face, I stared at her for a moment. I didn't deserve someone so beautiful, someone who always held out so much hope for me. I felt as though I was letting her down very badly. 'It won't be long now, Heather. Something will turn up. I can feel it in my bones.' I quietly closed the door and went off to bed.

I awoke the next morning curious. Rummaging through a few boxes we had tucked away in a small cupboard next to our bedroom, I found my old guitar case. Flipping it open, I grabbed the Fender guitar that lay quietly inside and sat down on a box. I caressed its smooth, shiny surfaces, letting my fingers lightly touch the strings at the top of the neck. I questioned if I could perhaps still play it, then I wondered if I could still play the piano as well. I mean, I hadn't played any music at all since I was in the band and that had been a couple of years back.

I began softly playing a few riffs I used to know. Shit! It was like riding a bike. The chords, I seemed to be just finding them with my fingers automatically. The rock'n'roll songs we would bang out to warm up just popped into my head. I strummed away. 'Johnny B. Goode'? Easy! It was only three chords, twelve-bar blues, simple, no problem. I thought of the talent show advertised in *The Stage*. What if I entered it? I wondered. I strummed a little louder. I imagined I was on stage, I was there. Yeah, I could do that, a couple of numbers on this, maybe one on the piano. Yeah, I could do that. If there's one thing I know, it's music. I was lost in my imagination for a moment.

But then a wave of doubt and anxiety swept through my entire body. I stopped playing. This is not for me, I thought, this is bullshit. I slammed the reluctant guitar back in its box and hid it away back amongst the junk and unpacked boxes. There was no way I was going to stand on a stage, no way. I felt stupid – you fool, Lee Evans, I said to myself, what you need is a proper job. I knew there had to be something that was right for me out there. I only wished I knew what that was.

But it wasn't on the stage.

I was utterly sure of that.

35. The Governor

A couple of hours later, after making sure Heather was fine, I was up'n'at'em in the call box, furiously calling the job vacancies that we had picked from the paper the night before. Most of them had already been filled, and it was only 10.00 a.m. Blimey, give us a chance!

I was used to rejection by now, so it was water off a duck's back that most calls resulted in bad news. I would just plough on, instantly going to the next one. Then I thought I'd call a random number, why not? It wasn't one we had picked out – it was a small ad tucked away near the bottom of the page and only consisted of a few words: 'Salesman needed. Potential to be very successful. No qualifications required. Start immediately. Earn good money fast.'

A man by the name of Jonathan answered. His voice was quite posh. 'Meet me at the entrance to Southend Pier, all right, in a couple of hours, say? Great!'

I went to meet him as planned, making sure I was prompt and ready. I was quite excited. He sounded very firm, concise and businesslike over the phone. His middle-class accent gave the impression that he must have been sitting in a leather-backed chair surrounded by plans, wall-charts and graphs. I think he may have been speaking to me with his back to a large floor-to-ceiling pane of glass tinted the same colour as my mum's Pyrex casserole dish. I imagined him looking out across a bustling floor of professional office workers.

I checked the time. I had to say he was quite late, but then I envisaged Jonathan arriving any second, probably in a chauffeur-driven Jag, perhaps climbing out to shake me by the hand and welcoming me to the company. I began to think he was being strategically late – maybe he wanted to play everything down, hold back. I mean, for all I knew it could have been a test, part of the interview. I only had to crack once and I was out. I could have been a time-waster. I had a little scout around, half-expecting to see a steamed-up car full of suits wearing sunglasses watching me. I was definitely getting this – he didn't want to show all his cards.

From what I could glean from our brief telephone conversation earlier, I reckoned this guy took no prisoners. Jonathan was mean and he was lean, and that's what he expected from me. I did my best to look dynamic, standing there under the arch of the blisteringly cold and exposed pier entrance, stamping my scruffy black trainers and rubbing my hands to keep warm. I felt a little as if I didn't quite fit the 'Potential to be very successful' mould in my now-nearly-threadbare-and-holding-on-for-dear-life Oxfam suit. I was also regretting opting not to wear the only coat I had at the time, a short red lumber jacket. But I knew it wouldn't work. 'Think dynamism, Lee!' – that was my mantra.

That's why I was initially taken aback when Jonathan eventually arrived, much, much later than the agreed time. I was lucky – any longer and I'd have lost at least a couple, if not all, of my outer extremities and I needed one of them if we were to try for kids again. I was on the point of having to marinate myself in a vat of boiling antifreeze for a week.

Jonathan had cut it fine, but I put his lateness down to his very busy schedule. Actually, I don't know what I put it down to; I didn't know anything by then, as I had significant brain freeze and probably, if asked, wouldn't even have been able to operate a spoon.

I nearly dismissed Jonathan at first as some poor beggar struggling to get up the seafront. As it was by now blowing a gale, he wobbled like a penguin along the freezing, abandoned promenade, his long black coat flapping furiously in the wind that howled in sideways and fired sharp rain like needles up over the seafront wall.

Disconcertingly, he appeared angry and frustrated with something as he shuffled towards me, all dishevelled, restless and spitting nails to himself. I noticed he was clinging on to something wrapped up in a carrier bag under one arm. Disrespectfully, I thought for a moment that he looked like a hobo who had just climbed off the bus down the road. But I immediately dismissed that as ridiculous – I was being unkind. I remembered our high-powered telephone conversation back at the call box, and rejected my preposterous idea right away. I reminded myself, this bloke takes no prisoners.

As we retired to a small, steamy café nearby, Jonathan dispensed with the formalities and launched straight into his pitch. 'There's no room for shirkers in my organization,' he blasted. Even though I desperately didn't want to admit it to myself – my mind was, like a bloodhound, fixed firmly on getting that job – he looked like a bit of a shirker himself.

He was a dumpy, besuited, untidy little man, well into his forties, with a bloodshot face, big, panda-like, dark drooping eyes and so many chins he looked like he was peering over a loaf of bread. He had been wheezing and short of breath when he hobbled up to me; he reminded me of one of those inbred miniature dogs you see under some large wealthy woman's flabby arm.

'Oh, I nearly forgot,' he smiled, with questionable sincerity. 'Did you bring the old money that I asked you to?' When he spoke, I was transfixed. I couldn't take my eyes off his chins, which all moved at different times to each other. They looked like those big red brushes that sway from side to side on a drive-through car wash.

'Yeah!' I enthusiastically replied, frantically searching for it in one of my trouser pockets, a task made all the more difficult by the fact that we were seated in a tight booth. Although I had started to warm up now that we had come in from the cold, my tingling hands still hadn't quite thawed enough to be fully operational.

'How much was it? I can't remember,' he said, feigning innocence. He didn't look at me when he uttered those words. It felt like he wanted to avoid eye contact. He occupied himself with moving objects around the Formica table. It was like he was playing chess. He never sat still for a second, cleaning his knife and fork with the serviette, placing them neatly next to each other at exactly the right space apart. The whole time he talked, he kept moving stuff, the salt cellar, the pepper pot, then picking up the sugar bowl and pouring so much sugar into his tea that I thought when he went to the toilet he was going to pump out candy floss.

'Twenty-five pounds, was it?' I enquired, momentarily stopping my search and desperate to sound like I knew what I was doing.

'Right, yeah. You'll want the Executive Kit, then.' He looked up from scanning the menu, slammed it on to the table, put his hands on top of it and now turned to look directly at me, smiling broadly once again. I squirmed – I was in his power. Blimey, I thought, that's how good he is, that's the aura he has. Just think, one day, I'll have that – although I'll perhaps pass on the ascending mountain range of chins.

To be honest, I was crapping it right then. I was finding Jonathan really intimidating and anticipated that demeanour might be something I would have to learn at some point if I were to become an equally go-getting hotshot. I was feeling a little like the Karate Kid, sitting at the feet of the Master.

Unable confidently to look at him directly, I sat cowering in the booth, flicking a glance up at him now and again to see if he was still staring at me. He was – in fact, he wouldn't stop. His eyes were boring into me. I was momentarily distracted when I noticed his teeth, every one of them a rotten dirty brown colour. They looked a bit like a series of badly painted pub signs flapping about in the wind. The gaps between them gave them the appearance of Stonehenge at dusk. He was probably too busy running his organization to worry about petty things like personal hygiene. Still, you could get your secretary to go out and get a toothbrush, surely. But who was I to question the great Jonathan . . . actually, thinking about it, I never got his second name.

I found the money in my back pocket and handed it to him. That's when he stopped staring at me and focused on the money. He quickly counted it and shoved it into the inside pocket of his heavily dandruffed jacket. He appeared to relax after that. He sucked in a deep lug of the steamy grease of café air and ran his fingers through his thick, oily black hair, then sat back contentedly, looking around the empty tables, picking up and sipping loudly on his sugary tea.

'Well, there goes my toilet-cleaning money,' I thought. But never mind, it was a shrewd investment on my part.

'Aaaaaaaaaaaaaaargh . . . Yeah, great!' he exclaimed, letting the air out in a whoosh of self-satisfaction.

I was trying to pluck up the courage to question him on what he meant by the 'Executive Kit'. I was intrigued as it sounded as if there was a choice of kits. Just then, the waitress arrived to take our food order. 'Riiiiiight, well, it's the Belly Buster Breakfast for meeee,' Jonathan announced. Then, unexpectedly, he brought his face really close to mine and added, quite unnecessarily: 'Cos I'm a fat baaasturd!'

His musky breath reeked of a thousand cigarettes. He then sat back upright and turned towards the waitress: 'And what will you be having then?' It was difficult to tell if he was referring to me or the waitress.

I felt a little embarrassed on her behalf, to be honest, so I tried to distract him. 'Oh, nothing for me, thanks.' But he took no notice. He slowly scanned her figure, his bulging eyes like an MRI machine, from her feet right up to the top of her bunched pineapple-esque hairdo. She definitely cut a sexy figure, her tight black leggings showing exactly what mood she might be in. But, for all that, she looked distinctly nonplussed by his overt leering.

Jonathan gave me a little sly wink. I half-winked back, desperately trying to join in. He then amorously widened his big baggy eyes, like a wily fox who's caught a chicken, and kinked an unsettling smile at me as though I was one of the boys. The look was made all the more powerful as it was accompanied at exactly the same time by a loud hiss of steam from the coffee machine, which made him appear frighteningly snakelike.

Just then, he poked his tongue out at me. I jumped violently off my seat which, just like a bouncy castle, made him shoot violently up into the air. He fumbled and hot tea poured into his lap. He yelped and jumped again from the shock, his stumpy little legs hitting the bottom of the table, sending condiments scattering everywhere. Jonathan quickly climbed from the booth. Grimacing in pain, he began frantically pulling at the hot wet patch around his crotch area.

The waitress gave me a little conspiratorial smile, but I pretended not to notice. I needed to remain firmly in the Jonathan camp, as there was a job at stake. I rushed around, ostentatiously trying to look helpful, grabbing rolling objects and putting them back on the table, as the gloating waitress looked on.

Jonathan snapped. 'You fucking idiot!' That was it – I had failed. He was angry with me. He handed the tea to the waitress. 'Get me another. I hardly had any of that, so I reckon that's a freebie, don't you?' When he handed the cup over, I noticed his fingernails were so thick with dirt, you could grow potatoes in them.

As he wiped the stain with a serviette, Jonathan gave me a smouldering look of disdain. I felt so dreadful, I scooped up as many serviettes as possible, dropped to the floor and began mopping his crotch. I hoped I hadn't ruined my chances. Now down on my knees in a very compromising position, I smiled up at him meekly.

'What are you having then?' he spoke down to me through gritted teeth.

I stopped mopping. 'Nothing for me, thanks,' I said again. I was too nervous to eat, plus I only had five more pounds in my pocket. If I got the job, I would need bus money to get around. The job entailed me going out and selling stuff. I didn't quite know at this point what, but it was definitely flogging something.

We both sat back into the booth. Then Jonathan's mood seemed to change. He began smiling, slapping me on the back and optimistically sounding more encouraging. 'Come oooon, yooooou,' he said, squeezing my shoulder tightly. 'Eat, you deserve it. My bestest employee can't operate on an empty stomach.' He then patted his huge pop belly. 'He'll have the same as me,' he said, then waved the now-scowling waitress away.

Good, I felt more at ease now. I hadn't upset him and, despite everything, I thought I'd just heard him call me 'his bestest employee'. To me, that sounded as if I was in. I had the job! I wanted to run home and tell Heather. 'It will only be a matter of time, Heather, before Jonathan is introducing me to some of the most exclusive clubs that the upper echelons of Southend society has on offer.' I found it hard to believe. How could I have been so fortunate to have met the great Jonathan? The gods have most definitely smiled upon me today, I thought, this sort of chance only happens once in a lifetime.

I was desperate to question Jonathan about what he meant by the 'Executive Kit', but I couldn't find the right opportunity. He chatted away machine-gun-like about his huge company and how, if I did get the job, I would unfortunately be without his personal back-up for a few weeks as he was off to spend the winter with friends and sample the new Golden Mile in Marbella.

But he gave me one of his cards. Well, I say 'card' – it was actually a small blue piece of well-worn paper on which he jotted down a number. He assured me that if I got a sale, I had to call the number on it immediately and the massive machine which was his company and which I had at my total disposal 24/7 would race into action.

'Aaaaand bam!' He slapped one palm of his hand with the other. 'A big fat cheque will be winging its way through the postal system to you.' And this was his exclusive advice to me: 'Newly opened platinum account, that's what I got. Listen, you might want to do the same. With the amounts of dosh you'll be bunging in there, mate, you'll want a little more bang for your buck, right?'

Very gently, I enquired what I might be selling. That was when he came in really close and whispered to me out of one side of his mouth, 'Aluminium shop-fronts.'

I was a little perplexed at first. I needed a moment to just take that in. I have to admit I was expecting something a little more dynamic, but there it was. I'm staring at the evidence right before me, I thought. Jonathan's clearly a multi-millionaire, so someone's doing something right around here, and it ain't me. I rest my case.

Just then, the 'Belly Busters' were dumped on the table, along with a fresh cup of tea for Jonathan. As the waitress walked away, he gave me a nudge and whispered, pointing at the tea: 'Hey! Why don't you throw that one at my cock and I'll get her to drink it later?' I laughed perhaps a little too loudly.

Jonathan immediately dived into the breakfast, scoffing it down without pausing for breath. Even when he was reaching for the ketchup and splurging it all over food, he still managed to stab with his fork at various sections and chomped away at the huge mound of lard on his over-sized plate.

In comparison, I was unable to bring myself to even touch what looked to me like a pile of dead animal bits on a plate, my stomach churning over with a mixture of expectation and excitement at the prospect of being just like Jonathan. I glanced over at him with admiration as he shovelled another lot of food into his mouth, washing it down with a slurp of tea. He smiled back at me as he wiped off some yellow egg that had dribbled down his chin.

'So, what did you mean, Jonathan, about the "Executive Kit"?' I asked hesitantly, a little reluctant to interrupt what was quite obviously the highlight of his week, if not his year.

He talked and ate at the same time, hardly giving the last lot of food a chance to go down before shovelling in another forkful. Every time he opened his mouth to speak, I could see the contents inside, swishing around like one of those industrial washing machines.

'Well, you've just shrewdly paid the deposit for the exclusive use of the Executive Kit.' He quickly squeezed the last lot of food from his plate into his mouth, reached over and grabbed his carrier bag. He placed it on the table and, like a magician, plunged his hand in, paused for effect and, as quick as a flash, pulled out what looked suspiciously like two triangular pieces of clear glass in a forty-five-degree angular piece of alloy window frame.

He smugly rested it on the palms of his hands, like those models might do on the game shows, displaying it to me and smiling. Yes, I could tell it was indeed a cutaway of a corner section of a window. I tried my best to look really amazed, as I thought any moment now he would show me a proper folder with all the bumf inside, a list of prices, recommendations from satisfied customers, photos of recent jobs. I surreptitiously looked around the table for other bits of the so-called kit – he would have it somewhere, I was sure.

'The Executive Kit,' he proudly announced. 'This is the very sales kit the company will loan to you and, when you finish, or are promoted even, we will give you back your deposit for it. By then, of course, twenty-five quid will be like a distant tab on your paying-in book.'

I mindlessly nodded and reached out to grab the proffered corner unit for a closer examination, but Jonathan quickly put it back in the bag and returned it to his side.

"Course, if you give me a little more, you get the use of what we all call back at the office . . . the Governor. Do you want that?' He pointed a fork at my plate.

I shook my head, 'No.' I was still trying to fathom what he was going on about as he swapped our plates and began feeding his face again. The fact that my Belly Buster was now stone-cold did not seem to bother him in the slightest.

'The Governor?' I enquired.

'Yeah, it's only a hundred quid. But that is for the use of the ultimate in sales kits. It's never missed a sale yet. I only let it out on loan when I think we need to make up targets for the month.' He stopped eating and gazed out of the window, all melancholy. 'Never fails. The Governor's helped me out of a lot of tricky situations. It earns an absolute mint. Anyway . . .' He returned to finish off my Belly Buster breakfast.

'Well, that's me out then, Jonathan,' I sighed with defeat and lowered my head. God, I wished I could have that Governor. 'Does it really sell that much?'

He dropped his knife and fork. 'Does it sell that much?' It was as if I had just insulted him.

'Sorry, Jonathan, I didn't mean to –'

'It's all right, don't worry. I tell you what, how much have you got, old chum?' He looked at me, peering out from behind his teacup as he sucked up the last dregs from the sugary bottom.

'Not a hundred, that's for sure,' I laughed nervously.

'Well, how much?'

'Another five pounds.' I produced it out of my pocket and showed it to him.

'Look, I'll tell you what. Give me that and I will loan you the Governor, and when you get your first sale, you can pay me the rest then, yeah?'

'Blimey, would you do that for me, Jonathan? Seriously?'

He nonchalantly took my five pounds, climbed out of

the booth, picked up the carrier bag and said to me, 'You wait there and I'll go and get the Governor.' He walked to the door, opened it and stood in the doorway. 'Don't you go away. I'll be a couple of minutes all right?' With that, he was off into the rain to get the Governor.

I couldn't believe it – I had a job! And, to top it all, I was now getting the Governor sales kit, too. I sighed with relief, congratulating myself. 'Well done there, Lee Evans! I'll tell you what, my son, Heather's going to be pleased with you tonight.'

I smiled over at the waitress, who was behind the counter wiping cups. I thought I'd try my new 'patter' skills out on her – why not? I was a fully fledged salesman now, with the back-up and the resources of a huge company all at my disposal. I raised my voice over to her. "Ere, I reckon your shop front, right, could do with a bit of, like, new bits and all that. What dew fink then, yeah?'

Amazingly, she was unmoved by my super-smooth spiel. She never even looked up from what she was doing; she just called out, 'Paul!' A short, stocky man – who looked like he'd just come from doing ten rounds with a life-sized Punch and Judy and they'd spent the entire time doing rope-a-dopes on his face – appeared from the back. He was wearing dirty chef's clothing and wiping his hands on a towel that was tucked in the front of his apron. He blinked his eyes under the bright strip-lighting.

'Yeah, what?' he asked and gave me a look.

'He wants to know about the front of our shop or something.'

'What about it?' He peered over the counter.

'I just wanted to know what you thought about it, that's

all. Nothing like . . . you know. Just wonderin', 'n that. Sorry.'

He bowled around the side of the counter and slapped the bill in front of me. Then he turned, but not before he looked back over his shoulder and said, 'No, we're all right.' He uttered the words quietly, but the menacing, deep sound of his voice reverberated around the whole café. I could hear glasses ringing in cupboards.

I flashed a little glance down at the bill on the table, then quickly looked back – with rapidly diminishing expectations – towards the door. Bollocks!

It was beginning to sink in, but I held on, hoping for the best, trying to convince myself that everything was going to be OK. I definitely recalled Jonathan's car – a Jag, I thought – being parked quite a way back down the seafront. It must have been, as I hadn't even seen him get out of it earlier, so I was sure he'd be back any moment and everything would be all – double bollocks!

I found myself anxiously tapping the table with my fingers. I knew I had to have nerves of steel if I was to be accepted into Jonathan's huge company, a worldwide operation, probably. Well, if this was part of the test, then I hoped I wouldn't crack on the final hurdle because now, I had to admit, I was starting to get just a little on the more pressing side of pant-crapping about where he had got to. I looked around and back over the counter towards the waitress. I was surprised to find her standing next to the chef. They were both staring intently at me.

'Can I go and check on me mate?' I pointed towards the door.

The chef showed me his teeth and snarled.

'No, you just stay right where you are, pal. I'm sure he won't be long.'

That's when I could hear the tim, tap, cling, clang, clong, in my head – it was the sound of a spanner falling, bouncing off the nooks and crannies then, clunk, eventually jamming in the works of my brain. I mumbled to myself as I fixed my eyes on the door. 'I don't think that Jonathan bloke is coming back.'

I bowed my head in shame. All I could see was my dirty trainers on a filthy tiled floor poking out the end of a second-hand suit. 'You fool, Lee Evans, you ridiculous, stupid fool.'

I peeked out the corner of my eye at the waitress and chef again.

'Do you have a phone I could borrow?' I called a friend and asked if he could go and get Heather for me.

I'm still waiting for Jonathan to come back with the Governor.

I was eighteen at the time. I am forty-seven now, but it's taken more or less that long, in fact, until quite recently, for her to forgive me for paying that Jonathan bastard bloke – her words, not mine – the last of any money we had in the world.

I say she has forgiven me recently – it was about an hour ago when she finally issued me with a proper pardon, and even then I am under strict instructions from the proper by-laws of our house not to go anywhere near anyone called Jonathan with a posh middle-class accent ever again.

36. Mrs Taylor Was Right

Trying to put the Jonathan humiliation behind me, I got straight back on the bike and was soon back at the Job Centre. But now my mood was changing. I was finding it all so hopeless. There were hardly any jobs on the boards, and when they appeared, they would be snapped up within minutes.

Even my usual confidence-boosting London Road job hunt was a hopeless exercise in rejection and self-doubt. I usually had a bit of a friendly banter with the shopkeepers, but even they recognized a marked change in my demeanour. If Dougal, our old dog, had been around, I might have copied my dad and threatened to boot him in frustration.

So I decided to sign on the dole. That was when I began to lose my self-respect. It had been something I swore I would never do, but there it was. I had to take a hand-out from the government, and so I spent the rest of that demoralizing day filling in forms, being told by people who didn't seem to care a rat's arse, sitting behind thick violence-proof glass, that I was either on the wrong floor, at the wrong booth or holding the wrong form. It was a demoralizing business, taking a ticket like you would at the cheese counter and sitting for hours with other depressed and gloomy people just like me waiting for my name to be called – just so they could tell me what I might be entitled to. I already had a rough idea that it was the princely sum of not much at all.

That night I huddled up with Heather on the couch, desperate not to show how low my spirits had become. She had just regained her strength and was going out the following day herself to look for a job, and so I didn't want to bring her down. I knew we were in trouble, otherwise she wouldn't be needing to look for work. But I didn't ask about any of this. As usual I blotted it out, choosing to live in my own bubble. Inside my head, I was dreaming of a day I would be able to afford some form of heating for our freezing cold flat.

The next morning I did my customary it's-a-new-day-let's-get-cracking routine. From very early, I was at the call box dialling up vacancies from the paper, but I quickly found there was nothing out there. I was either too late, or I wasn't qualified enough, or they just didn't like the sound of my voice.

I gently replaced the receiver, despondently walked from the call box and stood on the corner of the street. I was staring up at the phone lines above my head that criss-crossed the road, shooting off in all different directions. My eye followed the line to other telegraph poles, then angled off to buildings all the way down the road into the distance. I thought of all the places they could go, even under the sea and to other countries, across towns and cities, offices and factories, hospitals and police stations, everywhere. Then I thought back to where I was standing, right underneath one such line. It held all that potential and yet here I was, jobless and useless. I felt so insignificant. A nothing. I was throwing in the towel, admitting defeat. Mrs Taylor was right all those years ago. What those other pupils were looking at on that day was a failure.

I was officially a loser, a misfit who fitted in nowhere. Even if I managed to get a job, I couldn't hold on to it because I kept messing up one way or another. I spent my life trying to conform, going out of my way to meet other people's wishes. I was a happy-go-lucky bloke, always looking on the positive side, but to whom nothing positive ever happened. I was always friendly to people, but I had no close friends. I liked to be a part of everything, but I was a part of nothing.

I drifted off home, drew the lounge curtains and sat quietly on the floor. I tucked my face into my knees, covering my head with my hands to cut out the world and began to cry.

It might have been hours later – it felt like late afternoon – when I heard the curtains being pulled back violently. Bright light ripped into the room. I blinked my eyes open and standing over me was Heather.

'What do you think you are doing?'

'I'm sorry, Heather, but I have let you down. I can't find a job. I am nothing, a failure. You can throw me out if you like. I would completely understand. That's how it is.'

'No, let me tell you how it is. They're cutting the electric off tomorrow if we don't pay the bill. We had the last red one yesterday. It's the same with the gas. We haven't paid for the flat in months, and we have survived on clocking up money on a credit card which needs paying off. Plus, the bank that likes to say yes have just told me no. So I want you to get up off your arse, get out that door and find something. Please!' Suddenly, she cracked. She slumped on to the couch and burst into tears. I gave her a hug. I had known we were in serious trouble, but as usual I had blocked out the full extent of it.

I got to my feet and stormed out of the door with a new sense of determination. Heather was right. What was wrong with me, I thought, giving up like that, after what she had just gone through? I should be ashamed.

I reached the call box, dived in, plunged my hand into my coat pocket and whipped out a torn corner piece of newspaper. I slapped it against the back wall just above the phone and stared at it for a moment. It was the scribbled note I had written a few days earlier from *The Stage* newspaper while Heather slept next to me: 'Talent Show'. Underneath, I had hurriedly copied out the telephone number in South Woodham.

I hesitantly lifted the receiver, jammed it under one side of my chin and began dialling the number. I was concerned as the competition was to be held that night, so I hoped I wasn't too late to enter. The man on the other end of the phone informed me there was only one place left and asked what he should enter me as. I hesitated. I didn't know what I was, so I just blurted out, 'A singer, aaaaargh? A singer-instrumentalist.' He sounded quite impressed. I asked if there would be a piano; he said that there would be and that he would mic it up for me ready to play.

I calmly thanked him and gently replaced the receiver. I stumbled out from the call box on to the pavement in a daze. I bent over, putting my hands on my knees. I felt very light-headed and thought for a moment I was going to throw up. My whole body began to tremble. Thoughts began to whizz around inside my head. What I was doing? Basically, I had just lied to that man. I'm not a singer-instrumentalist, I thought, I'm a nothing. I have never performed in my life. Oh sure, I'd had seen acts all right, lots of them. I had been around performers since I was a sperm. But that didn't mean I could get up there and do it myself.

I spent the walk home thinking through various scenarios. 'I will open with perhaps a guitar number. Then maybe I should get on the piano and do a bit of twelve-bar blues to get the place jumping. To finish off, I should get back on the guitar and work up a bit of a sweat.' I tried convincing myself everything would be all right. 'I mean, I only have to perform a ten-minute spot – what's that? Three songs, I could do that easily.' But then doubt would creep in. 'Why are you doing this, Lee, you fool?'

I didn't know what might happen. There would be no time to rehearse. It was a gamble, but at least I felt I was doing something. By now I didn't even care why, how, what or where. I suppose I had nothing to lose. What did it matter if I was booed off the stage, chased out of town? At least that would be one step up from where I was right now: nowhere.

Even if I never set foot on a stage again, it was a throw of the dice that was worth trying. A little voice in the back of my head kept egging me on. Despite my wavering, somehow it felt perfectly natural to be on the edge, in a situation of uncertainty. I liked the feeling, the buzz, the risk. I hated the awareness that I might suffer the humiliation of failure, but at the same time that was the whole point. It was like stepping over a border to see what might be on the other side.

This felt like something I knew about, a world I had dwelt in. For the first time in my life, I reckoned there was a minuscule bit of good fortune in my favour. At the same time, I knew I might have to suffer some form of hardship or even humiliation to get it. But I liked the idea of punishment; I had to suffer in order to get something. I felt much more comfortable with the idea that if anything decent should come my way, I must first be afflicted by some kind of sacrifice, otherwise I wouldn't deserve it. I was used to failure, to being knocked. I was an idiot, a disappointment, a loser. I was so used to that tag, I damn well expected it. If I was to be treated as a fool, I would act like one.

At the front door to the flat, I slammed the key into the lock. Before entering, I paused for a moment. 'Right, I shall go inside, have a quick wash, grab my amp and guitar, then head off to South Woodham.' I gave a little careless shrug of my shoulders. The only thing I was doing was gambling the bus fare to get there. In the end, I thought, if it all goes wrong and is a huge embarrassment, so what?

I didn't care any more. I was fed up with being kicked in the teeth. I'd had enough indignity, shame and struggle to last me a lifetime. I stamped my foot on the front step and looked briefly up to the sky. 'Enough, enough now.'

I turned the key and entered the flat.

37. What Was This Strange Feeling
I Was Experiencing?

Everyone was there, the managing director of the brewery, the local newspaper and an audience of several hundred packing the venue to the rafters. Then I noticed the pub door opening and Heather enter and search the room for me. She needn't have bothered looking; she was about to see me – everyone was.

'He says he's a singer-instrumentalist – let's see if he's right! Let's hear it, ladies and gentlemen, for the last act in tonight's competition . . . Mr Lee Evans!' the compere announced. As I lurked nervously offstage at the back of the venue, I heard it booming out, vibrating, shifting the hot, heavy, thick air around me. The sound was resonating from two huge speakers pitched on stands either side of the stage like sentries that marked the gateway to another world.

'About time, too,' I thought, 'thank God.' I was relieved, just wanting to get on with it and over with. I was on the verge of exploding after having to mill around at the back of the jam-packed, lively room the whole night. The fact that it had dragged on so long had only added to the tense, rowdy atmosphere in the venue. The extra time had given the rammed pub more opportunity to get cheap promotional beer down as many necks as possible.

My ears were attuned to every shriek, shout and heckle

that the last performer had had to battle through. Every fibre in my body now racked with nerves, I held my hand up just to confirm to myself that it was shaking. I had waited for my turn, half-watching all the other acts as they had done their ten minutes. Mostly, though, my head had been dipped and my eyes had been fixed upon the floor at my feet, not really able to face what would eventually be my fate.

Instead, it felt more comfortable just to listen, assessing my own chances as, one by one, the acts got better and better. This only fed the growing voice of doubt which was now so easily drowning out what had been the whisper of such certainty and hope on the bus on the way there. I remembered when I was a kid, standing, waiting, watching by the side of the stage, and thinking it was all so magical. But not now, not from where I was standing – this was a different story.

I used to wonder why almost all performers looked so solemn and their eyes seemed so fixed and concentrated while either waiting to go on or just coming off the stage. Now I knew. That's when they began to doubt themselves. I hadn't known that was how they felt.

When I was a boy spending months travelling theatres and working men's clubs with Mum and Dad, I only felt the excitement, the wonder, skill and brilliance of all those comedians, singers, dancers and musicians. If I wasn't there watching from the wings, I would be tucked away back in some seedy dressing room, listening to the muffled sounds of what I imagined was going on out in the club, and which always sounded so intoxicating. Now I was experiencing the reality.

After announcing my name, the compere pointed to where I was standing at the back of the room, and the crowd parted like the Red Sea to allow me a passageway through to the stage. They began their exuberant beer-fuelled whooping and clapping. I felt I was a lamb to the slaughter as I stood trembling, still pinned against the back wall, hair ruffled up like a hairdresser had just finished drying and lifted the towel off.

The image was not helped by my faithful but rancid Oxfam suit, which was now showing signs of real wear, with one leg shorter than the other, one arm hanging off, a torn pocket and a gaping hole on the underside of the trousers bigger than the bomb-bay doors of the Enola Gay. It would have been more humane to have taken the damn thing outside and given it a fatal injection of dry-cleaning fluid. I gripped my old cumbersome Vox amp in one hand and held on for dear life to my electric guitar in the other.

This was it. I couldn't even think of how badly we needed that money – the only reason I was there. No, I would have gladly swapped any amount of cash not to be where I was at that moment. I wouldn't have even cared if we had been thrown out of the wretched flat and made to sleep under Southend Pier for the rest of our lives as two mumbling hobos.

It felt as if I was held to the wall by Velcro, but some-how I found the strength to peel myself off it. I forced my feet out in front of me to make my way along the corridor of people, all their eyes now fixed on me. I almost sleep-walked towards the set of three steps that led up on to the stage where all the lights were focused.

I could see everyone clapping and shouting, but I couldn't hear anything at all. My body was so on edge, my senses now completely in tune with the situation. The only sound surreally audible was the rustle of my suit as it bent and twisted with my movement – that, the sole of my shoe thumping against the ground and the loud deep gasp of air forced in to fill my lungs before rushing out again.

Time seemed to slow right down. People's voices sounded like a record with someone's finger pressed upon it. I pushed out another debilitating step in front of me. I felt as though I was wearing an anvil as a shoe; my knees wobbled and bent around in their sockets as I had to concentrate to find the strength to hold them in place. I was sure they would buckle from under me at any point, weighed down as I was by the amp and guitar that now felt like huge, great, cumbersome boulders. Every muscle had now turned to blancmange; the blood had drained off and left them as soon as my name had been called out and was now probably languishing somewhere around the Kursaal Ballroom on Southend seafront, doing a lively version of the mambo bop de do da friggin' day.

I forced another step forward, then another. I would only have to climb the three steps and I would be there, in front of all these people. My heart was now in my mouth, pumping at full steam ahead as more coal was thrown on the furnace. I heaved myself up the first step, my stomach bubbling away like it was a Jacuzzi at a swingers' party.

I took another step; just one more and I'd be on the stage. I was hardly doing anything that physical, but sweat, as though it were abandoning a sinking ship, poured out from every nook and cranny of my body at such a rate that my suit and shirt were drenched through. I was starting to resemble someone who had just got off the wet and wild ride at a theme park.

I lifted my leg up to take the final step, but then something unexpected happened. The compere who had just introduced me turned to exit the stage. He was obviously leaving me to it, but as he swished past me at speed, my instincts now having been heightened to such a degree, it made me jump. I didn't quite know what it was – he was simply a blur that came out of nowhere, unexpectedly rushing towards me. Just catching him out of the corner of my eye like that made me flinch.

It put me off my concentration and, as a result, my feet did not quite clear the lip of the top step, but instead struck the front of it. The top half of my body then toppled over and the sheer weight of the Vox amp shot me forward like an out-of-control firework. So, I imagined, there I went, straight into the losers' basket, arriving like some mal-coordinated lunatic on to the stage and then, just as suddenly, disappearing again below the heads of the audience like a drowning maniac.

On the way, I had managed to crash face-first into the microphone stand, which had now joined in the proceedings. I, along with the mic stand and everything I was carrying, then careered like a panicked pack horse of electrical equipment across the small, temporary platform into a loud amplified thumping pile just beneath the massive banner stretched across the stage that read: 'Talent Show. Winner gets £250'. Well, I thought from my crumpled heap underneath it, that's me out then.

My face now buried on the stage beneath a pile of equipment, I could hear only silence. The whole room seemed dumbstruck, trying to fathom exactly who, what or even where I was.

Deeply frustrated, I winced at my embarrassment. This was not a good start. I had blown it completely. I imagined what Heather might be thinking. Having asked her friend to drive her there, she had obviously wanted to follow me after our small row earlier. I had stormed out of the door with my guitar, and she, of course, had demanded to know what I was up to. I told her, 'I don't know, but I just need to do this!' I had left her looking annoyed and perplexed. Now here I was, a heap on the floor, our only chance of keeping anything we'd ever had abandoned at that last step.

I scrambled to my feet and, in a futile attempt at covering my initial mistake, I carried on setting up the amp and guitar as if nothing had happened. I was under the impression that if I could get that going and start playing something, then maybe I had the narrowest of chances of getting away with it. But I panicked, thinking there was too long a silence during which something should be happening. I felt the audience becoming a little impatient and everything began getting all muddled up.

I slammed the plug of the amp into an extension lead at the back of the stage, but then from sheer nervous energy started manically leaping around the tiny stage area, trying to organize my guitar. Its lead had become a frustration as whenever I tried plugging it into the amplifier, the volume was inadvertently turned up way too loud and just shrieked with feedback, causing me to jump back with fright. The noise of me landing would then rattle the echo-springs inside the archaic amp, resulting in another loud burst of ear-splitting racket. Another leap back then loosened the strap on my guitar, which fell to the ground just before I attempted a strum.

By now things had got so out of control, I didn't know what I was doing. I was all over the place and could see any hope of even remaining on stage fading fast. I looked for help at the side of the stage, where I knew the compere-stroke-DJ stood behind his record decks. But he appeared to be laughing so hard at my misfortune that I couldn't get any understandable response out of him.

I felt so deflated, mortified at being laughed at. I couldn't believe how badly it was all going. I just didn't envisage this happening at all. Eventually, the compere jabbed his finger towards the piano on the other side of the stage: 'Get on that, you nut case!' he cackled over the now-growing laughter from the crowd before dissolving into a fit of hysterics again.

As I stumbled over towards the piano, I picked up the mic stand on the way. I was going to use it to sing into, but it was now just a mangled, floppy, useless piece of uncontrollable metal in my hand, all the tightening screws having been loosened in the commotion.

I tried desperately to find some dignity at the piano, but it was made completely impossible by the continuing unpredictability of the mic stand. Every time I tried tightening it into one position, another joint would somehow loosen and it would fall to pieces again. At the same time, I was trying to position the piano stool, but was frustrated that I was unable to get it to the correct height.

One moment I was sitting at the keyboard like a small child, the notes just below my chin; the next, after desperate attempts to raise it, it looked like I was sitting on a bar stool and the keys were so far away I couldn't even reach them.

Most annoyingly, every time I would turn around to adjust the stool, my backside kept hitting the notes. Then I had to start all over again with the mic stand, which had fallen forward between the lid and the piano. It forced the lid to slam on to my fingers just as I was about to play, making me look like an idiot. I had to stop, dazed and confused about where the microphone had disappeared to, my hands jammed uselessly under the lid. The whole act descended into a shambolic disaster. Even though I did my best to plough through, I accepted I had failed miserably. I was bombing big time. It was a car crash.

But in the midst of this dreadful, failing performance, something odd started to happen. It was odd because, instead of feeling as though I was failing, I suddenly felt quite positive. No, more than that – I felt euphoric. I was starting to like being on stage. But, even better, there was a sense that the crowd, curiously, were starting to like what I was doing. What was this strange feeling I was experiencing? Was I starting to be – whisper it – a success?

As I fumbled and blundered my way through the act, getting all muddled along the way, as I fought with the inanimate objects around me that never seemed to do what I wanted them to, there was no doubt something was stirring in the audience. It was a notion that was slow at first, but then grew from a ripple that gradually spread across the entire room, building and building all the time into a massive wave. Laughter! It appeared that the more I struggled to get something right and hopelessly kept getting it wrong, the more the audience roared and howled at my unfortunate situation.

My head began to clear and, as I looked around the room, I realized everyone in the audience was killing themselves with laughter. Why? I was getting it all wrong. I couldn't understand why they were all in fits – the man from the brewery, the compere, the audience. In fact, the only person who wasn't doubled up with laughter was Heather. I could just pick her out under the lights and saw she was just as dumbstruck by the whole thing as I was. She was clearly bewildered that I was, in fact, not dying, but going down a storm.

That was when everything seemed to click into place. I couldn't help myself. For the first time in my entire life, I felt at ease. Indeed, I felt happier to be where I was, on a stage, than out there in the world, a place that appeared only to want to treat me unfairly, a world that never understood me. The feeling was mutual.

Here I was, getting it all so wrong, and yet – ironically – getting it all so right.

The cage was open. I unruffled my feathers and began to fly. I was enjoying myself now, soaring around the stage, improvising, getting tangled in the microphone wire, the stand. My amp became something to stand on, jump off. I played with the curtains at the back of the stage. A massive roar went up when, having never actually played the guitar, I used the strap around my neck to twirl it like a hula hoop around my head. As I stood there, swirling about like a crazed whirling dervish, the crowd went wild. Then, in a pool of sweat, my soaked clothes hanging from my buzzing, shaking body, completely exhausted, the stage littered with debris, I dropped into a bow and felt the electricity that ran through the room.

I straightened up and quickly searched the cheering, applauding crowd for Heather again and was so elated to see she was clapping with pure joy. The lights from the stage caught the tears in her eyes, making them twinkle as she beamed so hard I thought any moment she might burst.

38. The End of the Pier – and of Our Story

Afterwards, as we climbed out of the back of her friend's cramped Ford, Heather and I asked if we could have a little time to reflect on what was a pretty eventful evening. Heather's friend sped off along Southend's gusty seafront after kindly promising to drop my guitar and amp off some time the next day.

We wanted to take a walk along the pier. It had become a special place for us. It was somewhere we always liked to go on a Sunday, when the sun was shining and glistening off the sea. It was a beautiful spot to spend a couple of hours forgetting all our troubles. Plus, it was free!

We hardly ever noticed how long the pier is – they say it goes a mile into the sea, and it's billed as the longest pier in Europe. But we were oblivious to that, so engrossed were we in each other's company as we nattered away to each other about our hopes and dreams. We would always end up sitting right at the end of the pier with our feet dangling over the edge above the sea, not saying a word, just content. We were comfortable with our silence, as long as we were together. Now and again, one of us would look up and cast out a fantasy for the other's benefit. It almost always revolved around a favourite dish we hadn't been able to afford, or a place we longed to go, or an ideal home we dreamed of buying.

Tonight was different, though. There was an unusual mood between us, something we hadn't experienced for quite some time. As we stepped on to the planks of the pier, we linked arms. We squeezed each other closer and headed down the walkway. Our heads were bowed forward and we had to lean at times into the squally but warm winter wind. The breeze would suddenly rush up through the old blue and white Victorian railings as it went whirling off across the pier. It would sometimes catch us by surprise as it rushed at our backs, forcing us to quicken our step along the wet shiny slats. The pier was lit up by the swaying illuminations looped up on each lamp post that went along the entire length of the pier. It looked like one of those adverts you see in the magazines for some posh perfume.

The fresh air felt such a relief. It was so bracing after the intense, claustrophobic, intimidating atmosphere of the talent show where, just half an hour earlier, I had been struggling away, hoping against hope that the purgatory of my ten minutes – which, to begin with, had seemed like ten hours – would soon be over.

'I knew you could do a bit of music, but I didn't know you could do all that other stuff back in the pub,' Heather said proudly, taking in the magnificent view of the estuary in front of us.

Although I wanted to explode with delight when she said it, I dismissed it straight away. 'What? I can't do anything. I was an idiot. I failed.' I wanted to stay calm, so I replied to her playfully. But, of course, I knew it would only draw more praise.

Then I swallowed a deep bellyful of fresh sea air, as the two of us reached the very end of the pier. We held the top railing with both hands like you might a windy motor-bike. We just let the warm wintry breeze whip up and dance around and through our clothes. It certainly felt like it was blowing all the cobwebs away. I closed my eyes for a moment, my thoughts racing back to the talent show.

They had us all lined up at the back of the stage, firing-squad style, as the compere read out the winners. The mood in the pub went very tense and quiet. It had been a long night. With eight acts to sit through, the audience must have been feeling just as tired as some of us up on stage.

By now the room had become hot and sticky. A lot of booze had been drunk, bolstering people's enthusiasm for their favourite acts. So there were some pretty loud, intoxicated characters amongst the crowd. But no one was leaving; they had invested their support in their favourite performers, and they were not budging until they saw who had won. Although the stage lights were almost blindingly bright, you could just see the ones that had been on their feet most of the evening along the back wall and leaning wearily against the bar – from where, now and again, an impatient shout would emerge: 'Hurry up, mate, Give us the results, for Christ's sake.'

'And in third place . . .'

I looked up at the ceiling. 'If I'm not third,' I thought, steeling myself for the worst, 'then I'm nowhere.' And that prize was worth twenty-five pounds, meaning we could pay at least the electricity bill and maybe the gas. It would be compensation for the money that Jonathan ripped off. I put my hands behind my back and crossed my fingers.

From where we stood on the pier, you could look out and see the mass of lights like some giant metropolis that lit up the huge oil and gas refinery about thirty miles away across the Thames Estuary on Canvey Island. Next, you would take your eye along to the right where the lights got denser. They would then flicker as they got further and further away, up the river Thames inland to the Isle of Dogs and the financial towers of new money that stick up like miniature Christmas trees. The whole mass of lights play a trick on the eye, as it seems to hover like a space ship on the horizon.

Then you would turn your face into the dark, cooler wind that whips up off the unlit, ominous, open ocean just outside the gaping mouth of the estuary. It looks lonely, vast and black as it opens out wider still into the English Channel. Tilbury is still a busy port, so even at night you can watch the lights of mammoth, lumbering cargo ships as they slowly disembark, make their way past the pier, then break cover into open sea. Out there, they get smaller and smaller, becoming just dots of light as they position themselves in the busy shipping lanes of the English Channel before disappearing off across the world.

It really feels like you could be out at sea, you are so far from Southend – too far away indeed to hear the slightest noise of a moving car. The only things you can hear at the end of the pier are the deep rush of air as it whisks and beats past your ears and the waves as they crash and mingle amongst the great ironwork legs below.

'Well, I thought you were the best there,' Heather beamed, interrupting our reverie. She leaned back on the railings and smiled. She looked so beautiful. I loved the way her hair flipped and flapped around her eyes, which were flickering and watery because of the wind.

I tried to banter with her. 'How do you know? You didn't get there until I went on. You didn't see any of the others.'

Heather didn't respond. Rather, she stared out to sea. That was all right. Let's be honest, I hadn't done much that could be considered useful to anyone recently, let alone her. All I had brought her was bad news – and that was on top of losing the baby, which she still hadn't really spoken about. So, at last, I felt I had done something, even if it wasn't much, to lighten things up for her a little.

'I never doubted you, Lee,' she replied at last. 'I know you always think people are against you. And I know that you have no self-confidence and that makes you get all in a muddle. But I believe in you, even if you don't think I do sometimes. I know we've had some pretty bad things happen lately and, well, what I'm trying to say is . . .'

I turned to her. I had to – I was getting embarrassed. She had never spoken to me like that before. I could feel tears welling up in my eyes. Covering my face, I changed the subject. 'I'll tell you what – that wind, it makes your eyes water, doesn't it?'

Also, I didn't want to take any credit. As far as I was concerned, I hadn't done anything. I had just been my usual stupid self. It was Heather who had suffered so much. It wasn't about me, it was about us.

I stepped forward and tried kissing her but, as so often happens at times like that, the wind changed, creating an awkward moment when her friggin' hair flopped across her face. So she was suddenly wearing a kind of woolly-mammoth-Chewbacca-from-*Star-Wars*-hairy-face mask. We both became instantly engulfed in her hair as it flapped about between our faces like a frizzy sandwich. We broke off and started spitting hair balls.

I gathered myself. 'I know what you're saying and I'll never let you down again, and . . .' I searched for the right words to give her some hope, faith in me for the future. 'I promise that next time . . . I'll . . . erm . . .'

'Get on with it, you twat,' she joked. 'I've grown a beard waiting here.'

The compere left as big a gap as humanly possible in order to build up the tension before announcing the runner-up. However, the only tension that was building – to perhaps a critical point – was amongst the gathered number of near-to-bursting bladders that needed to be emptied. Then, of course, there were the other lot who were getting impatient for the winner to be called out, so they could start getting the pints in again.

By this point, I was desperate to get off the stage. The suspense had gone for me now. I had crossed the line the moment I had walked out in front of an audience and managed to perform a ten-minute set, even if it was completely disorganized and manic.

I hadn't made the third place I had dared to hope for.

So now I knew I was out of the running. I was really disappointed, as Heather and I wouldn't be able to pay any bills. I'd given up, resigned myself to being back to square one. It had only been a throw of the dice anyway. The adrenaline had slowly seeped from my damp body, rendering me dead on my feet, not from the performance, but the damn nerves. The unrelenting adrenaline that possesses your body like some mad spirit uses up all your body fuel in one go. Then, selfishly, after it's had its fun, it walks away, leaving you physically drained and shaken.

'I have thoroughly enjoyed the experience, though,' I reflected as I stood on the stage, waiting in line with the other performers. I had got a few unintended laughs that had completely converted my mindset. I felt the experience had somehow transformed me. I was on an entirely new bearing. It was nothing serious – it was just that I felt I had somehow crossed an invisible line. There was no doubt, I had been infected by something that had caused a disorder in the whole structure of my expectations. I was aware that I'd always had the symptoms of it, but didn't know what had made it flare up like it had that night.

All my life I had been a fool, an idiot, picked on, frowned upon, vilified by whoever I came into contact with. Yes, I do mean you, Mrs Taylor. But onstage, I was allowed to be whatever I wanted: a fool, an imbecile, a comedian – with none of the attendant rejection. I was accepted, I was free. Instead of being the victim, in my mind I suddenly became the hero.

'And in second place . . .'

I looked up to see the chairman of the brewery getting

all fired up by the excitement that was now growing and beginning to take hold of everyone. He stood clutching a bottle of champagne for the winner. Next to him were a photographer and a journalist from the *Evening Echo*, the local paper. The photographer smiled over at me and winked, as I nervously gave him back a half-hearted grin.

That made me wonder. If I hadn't come anywhere in the competition, would they still put my picture in the paper? If they did, I decided, I would do my best to hide behind someone else's head. If I lurked towards the back, I thought, then I'd surely go unnoticed. As soon as any-one mentioned cheese – kazam! – I'd be gone.

I knew my mum and dad read the *Echo*. They got it religiously every day. The headmaster at my last school in Billericay always read it too. At lunch breaks, as I passed the staffroom on my way to getting up to no good, I'd always see him devouring the paper. Gary also always had a copy of the *Echo* tucked down his dash in the front win-dow of his white van.

Then I wondered if Jonathan, that bloke who had conned us out of our last twenty-five pounds, might catch a glimpse of the paper as he was sitting in the café under the pier with some other poor sucker and feel a twinge of guilt about cheating a potential comedy star.

Heather and I turned back to face towards Southend. It felt as though we were so far away from land, it was like we were on a boat drifting offshore all alone. We were like ghosts observing the world from afar, disconnected from everything. There was only us.

From where we were, we could see the whole of the

seafront from one end to the other. We could just make out the odd person wandering around beneath the dancing bulbs hung along the front. The main drag is illuminated by flashing signs luring people in with quotes from Las Vegas or announcing an impending gold rush. The slot arcades, the discos, the pubs, the fish and chip shops, the bingo halls, all that fun and diversion, is pretty exciting stuff – you just can't get that if you go abroad. It all looked so romantic as its reflection flickered beautifully and skipped around upside down in the water just below the sea wall.

At one end of the sea front, like a great bookend, stands a club marked by huge lettering: 'The Kursaal'. It boasts the only sprung dance floor in the country, for better bounce when dancing. Then, at the other end of the sea front, you look up to the red flashing warning lights at the top of the helter-skelter in 'Peter Pan's Adventure Playground'. Perhaps the lights are a warning to the planes that take off from Southend's small airport.

Just above that, the Cliffs Pavilion theatre is perched high up on the clifftop, dominating the entertainment below. The Cliffs is home to real show business, people off the telly, even from Las Vegas. They have all the big stars coming to visit. The venue packs 'em in. At that point, Heather and I had never been there. We couldn't afford it, but I recognized some of the names from when I was a kid. I might spot an advert in the paper and think, 'Blimey, I remember him,' or, 'I know her. I watched her when I was a nipper.' I always kept it to myself, though. Somehow that sort of talk seemed frivolous and pointless, a world away from where we were in our flat.

By now it was late. It was winter, so the sea front was empty. I love that. The winter months in a seaside town are the best; I can't stand it when it gets all packed in the summer months. The off-season is when the locals get Southend back for themselves. They can enjoy their town without the hassle of coachloads of marauding pissheads on a weekend beano, or the day trippers who flood in by their thousands. These visitors always head for the beach, take all their clothes off, put up with the brisk, freezing wind as long as physically possible without turning blue, then slowly but surely begin to put more and more clothes back on as they fight off the symptoms of severe pneumonia.

Quite unbelievably, they also endure a phenomenon where, through what's called sun seepage, people wearing more layers than Scott of the Antarctic appear to go a bright traffic-light red, mostly at the back of the neck. Then, even though they are by now suffering the initial symptoms of frostbite that, if left untreated, would undoubtedly send a person into the screaming ad-dabs, they want to buy a freezing ice-cream cone before boarding the cattle train home.

'I'm sorry for shouting at you, Lee.' Heather smiled at me in a conciliatory way. 'You know, all that stuff about "get off your backside". I was angry, not with you, but with how everything is at the moment, and I think it all just came out. I'm sorry.'

I looked over at Heather. 'That's all right. I'm glad you did in a way. It made me do something. You made me see what a sad state I had got myself into. I'm sorry for giving up. I feel ashamed. I promise, right, from now on, I will buckle down and stop feeling sorry for myself. Starting from tomorrow, I'll go all out to get a proper job with real prospects, something solid. I will never just walk off without you knowing where I'm going. That was such a stupid thing to do.'

'And the winner . . .' The compere paused and gave the audience a little wry smile. There was absolute silence in the room as people waited on tenterhooks for the victor's name. The MC waved the cheque for £250 in the air. I looked at it longingly. White light bounced off it like a lure in the sun. I swear I could hear the paper folding and flapping as he brandished it in the steaming hot air. '. . . will receive this cheque for two hundred and fifty pounds.'

I put my arms around Heather. The wind was whipping up a little more now, and it was getting colder. We would have to make the walk back along the pier any moment. We held each other close, our faces pressed together, our arms wrapped around each other. I begged Heather. 'Please!'

'No,' Heather snapped back at me. 'I know what you're like you.'

I persisted in pleading, a little more strongly this time. I knew she would give in eventually – she always does. 'Just one look.'

Heather rolled her eyes and felt down into her coat pocket. She narrowed her eyes, concentrating hard. Then suddenly she whipped her hand up, held it right in front of my eyes and beamed at me with a smile so bright I swear it illuminated my whole face in a haze of white light. It was the cheque for £250.

'Lee Evans!'

It was like an earthquake. An almighty roar from the audience ripped through the room. They went wild. While I stood stockstill, frozen to the spot, my body jammed into a complete state of shock, the other performers gathered around me in a clinch. Cutting out the light, they smiled and congratulated me. Yes, I saw their mouths moving, shouting at me, but it was like I had my fingers in my ear. All I could hear was a muffled hum.

So I just stared at them, dumbstruck, unable to move my lips or speak back. My mouth had become so dry, it was like I was swallowing sand. My tongue had quite literally stuck to the roof of my mouth. I was trying desperately to fathom what was happening. At that moment, I spotted Heather in the crowd. I looked to her for some sort of guidance, as my head was not yet able to take in the situation.

The crowd of performers parted as the MC stomped forward and, with a little too much enthusiasm, began to pat me quite vigorously on my back. In fact, he was slapping me so hard, I lost any oxygen that was still lurking in my lungs. Then, before I knew it, the chairman of the brewery was at my side, shaking my hand with gusto. My limp arm just flopped around like a puppet's – it felt that at any moment my wrist might snap. It was all happening so fast, I couldn't keep up.

The chairman then handed me the cheque and the bottle of champagne. Suddenly there was a barrage of iris-burning white flashes from the photographer in front of us. He relentlessly clicked and clacked his camera at us while shouting out orders: 'Stand there, Lee. That's great. Look like you're drinking the champagne. Brilliant! Make one of your faces. Bite the cheque. That's it. Right, Mr Chairman, you hold the cheque. Lee, make it look like you're trying to take it from him. Great, very funny! I'll tell you what, let's have Lee and the chairman doing a tug of war with the cheque. That's fantastic!' I just did whatever he said – I was too dazed to argue.

Then I looked for Heather again. I was getting impatient. I couldn't see where she was. After all, it was beginning to sink in that we might actually be able to get the gas turned back on, and maybe even restore the phone line that had been cut off months ago. I searched for her across the crowd who were still going nuts, clapping, cheering and shouting.

At the end of the pier, I tried to focus my eyes on the cheque Heather was holding in front of me, but I couldn't. It was too close to my face and all the writing was fuzzy. With a smile, I reached up to grab it so I could get a better look. But just before my fingers could get a grip, there seemed to be a momentary lapse of communication. We both got mixed up about who was actually holding it. Suddenly, there was a fumble, and the cheque slipped out of our fingers and floated up into the air.

I instantly let go of Heather and began jumping around the boards of the pier, chasing the cheque as it flapped, twisted and flipped around above my head. I took a quick glance over at Heather – she still hadn't moved. She seemed amused at my physical contortions, as I desperately reached around in the air but kept missing. My hand snapped and grabbed at the dancing cheque.

I stretched up as far as I could on the very tip of my toes as it fluttered and jumped on the various currents of wind. Then – no! – it was too late. There was a quick, strong, sideways gust, and in a flash the small piece of paper was vaulting beyond the railings out over the sea. It hovered for a moment, as if to say goodbye, then with a little flap of its tail it made a roll. Then it dipped violently and was swallowed by the darkness beneath the pier. Gone forever.

I spun around to see Heather's reaction, but she was just standing there staring intently, examining, calculating and yet still smiling. Then she calmly raised her eyes up to a parting in the clouds through which suddenly shone a blanket of stars. We were both caught up for a moment in the beauty of the vast twinkling lights. But then she just shrugged her shoulders and chuckled to herself. I searched for some guidance, as I was sure she must have seen what had happened. But her mind, amazingly, appeared to be some place else. Had she not seen the disaster that had just occurred?

'Everything all right, Heath?'

'It could work, you know,' she said, dreamily. She looked deep in thought. Her mind was mulling something over. I had no idea what, but, quite frankly, I didn't care. I started pointing, angrily jabbing and shaking my finger out to sea. I was just not getting her calm reaction, because I, for one, was devastated.

'I've just lost the . . . ? Did you?' I was still not getting the response I expected. So, tactically, I went on the defensive and raised my voice a little, making sure I gave a convincing performance. 'Do you know what, right? That about sums it all up for me! Do you know that we had it? But then, oh no, we're not allowed to get ahead. It's all right, you don't have to say anything – I know I've messed up. Why is it that everything I touch turns into a catastrophe? I mean, we had it, but somehow it wasn't quite real, and now it's gone.'

Still remonstrating, I slumped dejectedly on to one of the wooden benches. 'The story of my life, that is! Why can't we just have one bit of luck, just a bit? That's all I'm asking for, a sign. You know, like some sort of sign.' I held my head in my hands.

Suddenly Heather was sitting there next to me. I looked up to find her still smiling at me. 'We have had a sign,' she beamed.

I didn't know what she meant. I shook my head, confused. 'What?'

But, frustratingly, she changed the subject again. 'It's all right, Lee, we can get a replacement cheque.' She put her hand under my chin, pulled me gently up towards her and kissed me on the lips. She whispered, 'Don't worry. Everything's going to be all right.'

We linked arms and began walking back down the pier.

'You know, Heather,' I said with a smile, 'I'll be back down that Job Centre tomorrow. Don't you worry. You leave it to me.

'I promise I'll get a proper job.'

Epilogue

Lee Evans is the most successful stand-up comedian in recent British history. He has performed to millions of people throughout the world and has sold more DVDs than any other stand-up comedian over the last twelve years. He entered the *Guinness Book of World Records* for the highest number of people at a solo stand-up comedy performance.

He has starred in films such as *There's Something About Mary*, *MouseHunt*, *The Fifth Element*, *The Martins* and *Funny Bones*, which have so far grossed in excess of 700 million dollars worldwide. He has also headlined in the hugely successful musical *The Producers* and plays such as Samuel Beckett's *Endgame* and Harold Pinter's *The Dumb Waiter*, scooping a mass of awards and critical acclaim along the way.

And yet, even as he sell outs 15,000-seater arenas, he still insists he hasn't actually found a proper job yet.

Well, one day, eh?

Only a small boy,
Just a small boy,
But he stood tall, as tall as a man,
As tall as a small boy can.

Only a short life,
Just a short life,
But he led a life of one hundred men,
No, of one thousand men.

We gave you all of our love,
But they came from above,
And took you from us,
A star called Max in memory of.

CHORUS
And let that be
A lesson to
To you and me.

Live your life,
As if you're gonna die,
La, la, la, la,
See you on the other side.

Lee Evans,
Billericay, 2011

RUN AND GET A COPY OF LEE'S BIGGEST LIVE SHOW YET!

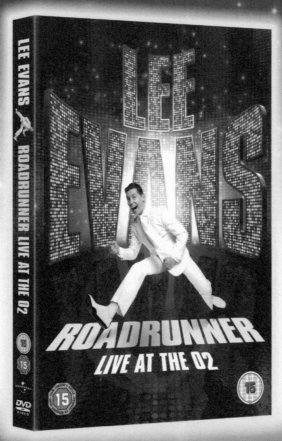

OUT 21 NOVEMBER
Pre-order Lee's New DVD Today